A New Westminster Album

To our ancestors,

To those of us who are still here,

And to those of us who are yet to arrive.

A New Westminster Album

Glimpses of the City as It Was

Gavin Hainsworth &
Katherine Freund-Hainsworth

DUNDURN PRESS
TORONTO

Copy-Editor: Andrea Pruss
Design: Jennifer Scott
Printer: Transcontinental

Library and Archives Canada Cataloguing in Publication

Hainsworth, Gavin
A New Westminster album : glimpses of the city as it was / Gavin Hainsworth and Katherine Freund-Hainsworth.

Includes bibliographical references and index.

ISBN-10: 1-55002-548-1
ISBN-13: 978-1-55002-548-4

1. New Westminster (B.C.)--History. 2. New Westminster (B.C.)--Biography. I. Freund-Hainsworth, Katherine II. Title.

FC3849.N49H34 2005 971.1'33 C2005-901765-1

1 2 3 4 5 09 08 07 06 05

We acknowledge the support of the Canada Council for the Arts and the Ontario Arts Council for our publishing program. We also acknowledge the financial support of the Government of Canada through the Book Publishing Industry Development Program and The Association for the Export of Canadian Books, and the Government of Ontario through the Ontario Book Publishers Tax Credit program, and the Ontario Media Development Corporation.

J. Kirk Howard, President

Printed and bound in Canada.
Printed on recycled paper.

www.dundurn.com

Dundurn Press
8 Market Street, Suite 200
Toronto, Ontario, Canada
M5E 1M6

Gazelle Book Services Limited
White Cross Mills
Hightown, Lancaster, England
LA1 4X5

Dundurn Press
2250 Military Road
Tonawanda NY
U.S.A. 14150

Table of Contents

	By Way of Introduction to Our Town With a View	7
Chapter 1:	A Fair Exchange	17
Chapter 2:	Our River of Life	27
Chapter 3:	Home and Hearth	41
Chapter 4:	Circle of Life: From Cradle to Grave	55
Chapter 5:	Arts and Culture: Food for the Soul	73
Chapter 6:	Ours Is a City of Champions	81
Chapter 7:	The Fruits of Our Own Labour	89
Chapter 8:	Buildings of Community	97
Chapter 9:	In Case of Emergency Call…	113
Chapter 10:	The Great Fire	121
Chapter 11:	"The Robbery of the Century"	131
Chapter 12:	Ever on the Move	135
Chapter 13:	A Storekeeper's Intimate Knowledge	145
Chapter 14:	A Cause for Celebration	157
Chapter 15:	The Great Fair	175
Chapter 16:	Guests of Renown	185
Chapter 17:	The Change of Roles in Wartime	195
Chapter 18:	Changing Streetscapes	209
Chapter 19:	Built Glories Lost	217
Chapter 20:	This Single Moment	227
Afterword:	Our History Is a Shared Legacy	239
Bibliography		244
Index		250

By Way of Introduction to Our Town With a View

The Lay of the Land

Imaginary visitors looking down upon the landscape that would become today's New Westminster would see before them topography both familiar and foreign. They would see a rolling bench land rising steeply northwest from a southwestern bend on the Fraser River. Varying in elevation from three hundred to four hundred feet above sea level, this bench land is dissected by numerous minor and a few major creeks, their canyon courses draining into British Columbia's largest river. The Fraser River carries its combined flow from half of the province's vastness past what would become the city of New Westminster.

~ 1 ~ *Looking southeast from the north end of the Queensborough Bridge. This aerial view was photographed by Don LeBlanc sometime within the last few decades, and other than a recent boom in construction, the city remains geographically much as it has been for thousands of years. The Fraser River flows from the upper left to the lower right, or westward. The heavily treed island in the middle is Poplar Island. The distant horizon is the city of Surrey, and the city of New Westminster includes all of the land on this side of the river. To the left of Poplar Island, forming a bracket around it, is the western end of New*

1

Courtesy New Westminster Public Library #456. Photographer: Don LeBlanc

Westminster. The downtown is in the upper left. The Queensborough Bridge crosses from left to right and connects to the neighbourhood of Queensborough (the easternmost part of Lulu Island). At the tip of Queensborough in the upper centre of the photograph, the Fraser River splits into the North Arm, which flows under the bridge, and the South Arm, which flows in the Fraser's main delta region, approximately twenty-two kilometres away.

From its high point at the split of the river's channels, the city has an uninterrupted view, both up and downstream and across to the south shore. It makes a commanding landmark to anyone travelling the river or wishing to monitor those who travel so.

Foreign to such visitors would be the extreme density and profound size of the trees and natural undergrowth thickening and entangling the high ground, obscuring the views so enjoyed by those in the city today. First growth Douglas fir and Western cedar tower where there are now quiet residential streets and homes, apartment towers, and commercial buildings. Swamps, marshes, and wetlands would be clearly visible along the river's shore, rich in birds and other wildlife that feed upon the abundance of this inter-tidal and floodplain region. The opaque brown Fraser, carrying nutrients along its tributaries, has mined and carried in this area since the end of the last glaciation ten thousand years ago.

Only fourteen thousand years ago the Cordilleran Ice Sheet covered most of British Columbia to a thickness of two kilometres. The Lower Mainland, including New Westminster, was buried under seven thousand feet of ice, enough weight to compress it below sea level. The land rebounded when relieved from this burden, and the ice melted back eastward up the Fraser Valley. The melting ice and the shifting courses of the Fraser deposited the surficial geological materials that created our recognizable physical landscape. The future city of New Westminster would be granted a complex blending of glacial drift detritus with river and marine deposits. These geographical elements would present both comfort and challenge to those who would come to make this place a home.

Our Earliest Beginnings

The portion of this high north river bank that became the city of New Westminster is extremely small, at only nineteen square kilometres, yet it is densely historic, as the oldest incorporated city west of the Great Lakes. However, it also has a much wider and more ancient past. The Salishan First Nations of the south coast hunted, fished, and settled throughout the Lower Mainland, occupying the New Westminster river shoreline and Poplar Island and harvesting the vast, seasonal runs of salmon and oolichans. They also hunted the enormous white sturgeon that swam the murky Fraser depths — such hunts looming as large in their mythology as the ghostly animal itself. Living close to the river, these Coast Salish used the river as a watery highway, perfecting their knowledge of the river's moods and utilizing its bounty in all aspects of their lives for over nine thousand years.

On July 2, 1808, Simon Fraser journeyed past the wooded hillside as he made a right turn at the fork below the future city site. He headed down the North Arm of the river that he mistook for the Columbia. The Columbia River also originates in British Columbia but swings much further south, arriving at the west coast at the border between the states of Washington and Oregon.

The nations of Europe kept the remoteness of B.C.'s coast un-colonized and unoccupied by the Western powers for over fifty years after its exploration by the English and Spanish in the 1770s. This remained until the establishment of the first land-based fur trading post at Fort Langley in the summer of 1827. During the intervening period, a mutually lucrative marine fur trade had developed on coastal waters between First Nations and private merchant ships. Sea otter pelts were traded from 1785 to 1825, when the otter population collapsed.

Founded by the Hudson's Bay Company, Fort Langley was located first at a site known as Derby, just thirty kilometres upriver from what would become New Westminster. Work began here on the company's first west coast trading post on July 30, 1827, but the fort would be relocated and rebuilt twice more. In 1839, the fort site was moved eastward five kilometres further upstream, to make use of the greater access to fertile land, and when this second fort burnt down a year later, a third Fort Langley was built nearby in short order. The company opened another trading fort, Fort Victoria, on Vancouver Island in 1843. Vancouver Island became the first crown colony on the West Coast in 1849, with former HBC First Factor James Douglas becoming the first governor. The province's mainland now had to wait nine more years before gaining its own colony status.

1858 was the most important year in the history of British Columbia. In February, the Hudson's Bay Company sent gold from the Thompson River south to San Francisco to be coined, starting a B.C. gold rush. This overwhelmed both the colonial administration and local merchants. Thousands of gold seekers needed provisions and rapidly increased the non-native population beyond manageable and taxable levels.

On June 19, Governor Douglas asked the British government for military aid and increased legitimacy, a request that was granted in part on August 2 with the creation of legislative government for a second crown colony, British Columbia. Sir James Douglas would be governor of both, with the official proclamation of British Columbia as a crown colony read out on November 19, 1858, at Fort Langley. On Christmas of that year, Colonel Richard Clement Moody, in command of the Columbian Detachment of Royal Engineers, known as "sappers," arrived in Victoria with a mandate to assist with the physical development of colonies and with the selection and design of the capital of British Columbia. Their arrival would set the stage for the birth and future development of the city of New Westminster and the province of British Columbia.

~ 2~ *William McFarlane Notman, the son of William Notman, photographed this postcard in 1887. Postcards were frequently used to send short messages. Where we today would pick up the phone or e-mail someone to say, "How are you?" "Remember me?" or "I haven't forgotten you," people in the past would send postcards. However, the date a postcard's photograph was taken should never be determined*

Courtesy authors' collection. #1N.PC.1. Photographer: W.M. Notman

2

solely by the postmark; there are other factors to consider. The postmark on this otherwise dateless card is obscured, but it still gives information through its stamp. The stamp is of King Edward VII (who reigned 1901–1910), and during this time stamps were only valid if bearing the image of the reigning monarch. If the postcard had been sent after King Edward's death, the sender would have needed to exchange the old stamps or purchase new ones with the new king, George V, on them. However, this is only the first step in determining when this photograph was taken. Notman Sr. started to build a photographic business in Montreal in 1856, and eventually he had more than eight studios in Canada and the United States. His studios are known for their beautiful portraits, landscapes, city scenes, and composites, all done until 1935. Between 1884 and 1909, Notman Jr. ventured across Canada to B.C. taking photographs. When the CPR line came through New Westminster in 1887, so did its Photographic Car No. One, with Notman Jr. on it. The train followed the line, stopping for photographs to be taken under contract to the CPR. Notman Jr. got off the train in New Westminster and took this photograph with his large-format camera using sixteen-by-twenty-inch plate negatives. With this specific information, the year this image was taken can clearly be determined as 1887. Images like this were frequently sold as postcards.

~ 3 ~ *This is New Westminster in its beginning, when it was nicknamed "Stump City." It is 1865, and the downtown area is showing signs of growth. In the* Columbian *newspaper of February 15, 1908, this picture was run with the following caption: "The above picture was taken from a large sandbar which ran from Lulu Island to Brownsville." Lulu Island and Brownsville, where the city of Surrey now sits, are both on opposite shores across the river from New Westminster. The left side of the frame is just this side of Church Street, and the right side of the frame stops where Merivale Street crosses Columbia. Royal Avenue is just below the*

Courtesy New Westminster Public Library #279.

3

top of the hill, and just above the length of the wooden pier in front is Front Street. Shown here is the land clearing of New Westminster, allowing more homes to be built up the hillside. The wide, two-gabled building on the left just under the top of the hill is the Royal Columbian Hospital at Clement Street (now Fourth Street), which spills down just to the right side of the middle of the photo; Agnes Street is on the north corner. At this time, a Board of Management hired Drs. Black and Jones to maintain healthcare at the hospital for a salary of $250 annually. A patient's weekly charge was $15, but this did not cover the hospital's basic operating cost. The hospital had taken over operations with the furniture and supplies from the makeshift sapper's camp hospital. The RCH, founded in 1862, is the oldest hospital in the province. It relocated to its current Sapperton address in 1889. Seen sitting just to the left of centre, near the edge of the still standing trees, is the Irving family home. Merivale Street runs down the other side of the Irving home, and the photograph captures a block or so running toward what will become Peele Street.

Just below Irving House is St. Andrew's Presbyterian Church at Blackwood and Carnarvon streets. The church opened on December 20, 1863, with the Reverend Robert Jamieson as minister, after having services held for a year or so in the courthouse. The building seen in this photograph today houses the Emmanuel Pentecostal Church's hall, with the church located at 321 Carnarvon. On Columbia Street (the line sloping parallel with the river), between Blackwood and Merivale streets, was St. Charles', shown here above the head of the man sitting in the canoe. The building along the left side of Clement below the Royal Columbian belongs to the Church of England, possibly used as a residence for clergy. The long wharf buildings in the foreground are roughly at the foot of Church Street, and the large three-storey building is said to be Collins's Overland Telegraph Company building. The California State Telegraph Co. sponsored a cable to New Westminster, and the first telegram in the city was received by Collins's on April 18, 1865. The message was about the assassination of President Abraham Lincoln. In August, Collins's connected itself to other parts of British Columbia. The first telegram received on this cable line was to make sure a bottle of wine had been delivered to their office congratulating them on this occasion. The photographer would have had to hire someone with a boat to get to the other side of the river to capture this view. There are other photographs of New Westminster like this, taken during the city's first growth spurts, in the public library and museum and archives collections. Most of these have in the foreground a man or two sitting in a canoe, no doubt serving as both prop and transportation.

~ 4 ~ *The home of Captain William Irving (1816–1892) is at 302 Royal Avenue. In this photograph of the Irving family's house circa 1880, Mrs. Irving and the Irving daughters are standing at the gate, and perched on the balcony railing is their son, John. This fine home was built by members of the Columbia Detachment of Royal Engineers and was completed by 1865 under a contract with Captain Irving, a prominent pioneer riverboat captain. Many who knew him described him as an*

Courtesy New Westminster Public Library #254.

4

intrepid navigator and steamboat man. He was a resourceful businessman and was very charitable to the less fortunate. The house remained within the family until 1950, when the city purchased it to house the Irving House Historic Centre. It has been reported that the foundation of the house still sits upon its original footings. The footings are round, not squared off like they would be today. They also have signs of hand chiselling, indicating that they were not altered far from their original tree state. At the back of the property behind the house the New Westminster Museum and Archives is located. The home still contains original Irving family furniture and décor.

~ 5 ~ Here is another view of New Westminster, possibly from within a canoe on the river in front of Brownsville, in 1881. The postmark on the postcard is December 12, 1907, 11:30 a.m., and this, together with recognizing buildings present in the photograph and their completion dates, can narrow down the photograph's date. For example, the Carnegie Free Library is present, and the year this building was completed was 1904. Therefore, this postcard was printed after 1904 and before 1907. In establishing details of stamps, landmarks, and postmarks on any postcard, an approximate date can be figured out.

~ 6 ~ This is a view of the city from Brownsville, circa 1905–10, with another canoe in the foreground.

Courtesy authors' collection. #1N. PC.2.

Above: 5 Below: 6

Courtesy authors' collection. #1N.PC.3

This view is roughly around the same time period as the previous postcard and is still facing the same direction, but the boat that the photograph was taken from is further downstream. In a close comparison, the landmark buildings seem almost the same. The only real difference is that this card has fewer trees scattered around than the first one does and more small buildings.

~ 7 ~ *Goad's* Atlas of the City of New Westminster, British Columbia, 1913 *is a fire insurance map produced to show the street configuration of 1913. It contained more than forty plates dividing the city into close-ups upon which descriptions of buildings, their heights, the materials with which they were constructed, and at times the nature of the business were written. It was used as a city-wide land survey. In the event of*

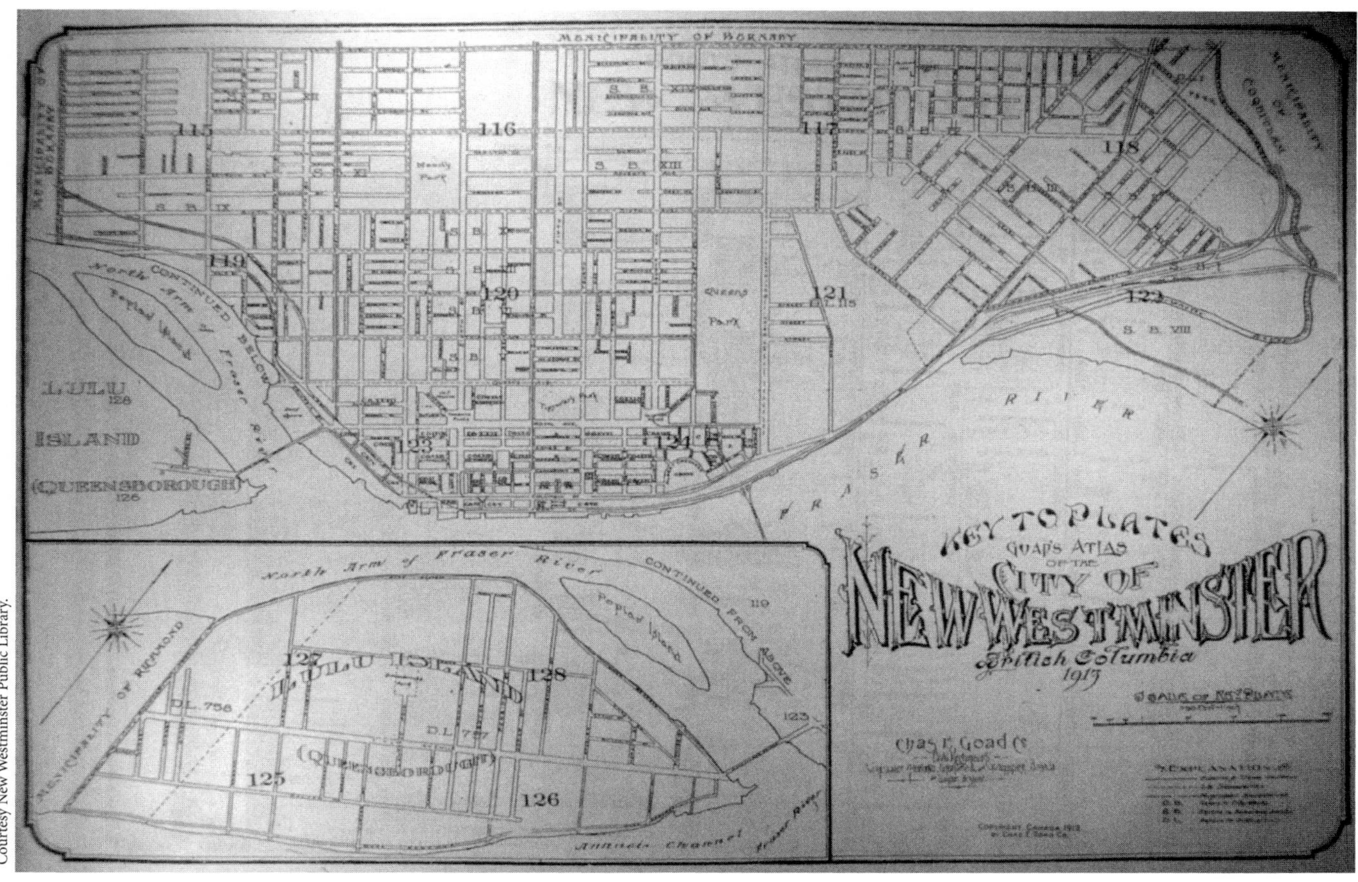

Courtesy New Westminster Public Library.

7

a large-scale catastrophic fire, the appraisal value of a lost or damaged building could begin to be determined from these maps. Today, maps such as these are a valuable research tool for people interested in seeing how land was used in the city at that time and in determining their own home's genealogy.

CHAPTER 1

A Fair Exchange

Sappers

~ 1 ~ *Dr. Seddall was a member of the Columbia Detachment of Royal Engineers who helped with the formation of the Royal Columbian Hospital. Men like Dr. Seddall were from a select detachment of Royal Engineers sent from England, and they included more than just engineers and blasters. There were medical professionals, architects, draughtsmen, surveyors, accountants, masons, and carpenters as well. They had been called sappers since the seventeenth century.*

Courtesy New Westminster Public Library #996.

1

If Governor Sir James Douglas thought he could entirely control the directions and outcomes of the arriving Columbia Detachment of Royal Engineers and shape the development of the two colonies to meet his own desires, he did not yet know the manner nor the measure of Colonel Clement Moody, their commanding officer. The sappers had left England with a mandate, clearly articulated to them by Lord Lytton, British Secretary of State. Part of Lord Lytton's address to the 165 departing members of the newly created Columbian Detachment of Royal Engineers is quoted within Terry Julian's book *A Capital Controversy*: "Christian cities will dwell in the land of which you will map the sites and lay the foundations. You go not as the enemies, but as the benefactors of the land you visit, and children unborn will, I believe, bless the hour when Queen Victoria sent forth her sappers and miners to found a second England on the shores of the Pacific." (p.106)

"Laying the foundations" included restoring the new colonists' faith in the fact that England was committed not only to ensuring law and order by supporting the legitimacy of the new government in the face of American expansionism but also to defending against possible invasion with a network of roadways, a military headquarters on the mainland, and a defensible permanent city capital.

As he read the official proclamation of the crown colony of British Columbia, Douglas had already chosen the location of the new capital: the area known as Derby, on the south side of the Fraser River and the site of the first Fort Langley. A public auction in Victoria was held for the sale of land lots in Derby within a week of the proclamation. The 343 lots, selling to speculators for an average price of $200 each, left the colonial government with more than $60,000 profit from the sale.

However, Colonel Moody favoured a new capital being located on the Fraser's north side, so that the river itself could act as a natural barrier and an added defence to the fortifications he'd planned for the new capital.

In early January 1859, Moody and members of the detachment set out to examine the Fraser's north shore nearer to the river's mouth with an eye to finding higher ground, navigationally suitable for a seaport and defensible as a seat of government. Their choice became New Westminster, and in *New Westminster: The Royal City*, Barry Mather describes Moody's report to Douglas, offering a site with the most desirable attributes:

> There is an abundance of room and convenience for every requisite in a seaport and the capital of a great country. There are great facilities for communication by water, as well as by future great trunk railways into the interior. There is good land for garden ground, if one may judge by the forest and rich meadow lands surrounding it.
>
> It is raised above the periodical floods, and yet the low lands (which will be most coveted as commercial sites, docks, quays, etc.), are close adjoining and easily made available.
>
> From the advantageous circumstances of the locality it is easily rendered unapproachable to any enemy. As a military position it is rare to find one so singularly strong by nature, in connection with its adaptation as the capital of a country.

While Moody's choice made him enemies amongst the land speculators of Victoria, and disappointed Douglas, his case was undeniable. The sappers began surveying the new frontrunner for the mainland colony capital, which Moody had dubbed Queensborough. The grumbling Derby investors were allowed to give up their devalued lots in exchange for what they paid for them so they might purchase lots in the new capital during a new auction on June 1, 1859. This auction netted the government a profit of $90,000. There was some dispute over the name for the new capital prior to the formal proclamation in which Queen Victoria made the final choice. Due to this decree, New Westminster can lay claim to being the first city west of Thunder Bay, and the first to adopt the appellation "Royal." On July 16, 1860, Queen Victoria herself decreed that "the city of New Westminster" would be the new mainland crown colony's capital. This capital of Lytton's second England was therefore given the authority to call itself the "Royal City." Four days later, Douglas himself formally recognized it as a city by reading the queen's proclamation. The final step of full incorporation of New Westminster as a city occurred in 1871.

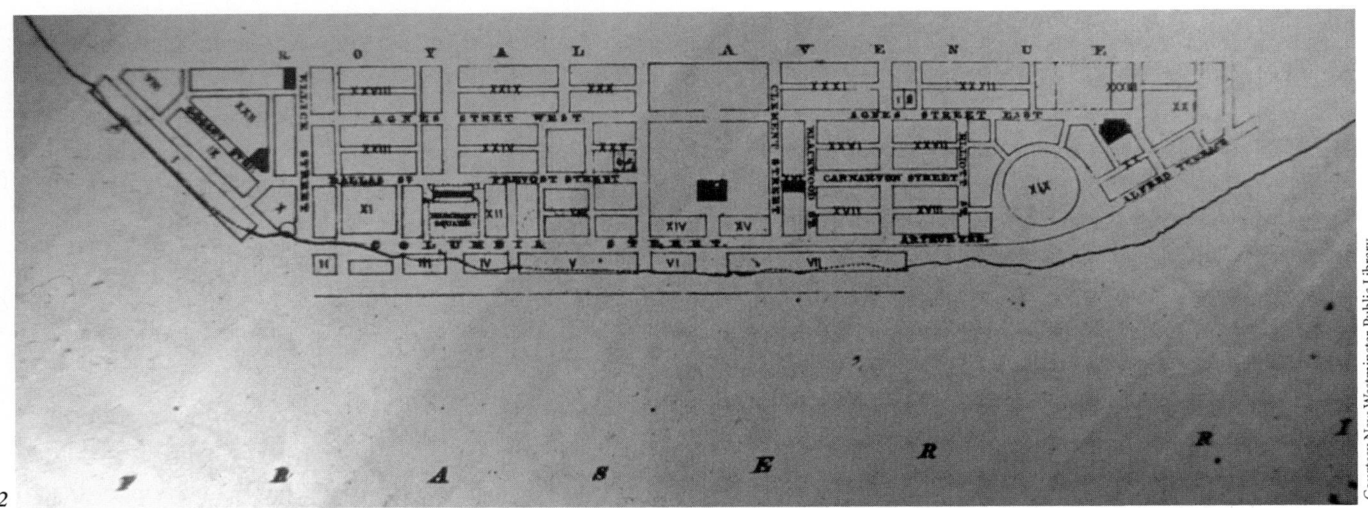

2

Courtesy New Westminster Public Library.

~ 2 ~ *"Lithographed under the direction of Captain Parsons, R.E. New Westminster, July 1862."*

Colonel Moody's original design for New Westminster had a cross as its focus, with the main axis rising directly from the river. It began with the Anglican Church and a garden in behind it, with government offices and the parliament buildings at the cross's centre. Parks would be located on either side, with St. George's Square located behind them. The neighbourhoods would be class-defined, with elite housing on the eastern waterfront and the lower classes and Chinese on the western side. The central waterfront would be commercial. The street grid was laid out, but Moody was not able to complete his vision for New Westminster due to the enormous workload the Royal Engineers undertook building roads to the gold fields and maintaining law and order. Both New Westminster and Victoria were battling declining revenues as well. The sappers had accomplished a great deal, including building Government House (through the enlarging of Colonel Moody's residence) and the Ark, the meeting place of British Columbia's legislative council from 1864 to 1868.

~3 ~ *City Engineer Alan Stewardson displaying an unearthed piece of a twenty-foot segment of pipe*

3

Courtesy New Westminster Public Library #1043. *Columbia* Newspaper Collection.

that was under Agnes Street. This pipe was made out of a hollowed-out log to serve with the early water system. It is believed that the pipe was possibly made by the sappers. September 16, 1955.

The British government formally disbanded the Columbian Detachment of Royal Engineers on November 11, 1863, and although Colonel Moody returned to England, 130 sappers chose to stay and continue their lives in the Royal City. Declining finances and debt from the two colonies after the end of the Gold Rush, and the double costs of two colonial governments, caused the British Parliament to unite them into one colony, called British Columbia. On November 17, 1866, New Westminster was designated the capital, and Victoria lost its seat of government and capital status. The rivalry between the two major cities of the new colony became fiery, and after two years of bitter dispute and a few documented dirty tricks by Victoria's legislative members, it was New Westminster that lost out. The capital was transferred from B.C.'s mainland to Victoria on May 25, 1868, despite its distance from the majority of British Columbians and its smaller size. It was a crushing blow to the residents of New Westminster, and the first of many disasters.

Provincial Institutions

In 1871, the colony of British Columbia agreed to join Confederation, and the need for a federal prison to house long-term prisoners was apparent. The decision was made to place the penitentiary in New Westminster, and the plans were prepared by May 1874, under the direction of chief architect T.S. Scott. It was to have seventy-nine cells (sixty-seven for males and twelve for females), each of which would be eight feet long by four feet wide. The insane would also be housed within the new prison block. Arthur H. McBride, father of future premier Richard McBride, was the prison's first warden. However, even after the prison was completed it sat empty for eighteen months. The true reason for the delay is unsure; some documents indicate problems due to intergovernmental jurisdictional disputes, and others note some technical construction problems. However, on June 2, 1876, the penitentiary received its first unofficial prisoners, described as seven British, four Chinese, four British Columbians, and one Canadian. The institution's rocky start extended for approximately four years while on its way toward an unobtrusive official opening.

~ 4 ~ *These are the British Columbia Penitentiary guards in July 1914. The numbers around the men were handwritten on these photographs as part of penitentiary official records. Warden J.C. Brown (1907–22) is sixth from the left in the front row.*

~ 5 ~ *B.C. Penitentiary, 1960. With the federal prison not having a gymnasium until 1963, this small fenced-in yard with two tennis courts was the exercise yard. The inmates here are wearing kitchen whites because they work as kitchen staff — they are not wearing tennis whites.*

The British Columbia Penitentiary inmates' tennis courts were beside the first building completed

4

Courtesy New Westminster Public Library #1641. Jim Clawson Collection.

Courtesy New Westminster Public Library #1567. Jim Clawson Collection.

5

during the building project of the site, now referred to as the Main Block, also known as the Gaol Block. This building was in use in 1878 and was built of stone-backed brick, with a roof in the Mansard style. The walls had two courses of hooped iron in every course of brick, with a concrete floor and ceiling. The newspaper stated that even if a prisoner were able to remove all the cell's bricks and concrete, he would discover himself in an iron cage. After other buildings were completed it was used as the prison hospital until the penitentiary was closed.

Courtesy New Westminster Public Library #1558. Jim Clawson Collection.

Courtesy New Westminster Public Library #1582. Jim Clawson Collection.

Courtesy New Westminster Public Library #1627. Jim Clawson Collection.

Top: 6 Centre: 7 Bottom: 8

~ 6 ~ *The undressing area of the inmate shower room in Building B-4. All entrants were given a haircut and a shower or a disinfectant bath. December 1951.*

~ 7 ~ *The interior of the penitentiary tailor shop located in the industrial building (building C-1), where inmates could obtain training toward apprenticeship certification. Inmates could apprentice in barbering, auto body, auto mechanics, painting, carpentry, metal work, and welding. September 23, 1957.*

~ 8 ~ *Interior of the kitchen at the penitentiary, circa 1955.*

The inmates at this penitentiary ate in their cells, after lining up in a hallway to get a tray of food pushed through an opening. This was one of the few institutions where inmates were expected to eat in their cells. The penitentiary and the asylum tried to be self-sufficient by creating apprenticeship programs and by growing their own food and making as many supplies as they could on their respective sites.

Soon, the need for a second provincial institution for just the insane became apparent. This was delayed due to both Victoria and New Westminster angling to be its location. New Westminster won out, and construction began in 1875. It was troubled by building delays, cost overruns, poor design, inferior materials, and the firing of the first superintendent of construction in January 1878. The Provincial Asylum for the Insane expanded greatly over the years, accommodating more than one thousand residents in a series of

Courtesy authors' collection. 1.PC.04

9

Courtesy authors' collection.

10

buildings across its twelve-hectare site. In 1950 the hospital, now known as the Public Hospital for the Insane, was renamed Woodlands.

~ 9 ~ *The Public Hospital for the Insane, viewed from the western approach to the site, circa 1906.*

~ 10 ~ *Sprinkler taps and thermometer from Woodlands hospital's greenhouse. Constructed between 1911 and 1915, it was used in the occupational therapy gardening program.*

Both institutions officially opened in the same year: the Provincial Asylum for the Insane on May 17, 1878, and the British Columbia Penitentiary on September 28, 1878 (the first federal penitentiary west of Winnipeg).

After ten years, the old wounds and a sense of betrayal over the loss of its capital status were lingering grievances in New Westminster. As a result, the openings of these institutions did not receive great acclaim. Many people perceived them as a further symbolic insult to the city by Victoria's politicians. Notable newspaper editor of the *British Columbian* and future B.C. premier John Robson quipped, "To trade the seat of government for prisoners and lunatics, it is a fair exchange." Ironically, the penitentiary was built on the former site of the Royal Engineers' camp, and for a short period of time it was also the location of the colony of British Columbia's Government House, which was torn down in 1889.

~ 11 ~ *The front of the Provincial Asylum, viewed from the New Westminster Bridge, located in behind and above East Columbia Street. It is*

Courtesy New Westminster Public Library #7.
New Westminster Museum and Archives Collection #14P0348.

11

seen with Maple Lodge, which housed male patients, and the Nurse's Lodge to its right.

Both institutions added greatly to an already revitalized local economy that was based on a waterfront of shipping lumber and fish. Both provided an economic boom for the city during its construction years and steady employment for over a century. B.C.'s penitentiary released its last prisoner on February 15, 1980, and was officially closed on May 10 of that same year. The property was later sold off in phases as homes and residential towers. Only the Gaol Block and gatehouse were retained as heritage buildings. The Woodlands facility was gradually downsized, and eventually completely closed on April 3, 2003, the last shift of the B.C. Corps of Commissionaires. It was rezoned for residential development in 2004 with the thoughtlessly ironic name Victoria Hills.

Chapter 2

Our River of Life

~1~ *The schooner in the photograph appears to be anchored around the area where today's Westminster Quay Public Market is. It is the* D.L. Clinch, *and it departed to a thirteen-gun salute as it sailed away from New Westminster's port out of the country in 1859. It is carrying sixty thousand feet of cabinet wood and fifty barrels of cranberries, and it was the first vessel to leave this port with B.C.-produced products.*

The Fraser River was both the lifeblood and the highway of British Columbia in the 1800s, and New Westminster had the best seat in the house to reap its benefits while shaping its use. The river defined New Westminster, and the city was the gatekeeper to sailing ships. Some sailing ships of this time were the *Forest Friend*, the *Island Friend*, *Pamir*, *Tolmie*, *N.S. Perkins*, *Vickery*, and the *Thermoplya*. These vessels were multi-masted, and they likely carried a variety

Courtesy New Westminster Public Library #273.

1

of provisions into New Westminster while carrying lumber and other products out. Bundles of shakes, barrel staves, cabinet and box materials, and spars and uncut logs were loaded from local mills such as the Brunette Sawmill. The ships also carried cranberries, of which the Lower Mainland is still the third largest producer in the world. The ships were sometimes towed upstream to port and sometimes arrived under their own sails. These same ships, and the steamboats of this Gold Rush period, rarely travelled the river at night. The sailing ships waited at the river's mouth before setting off, while the steamboats tied themselves off to a tree or stump along the riverbank if they were already within the river channels and between dock moorings.

Courtesy New Westminster Public Library #805.

2

~2~ *This photograph of the steamer SS* Paystreak *on its inaugural voyage was taken on March 10, 1910. This voyage went up the Fraser to Langley and back to New Westminster with 189 guests invited by the Royal City Navigation Company (RCNC), an association of merchants and businessmen. They had the steamer built to travel between New Westminster and Chilliwack to promote trade along the river communities.*

The sternwheeler steamers were the most versatile due to their very shallow drafts. They could slide themselves up on a sandy riverbank and then slip back off into the flow. They could also manoeuvre around obstacles and run the upper rapids. Their captains prided themselves on their skill, speed, and the comfort they provided for their passengers. Most Gold Rush-era steamboats stopped overnight at New Westminster before carrying their gold seekers further up the Fraser. The riverboat captains (who owned their own ships) and riverboat pilots (non-owners, captains in all but name) were highly competitive. They ended up racing against each other to gain such reputations as being the fastest to the gold fields. They even pushed their boats to the breaking point just to attract more clientele, which sometimes led to boiler explosions or cabin fires. At the height of the Gold Rush there were more riverboats on B.C.'s Fraser River than along the Mississippi, and Captain William Irving was the most respected and well-known B.C. riverboat captain. Once the Gold Rush ended, these steam wheelers were adapted for the excursion trade, offering picnic trips upriver to Langley or downstream to Richmond or beyond.

Courtesy New Westminster Public Library #124. Photographer W.T. Cooksley.

3

~3~ *The townsfolk are aboard the SS* Beaver II *taking a day's excursion along the river in celebration of Dominion Day, July 1, 1905. The photographer had everyone pose for posterity in this amazing moment.*

~4~ *This is a colour-tinted postcard by A.L. Merrill of Toronto, Ontario. There is no date printed on the postcard, but the front says: "Ewen's Salmon Cannery, Near New Westminster. On line of C.P.R." On the back, the postcard is addressed to "Mrs. Thos. E. Rakestran, #1199 Kisty Ave. A., Detriot Mich., U.S.A." It reads, "Many thanks for the pretty card. It was Fine. Call again. M. Potts". It is postmarked Northfield, Ontario, and dated "Apr. [or Aug.] 30, 1907."*

Fishing and canning salmon was the second major river industry of the city. The fish were caught either off the mouth of the Fraser or, by smaller skiff gill-netters, near the New Westminster canneries. These canneries were highly profitable, and their owners became very powerful within the community beginning in the late nineteenth century. The first successful salmon canneries in New Westminster opened in 1871 on the city's waterfront. By 1881 there were ten canneries on the Fraser River that collectively exported 142,516 cases of canned fish that year. One of the cannery owners was Alexander Ewen of New Westminster, whose cannery began on Front Street but moved to Lion Island near Queensborough. By 1884, Ewen's Lion Cannery was the

Courtesy authors' collection. #2.PC5.

4

Courtesy authors' collection. #2.PC22.

5

Courtesy authors' collection. #2.LS175.

6

~ 5 ~ *This is a hand-tinted postcard made in Germany. "Unloading Salmon From the Scows, New Westminster. On line of C.P.R."*

~ 6 & 7 ~ *This lanternslide has had a print made from it and has been notated with information by the photographer or the assistant. These notations are typed very small on paper and glued onto the front and the edge of the doubled glass plates. This*

Courtesy authors' collection.

7

largest on the Fraser River, and he became one of the wealthiest men in New Westminster during the 1890s, when the number of canneries on the river tripled. Ewen invested his wealth in property and politics, serving on City Council for several terms and owning most of Queensborough, as well as other city property.

was the typical manner in which a photographer catalogued his or her work. There is nothing indicating who the photographer is, what the date is, or what cannery this is. There is not much room to attach labels, nor would it be a good idea to do so on this slide. There would have been a separate written record as well, a catalogue in which this information would be stored. This slide also indicates that someone has re-catalogued the slide, as in the upper right corner there is another number added over top. These slides came recently from England's Isle of Wight, where they were in a collection that someone had inherited from a friend. Another curious thing about this slide and its print is that a postcard was made of the same cannery at an angle a little to the right, showing the fish arriving. These were probably taken by a commissioned photographer at Ewen's Cannery and could have been taken for an assortment of reasons, besides being printed as a postcard in Germany. Unfortunately, the postcard was not sent to anyone through the mail, so it lacks other clues, but the fact that it was made from this lanternslide, and that the two came from different countries, is very interesting.

Courtesy authors' collection. #2.PL5176.

8

~ 8 ~ *This print image of a lanternslide of cannery workers in front of unloaded fish has a faint figure of a young girl in the background. She appears to be just wandering freely as the others work. She is not acting as though she is an employee, and she is very comfortable, and so it is not far-fetched to think that she is the daughter of this cannery's owner. This may be one of Alexander Ewen's daughters, which would make this a photo taken at the Ewen cannery. In the far end of the notated Ewen Cannery postcard seen earlier, taken from across the water, one can see what looks like the covered area shown here. The girl looks to be the age of Adelaide Ewen, who was fourteen in 1890. Adelaide is in a portrait with her two sisters circa 1890 in another chapter, where she appears to be about the same age as the girl here. It is known that she was born in 1876, but it is still only a guess that 1890 is the year this image was taken. This figure could also be of another Ewen girl at a later time. The Ewen Cannery was the largest and most profitable on the Fraser River at this time, and would have been a well-known local landmark; it definitely had photographs taken of it to have at least some postcards printed.*

In the early growth of photography, a three-and-a-quarter-inch squared positive image was produced. It was taken with the same bulky camera equipment, but with different size glass plates. Once out of the darkroom, the emulsion on the glass plate was sandwiched between another thin glass plate and taped together with a black paper tape, creating a slide. Lanternslides were designed so that photographic images could be enjoyed in the same manner as slideshows are today. Photographers benefited through their work being viewed by the general public, and the public gained the entertainment of experiencing beautiful images of far-off places and of what was familiar, all up on a big screen. Today, we get the same entertainment by flocking to the library to see slideshows of these now historical photographs taken of New Westminster. The New Westminster Historical Society's presentations are brought to life by the research of historians Archie and Dale Miller. Archie remembers experiencing a few lanternslide shows when he was a youngster, and he brings this to life in his presentations, albeit without the smoke and flame from a lanternslide projector.

~ 9 ~ This photograph shows Cleeve Canning Co. manager P.J. Venables standing on the right, circa 1902. The Cleve Canning Co. began operating under the B.C. Packers Association in 1903.

Courtesy New Westminster Public Library #790. Percy Venables Collection.

9

Other New Westminster canneries of note were St. Mungo Canning Co. Ltd., Monk and Company, and the Butterfield and Mackie Cannery. Alex Ewen began consolidating canneries under the B.C. Packers Association in 1901. He was the first president of the association and remained in that position until his death on July 8, 1907. Workers in these canneries were often non-white (Chinese, Japanese, or First Nations) and were paid at a lower rate than white workers while doing the messier jobs. Occasionally the canneries' fishing boats caught the enormous white sturgeon, a fish that must have seemed from another planet to the citizens of that era. These large fish were newsworthy monsters, but years of overfishing saw their size grow smaller and smaller and depleted their numbers to the point that they were listed as an "at risk species." Only recently have their numbers begun to rebound.

~ 10 ~ This is the interior of an unknown "salmon can-

Courtesy authors' collection. #2.PC6.

10

Courtesy authors' collection. #2.PL5748.

11

nery, Fraser River, near New Westminster B.C.," as the postcard reads. Note the man standing in the sea of caught fish and the work stations on the left.

~ 11 ~ *About three days' worth of catch waiting to leave a cannery — about sixty thousand cans. This lanternslide came in a collection from England and doesn't list the name of the cannery or the date the image was taken.*

~ 12 ~ *This photograph depicts curiosity and catching a sturgeon on April 22, 1925. This was not the first sturgeon caught here, nor would it be the last.*

Courtesy New Westminster Public Library #3226. New Westminster Museum and Archives. #1HP2930. Austin Lyles Collection.

12

This is M. Monk's wholesale and retail dealer at 531 Front Street. The great sturgeon weighed in at 1,015 pounds and measured twelve feet, eight inches. Of course the British Columbian Industrial Supplement *was in attendance to witness the catch of Silverdale salmon fisherman Pat Edwards. When the sturgeon became entangled in his gill net, he ended up calling on other nearby fishing boats to help him land it. He sold the fish to Monk and Company for $100, and the caviar was put up for sale. Dave McWaters and Sam Evans acquired the fish and planned to put it on a Canada-U.S. tour, and it was reported to have toured throughout British Columbia. Noteworthy in the photograph are Scotty McClew, a newsboy, standing in front of the post wearing a cap and with his hands in his pockets; Alf Monk, standing just to the right of the middle box label with his hat sitting back on his head; and Ed Seabrook, the barber in the British Columbia Electric Railway (BCER) building, on the far right in a dark suit and hat with a wide band.*

~ 13 ~ *The photographer of this 1889 photograph was E.C. Brooks. It is of New Westminster and Delta cannery owners. This was probably taken before or*

Courtesy New Westminster Public Library #281.
New Westminster Museum and Archives Collection.

13

after a cannery meeting, and it may have been taken in Delta at Ladner's Landing. The men who are looking out through the windows are cannery employees. Standing (left to right): M. Leary of Delta; H.E. Harlock of Delta; Thomas E. Ladner of Ladner's Landing; J.A. Laidlaw of the New Westminster cannery Laidlaw's; and Robert Matheson of Delta. Sitting (left to right): D.J. Munn of New Westminster; E.A. Wadhams of Delta; Alexander Ewen of Ewen's Salmon Cannery; Marshall Martin English of the New Westminster canneries English and Co. and Phoenix Canning Co., near Steveston; and B. Young. What an imposing group of important men.

~ 14 ~ Fleet of fishing boats working at the mouth of the river, circa 1895. The photographer, S.J. Thompson, took this shot from within a boat. With the number of boats out there, nothing could go unnoticed, and it is easy to imagine that help would be at your side if a sturgeon got caught in your gill net. At the same time, you can understand why there were so many canneries and why so many sturgeons got caught in nets.

Courtesy New Westminster Public Library #73. New Westminster Museum and Archives Collection. #1HP0359.

14

~15~ This hand-tinted postcard was printed by Photogelatine Engraving Co. Ltd. in Toronto. New Westminster's Fraser River saw the foundation of what is currently the Fraser Port Authority, which began as the New Westminster Harbour Commission in 1913. It improved the city's waterfront by extending the existing docks by two hundred feet, making way for increased railway tracks, roads, and new wharfs such as the Pacific Coast Terminals in the 1920s. The postcard reads, "Deep Sea Shipping in the Fraser River at New Westminster, BC – 9." In the background on the left, the B.C. Penitentiary can be seen on the shore. Today, Fraser Port is responsible for more than 22 million tonnes of cargo a year, utilizing 227 kilometres of shoreline, making it the largest river port in Canada as well as the most profitable, with a total annual economic output of $4.8 billion.

Courtesy author's collection. #2.PC7.

15

~16~ *This print shows the early waterfront's green timber stacks drying out, with a rail track running through. A rail car is on the tracks with timber on it, and sitting at its edge are two men. Each stack is atop a large log that protects the bottom layer of timber, and covering the top layer for weather protection is a portable roof. There are stacks as far as the eye can see in this shot.*

Courtesy author's collection. Lanternslide print 402-23.

16

~17~ *This photograph shows the timber rafts empty of drying timber, with men working on the right side. In the background on the left is Brownsville (now called Surrey), and on the right in the background are piers and buildings. On the front pier are stacks of timber waiting to be attended to.*

Courtesy authors' collection. Lanternslide print 401-31

17

Crossing the river has also been an important part of New Westminster's development. But before there were bridges in New Westminster, there were an assortment of public vessels. The first of these was the *K de K*. Its full name was the *Kynvet de Kynvet*, and its first sailing trip transported the citizenry of both Brownsville and New Westminster across the river. The *Mainland Guardian* on March 5, 1884, reported: "Steam Ferry, the last of the machinery for the steam ferry was expected by yesterday's boat, with luck it ought to be running by end of the week." An item a few days later read: "On Saturday last, the steamer made its first trip across the Fraser, and has continued to cross with passengers and freight; it's a public accommodation. A person residing in the city can saddle his horse next summer, cross the river, and ride to Yale — and New York." The captain

Courtesy New Westminster Public Library #979. Columbian Newspaper Collection.

18

Courtesy New Westminster Public Library #252. Suzanne Spohn donation, A.E. (Grant) Campbell Collection. Vancouver City Archives. #BO.P 275 N132

19

was Angus Grant, and he took up a contract with the city to build a scow that would carry teams of horses and foot traffic across by steamer. However, he built a larger scow that was powered on its own, utilizing its boiler, engine, and side paddlewheel system. The resourceful Gilley Bros. Co built New Westminster's landing at the foot of Mary Street (now Sixth Street). The *K de K* had scheduled crossings every hour during running times until 1889, when the city put into service a ferry steamer called the *Surrey*. Passage prices were twenty cents for an adult, ten cents for a calf, sheep, pig, or child, and up to $2.50 for a thresher and horse team.

~18~ *The frozen river in February 1929, before the Pattullo Bridge was built, as the New Westminster Bridge allows a vessel to pass through. The bridge's designer, who at the time was referred to as one of the world's renowned bridge engineers, affectionately called it the "Lucky Lady" because of its safety record. On the left is a timber raft not quite fully loaded. The waterway, frozen or not, was never still.*

~19~ *On this 1884 trip on the* K de K, *the only people identified are Dennis Lawler, the engineer (second from left), Malcolm Matheson, the trailer (fourth from left), and to his left William Forrester, a businessman passenger. The man in the wheelhouse can be assumed to be Captain Grant, but no information on him in this photograph has been found. Above the door is an advertisement for William Rae's dry goods and millinery store on Columbia Street, called The Globe House.*

~20~ *It seems fitting to finish this chapter off with one of the tugs that was built in New Westminster.*

Courtesy New Westminster Public Library #166. New Westminster Museum and Archives Collection.

20

The St. Clair *is a sixty-six-ton steam tug, built with river and coastal tug service in mind. This photograph's date is listed as circa 1898.*

Sometimes it can be a challenge to date a photograph. Looking at a photograph through a photographer's or a jeweller's loupe, or even looking at a modern slide made of the print then projected upon a big screen, can be fascinating, but it is only the first of all the bewitching steps. After the eyes learn how to see what's there, then comes the engaging research. It is just the beginning, and hopefully the discoveries of information and clues to new identities and associations will never end.

CHAPTER 3

Home and Hearth

New Westminster's Neighbourhoods

The city went through many cycles of residential boom during economic good times and consolidation or stagnation during the bad. Many of the town's wealthier citizens acted as land speculators and developers in addition to whatever other investments and industries they managed. Also, until 1948 mortgages were paid directly to the seller, and only after the land had been purchased outright was the title given to the new homeowner. Even today, it is possible to find homes in the city that were last purchased before 1948 and had not changed hands until recently, resulting in land title transfers not occurring due to this forgotten detail. Also before 1948, it was not illegal for one individual to act as developer, real estate agent, insurance agent, moneylender, and mortgage broker all at the same time for the same piece of property.

The Great Fire of 1898 encouraged many citizens to build further from downtown, along the new streetcar lines into uptown areas as well as further eastward and westward. The cost of servicing these new neighbourhoods represented a substantial investment in labour and money, especially when the local economy was white hot during the years from 1910 to 1912 and in the 1950s.

When Colonel Richard Moody and his Columbia Detachment of Royal Engineers laid out the first patterns of the housing settlement plan, the area east of Sixth Street and north of Carnarvon Street was designated to be the upper-class neighbourhood, and was later named Albert Crescent (after Prince Albert, consort to Queen Victoria). Housing lots with a grand view of the Fraser, with a circular Victorian-style park bounded by Albert Crescent proper as its centre, distinguished this neighbourhood. This park became the centre of annual events celebrating the queen's birthday with the firing of cannons.

Increased industry along the waterfront in the 1920s pushed the upper classes from Albert Crescent northward into the larger lots adjacent to Queens Park, and so began the crescent's decline to its current state; it has been sliced up in the Pattullo Bridge's exit and entrance routes. Home development also moved northward out of Moody's west-end area. It split into a new west end (west of Twelfth Street and its streetcar line into Vancouver) and the ritzier area around the Victorian-style Moody Park. Moody's former west end was now called the Brow-of-the-Hill, perhaps the most evocative and descriptively named neighbourhood in New Westminster. It wasn't until much later, after it was called Honeymoon Heights, that the current west end of New Westminster was officially named the West End.

Sapperton became a freestanding neighbourhood after the Columbian Detachment of Royal Engineers settled there, encouraging further settlement growth around them. When the detachment was formally disbanded, the 130 sappers and their families who remained formed the catalyst for future growth in the area. In 1889, after agreement by city officials, a new Royal Columbian Hospital was built in Sapperton. Even when former hospital structures needed rebuilding, the location has been the same, and the neighbourhood has continued to grow and develop.

What would in time become New Westminster's neighbourhood of Queensborough was not made a part of the city until October 1889, when the city purchased the area from the province. A bridge was built in 1891 linking the island to the area near the water's edge adjacent to the foot of the intersection of Twelfth Street and a section of Columbia Street that is now known as Stewardson Way. This was achieved largely through the efforts of cannery owner Alexander Ewen and others who wished to relocate their industries to Lulu Island's most northeastern and upstream point. Their investments enhanced the identification and reputation of this area. Ewen purchased most of this part of Queensborough parcel by parcel, making him the largest landholder and locking this area into agricultural use. His monopoly was such that his death in 1907 actually spurred a miniature land boom — which was further amplified by the streetcar line using the bridge to run from other New Westminster areas to Ewen Avenue.

Home

It has been a fascination in modern times to explore how people lived, worked, and travelled long ago. One way of gaining an understanding about people in the past is to explore their homes. Exterior house styles varied from neighbourhood to neighbourhood, and from era to era. Finding out how early residents furnished their homes' interiors can reveal many aspects of people's personalities in ways that would otherwise not be discovered. New Westminster has a wealth of this sort of heritage. In turn, we will be remembered and valued when we are only in the memories of our descendants, thanks to what we did and didn't leave behind.

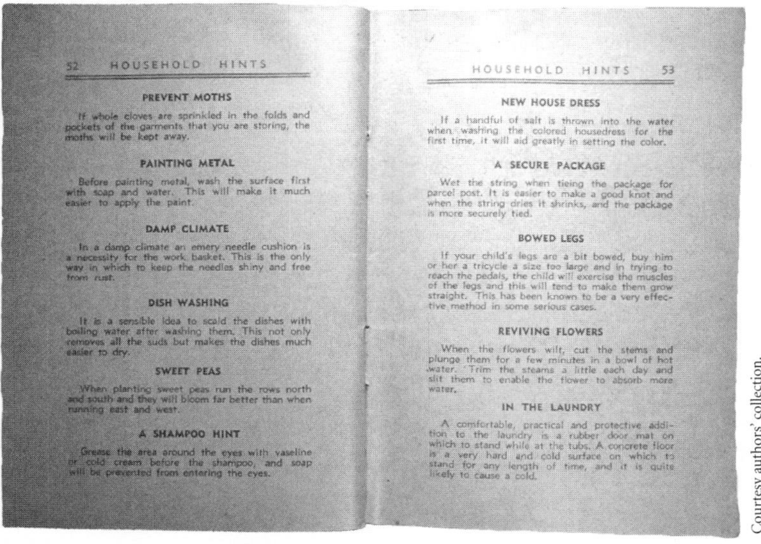

52 HOUSEHOLD HINTS

PREVENT MOTHS

If whole cloves are sprinkled in the folds and pockets of the garments that you are storing, the moths will be kept away.

PAINTING METAL

Before painting metal, wash the surface first with soap and water. This will make it much easier to apply the paint.

DAMP CLIMATE

In a damp climate an emery needle cushion is a necessity for the work basket. This is the only way in which to keep the needles shiny and free from rust.

DISH WASHING

It is a sensible idea to scald the dishes with boiling water after washing them. This not only removes all the suds but makes the dishes much easier to dry.

SWEET PEAS

When planting sweet peas run the rows north and south and they will bloom far better than when running east and west.

A SHAMPOO HINT

Grease the area around the eyes with vaseline or cold cream before the shampoo, and soap will be prevented from entering the eyes.

HOUSEHOLD HINTS 53

NEW HOUSE DRESS

If a handful of salt is thrown into the water when washing the colored housedress for the first time, it will aid greatly in setting the color.

A SECURE PACKAGE

Wet the string when tieing the package for parcel post. It is easier to make a good knot and when the string dries it shrinks, and the package is more securely tied.

BOWED LEGS

If your child's legs are a bit bowed, buy him or her a tricycle a size too large and in trying to reach the pedals, the child will exercise the muscles of the legs and this will tend to make them grow straight. This has been known to be a very effective method in some serious cases.

REVIVING FLOWERS

When the flowers wilt, cut the stems and plunge them for a few minutes in a bowl of hot water. Trim the steams a little each day and slit them to enable the flower to absorb more water.

IN THE LAUNDRY

A comfortable, practical and protective addition to the laundry is a rubber door mat on which to stand while at the tubs. A concrete floor is a very hard and cold surface on which to stand for any length of time, and it is quite likely to cause a cold.

Courtesy authors' collection.

1

~ 1~ *A page from within* Household Hints, *compiled from the column "Household Scrapbook," in the* British Columbian, *1950s. Notice the bowed leg remedy.*

In 2004, the New Westminster Heritage Preservation Society celebrated its twenty-fifth anniversary with its annual Heritage Homes Tour and Tea. The NWHPS was founded in 1974, shortly after the two prominent Hill Houses, Idlewild and Dashwood, were demolished in Queens Park. Each year since 1979, the NWHPS Heritage Homes Tour and Tea organizes twelve or more local homes and buildings to open their doors to the public in their annual fundraiser. Owners receive many benefits from this hard-working society. The fundraising allows the society to help owners of municipally designated heritage homes with restoration costs, through their grant program. Between the NWHPS, the Community Heritage Commission, and the City, owners of designated homes in New Westminster are given tremendous support and advice. The tour has become an annual tradition for many citizens of New Westminster and its environs. As these three groups continue together to celebrate the city's historical traditions, they will continue to jointly move New Westminster into the future.

~ 2 ~ *This is a front cover of the quarterly published newsletter of the New Westminster Heritage Preservation Society (NWHPS),* The Preservationist, *Vol. 9, Issue 2 (May–June 2003). The front cover drawing is of 902 Third Avenue in 1891, the C.W. Gillanders House in the Brow-of-the-Hill neighbourhood. The home is of a modest Italianate style with two-storey bay windows and cross-hipped roof.*

The PRESERVATIONIST

May-June 2003

The Newsletter of the New Westminster Heritage Preservation Society

Volume 9/Issue 2

Don't miss the 24th annual New Westminster Heritage Home Tour and Tea

Inside..
Home tour preview..page 2
Upcoming guest speakers...page 2
Write on the River...page 3

Courtesy New Westminster Heritage Preservation Society.
Copyright K.A. Freund-Hainsworth.

2

The NWHPS tour ticket takes the form of a booklet containing a researched building history, a current description of the restoration and upkeep, and a drawing of each building. Tour committee members and local researchers, writers, and artists make great contributions toward the collectible nature of the tickets, together offering an exceptional opportunity to experience New Westminster's built heritage, family histories, and neighbourhoods.

The authors of this book have both contributed to the tour through drawings, photography, research, and writing. This small selection of their own research and drawings of some toured homes is but a sampling of the heritage and the stories of family homes within this historical city, and of what the NWHPS offers through these tours.

Copyright K.A. Freund-Hainsworth.

3

~ 3 ~ *J.J. Johnston House, 125 Third Street, Queens Park.*

John Joseph Johnston was aptly known as "Mr. May Day." His home was originally designed by architects Charles Clow and Daniel Welsh and was built in 1905. It was renovated in 1912 through additions by the architectural firm Gardiner and Mercer, consisting of four rooms and the large front verandah.

Installed in the home are some very fine examples of Art Nouveau–style stained glass windows by H. Bloomfield and Sons. One of the sons, Charles, later opened Charles Bloomfield's Standard Glass Company, first establishing it in New Westminster in 1890. He later moved its lead store into Vancouver after the Great Fire. Bloomfield did, however, continue to create in New Westminster from Vancouver. When the home had a second-floor fire in the 1920s, it destroyed some of these beautiful stained glass windows as well as damaging other portions of the home. Repairs were made, but not all the stained glass windows were replaced.

After the deaths of all the family members, the home became a rooming house and had many of its beauties covered over and much of the original furniture sold. The home was later purchased and restored with great commitment to once more become a single-family home; some of the original furniture is still in the house today.

John Johnston, affectionately known as J.J., married Charlotte Mary Lake just after the house was built, and they had two children, John Gordon and Mona. Johnston's insurance sales business became J.J. Johnston and Son, and after his son began working there they became partners in the business. Charlotte died in 1951 at the age of sixty-five from cerebral thrombosis. John Gordon died in 1956 at the age of thirty-nine from an infection complicated by pneumonia, and Mona remained in the home until her death in 2001. J.J. lived to the age of ninety-six. During his life he had been elected a New Westminster councillor (1907–1911, 1915–1919) and mayor (1921–1922) of New Westminster. He died after the May Day celebrations of May 14, 1966, having been too ill to attend the festivities earlier in the day. This family's many branches have a long and interesting genealogical line still running deep in this city.

4

~ 4 ~ *John and Adelaide Jardine House, 318 Fifth Street, Queens Park.*

Built in 1908, the Jardines' Edwardian house was created in the Classical Revival style, and the home went on to have a rich and varied history. It was constructed for a noteworthy and prominent couple, John Buckle and Adelaide Jardine.

John Buckle Jardine rose from humble beginnings, making his fortune and then marrying up into the second generation of the wealthy establishment in 1900. He married Adelaide Ewen, the eldest daughter of cannery and land magnate Alexander Ewen. He had come to New Westminster from New Brunswick in 1890 at nineteen years of age, and he rose from his first job as a tallyman at the Royal City Planing Mills to the very top of the company. He increased his economic involvement in not only the lumber industry but also other businesses, including the Westminster Trust Co., B.C. Life Insurance Co., and the Crystal Dairy. He was a very wealthy man only ten years after he arrived in the Royal City.

Adelaide's father was one of the most powerful and wealthy men in New Westminster at the time of John and Adelaide's betrothal. It is likely that Alexander Ewen saw Jardine as not only worthy of his beloved Adelaide but also a man after his own heart. Jardine became an influential city councillor, serving for a total of fourteen years (1905–1910, 1913–1918, and 1921–1922). He was a member of the Westminster Club and served as its president in 1915. He was also prominent within the Knights of Pythias and the Masons (Ancient Free and Accepted Masons, or A.F. & A.M.), and served as president of the New Westminster Lacrosse Association.

At the death of Alexander Ewen in 1907, Jardine was listed as one of two executors in the will. The Fifth Street home was built for the Jardines one year after the settlement of the Ewen estate, and would have been a worthy addition to the already trendy Queens Park neighbourhood. Also serving the city as a councillor, Jardine likely used this home as a location for business meetings and social engagements. In April 1913, the home suffered a fire, resulting in damages in excess of $750 (a substantial figure at the time). The necessary repairs were made, and the Jardines went on to further success while still occupying the house.

The home was sold in 1921 to Dr. Thomas Green, who used the substantial residence as both his home and private surgery until 1931. From 1933 to 1936, the home belonged to Marjorie and Louis A. Breun; Louis was a technician at the Royal Columbian Hospital. Police Sergeant Eric Ewen Anderson and his wife, Annie, occupied the house from 1937 to 1939, followed by Canadian General Electric salesman Henry B. Thompson and his wife, Georgia, from 1939 to 1948. After this, the single-family home was subdivided into a seven-suite rooming house. It once again became a proud single-family residence and won a Royal City Builders' Heritage Renovation Award in 2000.

~ 5 ~ *Armitage House, 340 Fifth Street, Queens Park.*

5

Armitage House, a landmark English cottage in the Eclectic Revival style, was built by George Owen and Mary Armitage in March 1938. Owen Armitage (who was "never called George," according to his daughter, Marnie, who still lives in the neighbourhood) was the general manager for Valley Lumber Yards, which had its head office on Pacific Highway at the south end of the 1937 Pattullo Bridge. He and his wife had three children. Marnie recalls her neighbourhood then as full of fruit trees. In 1951, the Armitage family moved to 217 Queens Avenue, and their home was purchased by B.M. Bowell, a funeral director of the New Westminster funeral home service Bowell and Sons, which today is run by his descendants. Bowell eventually sold the house to the First Presbyterian Church at 7th Street, as a home for its clergy. The church had to sell the home in 1981, and they tried for some time to find a buyer in the then cooling real estate market, wishing to have the home retained as a single-family dwelling. Necessity won out, and the house was eventually sold to the provincial government. Their plan for it to become a care facility with safety and code requirements resulted in radical changes, including additions of interior exit signs and sprinklers and a large exterior fire escape on the back of the house. The house has since been restored and is once again a single-family home. Its owner's personal touches, which won it a Royal City Builders' Award for Heritage Renovation in 2004, make it a lovely example of its era.

6

~ 6 ~ *Edgar House, 415 Third Street, Queens Park.*

The manager of Tip Top Tailors on Twelfth Street, Elmer Albert Edgar, and his wife, Elveria Birdena, commissioned the house in 1926. Similar plans were used for a home on the same block, at 409 Third Avenue. The builder was F.X. Cormier, and the cost of the construction was $3,000 each. The Edgars lived here until 1934, when the second owners, Stepan Gudlaugur Peterson and his wife, Halla Rannveig, moved in. Halla's husband died before her, and after her death in 1950, her son, J.A. Peterson, inherited the home. He occupied the home until 1989, when it was sold to the current owners.

The housing boom that came to an end in 1913 started a downturn in house building that continued through 1919. The 1920s revival issued a shift in architectural styles away from traditional Arts and Crafts homes, toward a new fashion of Craftsman bungalow homes. These homes had a shallower roof pitch, while continuing the previous Arts and Crafts philosophy of integrating the home with its natural surroundings. This was achieved through the use of natural building materials both inside and outside the home. The homes also featured gardens, providing living space to be enjoyed throughout the seasons. Edgar House is an example of the Craftsman bungalow from the Roaring Twenties.

7

~ 7 ~ *Cheyne House, 435 Third Street, Queens Park.*

Robert H. Cheyne was a chief clerk at the Provincial Land Registry Office. In 1912, he employed architect B. Macaulay to build a home in the Arts and

Crafts style. Typical of this style are the home's low-pitched gabled roof and the varied uses of wood, including shingle siding and a clapboard-sided open porch that wraps around the house on one corner. Such porches were very popular in Craftsman homes, creating an open-aired "room" as an exterior feature celebrating outdoor beauty while protecting against rain and snow. Interestingly, a company that installed some interior woodwork in the house has been identified as the S.J. Kelly Woodworking Company. It is uncommon to be able to identify anyone other than the architect or possibly the builder of a house, but during Cheyne House's most recent restoration, the current owners found Kelly's name written in the window and door casings.

By 1935, the home was owned by William A. and W.C. Thompson. William Thompson was the manager of the Cunningham Trapp Hardware Co. on Columbia Street. In 1937, the home became the property of Harold R. and Edythe Wilkinson, who in turn rented it out to various tenants until the very early 1960s.

In the 1957 telephone book, there is a listing for a garage and gas station, Wilkinson's Shell Service, at 916 Eighth Street, with the telephone number LAkeview 2-2310. This could have possibly been the precursor to the Wilkinsons' home-based business. By 1965, the Wilkinsons were the proprietors of Wilkinson's Towing Service, which they operated from the house itself. The city would not allow home-based businesses unless the family had separate home and business phone lines. This was an attempt to hinder such home businesses within Queens Park. According to the current owner, the Wilkinsons thus installed an elaborate phone switching system, one line being the residential number, the other listed as Wilkinson's Towing Service and Car Repair. Another local resident informed the current owner that at one time there were as many as three tow trucks and a car repair garage at the residence. The current homeowners bought the home directly from the Wilkinson family. They have carefully and lovingly restored it, and have also had it designated as a heritage home.

~ 8 ~ *Chelsea Lodge, Alfred and Ruth McLeod House, 120 Fourth Avenue, Queens Park.*

8

Designed by architects Gardiner and Mercer, Chelsea Lodge is a fine example of the Arts and Crafts style, along with its Prairie-style features, including second-floor sleeping balconies. Built at a total cost of

$9,000, the home was featured in the *Columbian* newspaper. Alfred W. McLeod and his wife, Ruth, commissioned this home for themselves. McLeod was well-known in town as "The Insurance Man." After initially coming to New Westminster as a youngster, on leaving school he worked for the circulation department of the *Columbian*, and in 1898 he opened his first office for insurance sales. He also established a distribution centre for a rival newspaper, the *Vancouver Province*.

In 1907, McLeod made two big decisions in his life: to go into insurance exclusively, and to get married. At both, he succeeded admirably. Ruth Temple was the daughter of a noted California Supreme Court Judge, Justice Jackson Temple. After marrying on February 5, 1907, in Santa Rosa, California, the bride and groom returned to New Westminster. McLeod became very active in city life through membership in the Knights of Pythias, the Masons, the Westminster Club, and the Board of Trade. By the time the home was built, McLeod's was the largest insurance firm in the city. The *Columbian* of September 22, 1911, aptly describes the home's features:

> From the front, the house is entered from a wide verandah by means of a tiled lobby, which opens, into a spacious hallway from which various rooms open on either side. The stairway is approached through a spacious arch. The ceilings are white plaster and the hallway is beamed, as is also the ceiling of the dining room, which is perhaps the choicest room in the house. [...] The walls are paneled up to the six-foot level and large windows provide ample light. [...]
>
> The kitchen and pantry are a model of convenience, every facility being supplied. On the upper floor there are four large bedrooms, and two bathrooms. The attic is so arranged and lighted that it is admirably adapted for a billiard room.
>
> In the basement, which is the full size of the building, is the apparatus, which will heat the house by means of hot water, complete laundry equipment, and a hoist, which will raise the required coal and wood to the upper floors. [...]
>
> Taking all in all this new residence may well be regarded as one of the most comfortable and well planned of New Westminster's many beautiful homes.

Hearth

The interiors of homes in New Westminster's past were varied, serving the tastes and purposes of the residents. There was a great range of choices available to anyone with a sufficient budget, although some homes had only what was necessary and affordable.

Some brought their belongings whence they came, some ordered from a catalogue, some made things themselves, and some just went to the local general store (and later to the furniture makers in town) to special order or to buy what was available, new or second-hand. Furniture could be purchased at several local shops and factories like at Joseph Wintemute's before the Great Fire and in 1922 a shop called Reliable Furniture, located at 53 Sixth Street. Later, department stores opened and offered customers a vast array of smaller items for the home. Over the years, and according to the needs and fashions of the time, stores have adapted and sold housewares of all kinds. New Westminster residents have always created a place to hang their hats, while having practically nothing or having more than most would ever want or need.

~ 9 ~ *This is Alexander and Mary Ewens' parlour in their downtown Carnarvon Street home circa 1890. At the centre of this room is a large glass case encapsulating an array of stuffed and*

9

Courtesy of the New Westminster Public Library #2720. Isabel Macmillan Latta Collection.

mounted birds. Taxidermy was extremely popular in Victorian times; displaying the art of prepared, stuffed, and mounted animals as if alive fed a curiosity about the animal world. Homes of this stature had their favourite animals on display, and the Ewens' fascination was with birds. The Ewens also displayed French bronze figures, for example the horse and rider up on their mantelpiece amongst some of their ceramics. The little wicker child's chair in the back centre has a doll sitting in it that is now displayed at Irving House Museum. The doll belonged to Alexandria, the youngest of the three Ewen daughters. A direct descendant of Lexy's lovingly donated this doll to the museum and this and other photographs to the New Westminster Public Library. This doll would have been saved from the fire of 1898. Mr. and Mrs. Ewen would have woken their daughters from their beds late at night, after they were alerted to the fire that was ripping through both the downtown and waterfront areas. Eleven-year-old Lexy obviously grabbed her beloved doll, and one of her parents might have even grabbed a collection of photographs that included this one of their parlour. (Although Mrs. Ewen had a sister living in Ontario, and she might have previously sent photographs there.) The family escaped with their lives and what they could each carry before this grand home perished in flames. The New Westminster Public Library also has photographs of the Ewens' home before and after additions were made in the early 1890s as well as portraits of the family from the 1870s to the late 1890s.

In the Reference Department at the New Westminster Public Library there are many donations of photographs. It is a great privilege to have access to such gems as these, through the great preservation efforts that our public library, along with our museum and archives, offers us all. And this, with the wonderful inheritances of members of this community handed down through the thoughtful protection of ancestors, which are then granted to public organizations in the city, is how we are all able to have our lives enriched by the experiences of our past.

~ 10 ~ *This dining room is located in the 1907 vicarage belonging to St. Mary The Virgin Anglican Church on East Columbia Street in Sapperton. The Reverend Canon Frank Plaskett served as rector of the church between 1912 and 1944, and this photograph was taken just after his arrival. This photograph was donated by Joe Plaskett, a direct descendent of the minister who is also one of New Westminster's most famous artists. Joe has documented much of the built heritage of his hometown and has generously donated a wonderful collection of his early works of local subjects to the public library. As this photograph is reported to have been taken just after the Reverend Mr. Plaskett took up residence here, maybe photographs like this one were sent whence he came, showing his new home.*

Courtesy New Westminster Public Library #1890, Joe Plaskett Collection.

10

~ 11 ~ *This photograph is of Ron and Dorothy Bilton (née Spooner) in their living room at 912 Thirteenth Street, circa 1940. This comfortable New Westminster home was typical of its time, although untypical is the fact that its main structural beams were from the hall at St. Barnabas Church, located in the Brow-of-the-Hill.*

Courtesy authors' collection. 3.D.B.01 Dorothy Bilton Collection.

11

Dorothy's parents had a house built next door to the family home in 1926, and they rented it out until Dorothy and her new husband bought it in 1937 after they married. "Mother told Father that it was foolish to have the property sitting there with just a tennis court on it," Dorothy, age ninety-three, clearly remembers, "so they decided they should build a house on it in order to earn its keep." The church hall was torn down and replaced before this house was built. The wood salvaged from the hall was sold to Dorothy's father, Frederick Spooner, who then used it in the construction of this house. In the photograph, an occasion that warrants the silver tea service and good china to be brought out was occurring. This was an example of a Sunday with a "touch of the special," spent together in the home in which they lived for sixty-odd years. It is very common to find homes in the city that have been in the same family for many years, or to find long-time owners of the same place. This home, like many other New Westminster homes, houses the legacy of memories.

~12~ *A 1939 civic pride promotional pin.*

Courtesy authors' collection.

12

Chapter 4

Circle of Life: From Cradle to Grave

Written Portraits

In any antique store can be found the most personal and the saddest of all finds: old, unnamed and unnotated photographs, loose or in unlabelled albums, appearing like mute remnants of very personal lives. Questions like "Who are you?" and "Where did you come from?" rush to mind. Sadly, no one can directly answer these questions. It doesn't take long to start yearning for the answers. And perhaps these unanswered questions create an attraction, beginning with why a portrait of an unknown person is unforgettable.

How incredibly fortunate when these photographs do not travel too far from their homes, or when they leave a written snippet — a little sampling of the stories captured from within a portrait, or on the back of one. And thank goodness for donors of these treasures who pass them on to a place that allows the average person to see and learn from these records of the past.

~ 1 ~ *This is a portrait of Janet Lucy Peacock when she was only four months old, on October 25, 1889. She was the daughter of New Westminster Public Librarian Julian Peacock, who served from 1891 to 1898. Janet and her sister, Kitty, lived the rest of their lives together, as they both never married. Their sweethearts both went off to fight in the First World War but did not survive, leaving both Kitty and Janet broken-hearted. Both the sisters became schoolteachers and lived into their eighties, in Bude, Cornwall.*

Courtesy New Westminster Public Library #3230. Ted Woodruffe-Peacock Collection.

1

~ 2 ~ *Thompson and Bovill of New Westminster photographed this portrait of the Ewen girls circa 1890. The girls would have gone to the photographer's studio to have this done, as this background is seen in other portraits by S.J. Thompson and W. Bovill. On the left is Isabella May (born 1879), on the right is Adelaide, or Addy (born November 5, 1876), and in the middle is their little sister, Alexandria (born*

Courtesy New Westminster Public Library #2724. Isabel Macmillan Latta Collection.

2

Courtesy New Westminster Public Library #2085. Odin Collection.

3

June 28, 1886). Lexy was the May Queen in 1900, and then in 1901 was the maid of honour for her friend Aldyen Irene Hendry, who was May Queen. There are many photographs of the Ewen daughters available in the city.

~ 3 ~ *This 1897 studio portrait is of young George Frank "Gotch" Odin, born January 29, 1890, and died December 3, 1951. He lived at the same address at 1015 Nanaimo Street all his life. He married Mabel Ethel Purvis, and they had two sons and three grandchildren. It is said that Gotch was the first automobile driver in the city, the first wrecking truck driver in the Lower Mainland, and driver of the first May Day car in 1919. He was also an occasional chauffeur to the W.S.*

Collisters, whose family home was 617 Agnes Street. Gotch also owned his own garage on Front Street. His son Charles took after him in the 1950s; he was listed as having a service station at 428 Eighth Street, called Charles Odin Chevron Service. You could call him up to find out if your vehicle was ready and how much it cost to make the necessary repairs at LAkeview 1-2827.

~ 4 ~ *In this photograph is a little girl, Betty McMillan, sitting in a model airplane aptly named "The Spirit of Childhood." She is the daughter of David MacMillan, who was manager of a New Westminster bank. On the back of the photograph, someone has written that it was taken circa 1930. Thanks to our own public library's research librarians and the information received from photograph donors, a wealth of questions can be*

Courtesy New Westminster Public Library #3249. Andrew Herfst Collection.

4

answered, opening the door for more mysteries waiting to be discovered. Many pictures of other children in this same toy plane have been discovered. Unfortunately, some of these depict unnamed children, and most do not name this modest photographer. The plane is clearly modelled after Lindbergh's "Spirit of St. Louis," which had at that time heroically carried Charles Lindbergh across the Atlantic to Paris, and then to fame and celebrity. The portrait prop was an inspired act of playful marketing by the photographer and was clearly successful, by the number that still can be found. Such an image is universal and carries us away on planes of our own imagining, even if we do not know anything about the photograph.

~ 5 ~ *The graduates of the T.J. Trapp Technical School, Matriculation Graduating Class of 1926, were all fifteen years old. (Left to right) Miss Dorothy Spooner, Miss Augusta Brookes, their teacher, Mr. Johnson, Miss Sylvia Palm, and Miss Edna Wales. Asked what Mr. Johnson's first name was, Dorothy Bilton answered, "Well, to all of us, he was only known as Mr. Johnson, of course."*

~ 6 ~ *Dorothy Bilton and her husband, Ron, are in the backyard of his parent's home at 324 Eleventh Street, circa 1939. Dorothy had a successful career in the law offices of McQuarrie, Edmonds and Selkirk, which were located for a while in the B.C. Electric Building and then later in the Westminster Block, both on Columbia Street. Ron worked for Gilley Bros. as a shipwright for many years.*

Courtesy author's collection. Dorothy Bilton Collection. #4.DB2.

5

Courtesy authors' collection. Dorothy Bilton Collection. #4.DB3.

6

~ 7 ~ *The interior of the William Johnston and Elizabeth Burr Johnston home at 212 Queens Avenue. This is a family Christmas gathering. William is sitting on the floor and has a long beard, and Elizabeth is sitting on a chair and has her hand on her right hip. We know that this photograph was taken before June 1894, when William died. William and Elizabeth had four sons and three daughters. William Burr Johnston is standing in the back on the left side. Edward H. is leaning on his elbow reading what looks to be a postcard while waiting for the photograph to be taken. George B. is standing with his back up against the curtain, and Elizabeth is leaning against the curtain (she married William Stanley Collister a few years after this photograph was taken). Edith Louise, right at the back in the plaid dress, later married Harry Allen Bourne. Mary Anne is sitting in the second row with her cheek resting on her left hand. She was married to Charles Elmer Warwick, who is sitting just behind William Johnston. They had three chil-*

7

Courtesy New Westminster Public Library #2280. Mr. and Mrs. William Johnston Collection.

dren: William James Warwick (born July 19, 1885), sitting in between his grandparents in the front; Charles Elmer Warwick, Jr. (born December 18, 1887), to William's left on the other side of his grandfather; and Effie Lenore (born February 27, 1889), in the back in between Elizabeth and Edith. William Burr Johnston eventually married Annie Dalglish on November 29, 1911; they had three sons, William D., George M., and Alfred Lloyd. There is a Rebecca Johnston sitting in the back, in the left quadrant of the photograph, wearing a frilly blouse. She may be a niece of William and Elizabeth. On February 28, 1904, she married William Love. The only other person who might be identified in this photograph is the older gentleman sitting profile on the right, who may be William's brother John Johnston. The other six men in the photograph are unidentified at this time, but one may be W.S. Collister; another is more than likely J.J. Johnston (we know he was born in 1870); and the others could be future husbands or other close friends or relatives.

Courtesy New Westminster Public Library #2380. Mary Bovee Collection.

8

~ 8 ~ *This is a very interesting wedding party, because included in this photograph are many people who are talked about elsewhere in this book. Seated are the groom, Frank Thornton, a BCER conductor, and his bride, Lily Davidson Barr, on April 5, 1916. Frank looks extremely happy and proud. He was thirty-six years old, and Lily was twenty-two. Once married, they lived at 758 18th Avenue in Burnaby, close to a British Columbia Electric Railway line. They lived for twenty-seven years in this house together and raised two sons, Walter and James, who both went into military service. Frank and Lily both died in 1943 a few months apart. E. Stride, the best man, is standing with a flower in his buttonhole right next to Frank. Charles Stride is at the far right standing in front of the first step. At the time Charles was on the verge of starting his first photography business, Universal Photographers. The man standing behind him is John Mowatt, superintendent of the BCER. The maid of honour was named Claire, and worked at McQuarrie and Mitchell Milliners. The woman in the second row at the far left is Mrs. Clarence Webb, and she is holding baby Winnie. The man standing in the third row, fourth from the left, is Shorty Thompson, who also worked at the BCER. The woman to his right is twenty-*

Courtesy New Westminster Public Library #2109. Basran Collection. Edna Anderson Collection.

9

five-year-old Katie Campbell, who was also employed at the McQuarrie and Mitchell Milliners. The man to Katie's right is Clarence Webb. Standing up top in the last row on the right is another BCER man, Alec Wallace.

~ 9 ~ *It is September 4, 1932, and this group was photographed at the annual family gathering of members of the Sikh Temple on Boyne Street in Queensborough.*

In the process of studying the history of a community, having a photograph with some of the people identified either by the donor or by places like the library or archives can open many research doors. After going on-line or visiting the New Westminster Public Library Reference Department, the Bowell Funeral Home's Record Database, or B.C. Archives, it is easier to read what a photograph has visually written. There may still be some unknown people in the photograph, but often there is information to be found that can help to identify them.

~ 10 ~ *This funeral, held by the Masonic Lodge, honoured John Thomas Scott's life and achievements on February 18, 1908. He died on February 16 in Port Moody at the age of eighty-six. The elaborate funeral procession is going along Columbia Street, and the photograph was taken from the north side on top of a building in the 500 block near the corner of Sixth Street, looking west. Scott's life in the new colony started after he arrived in the province with the influx of the gold rush of 1858. He was a sergeant in the U.S. Army, but was referred to as*

Courtesy New Westminster Public Library #186. Clerihue Collection.

10

"the colonel." He was one of only a handful of business operators to open in Stump City, and over time he started a number of saloons on the waterfront. He made quite an impact on the young city, as he seemed to be involved in just about everything, even if only in the background. He had a cannon that he fired into the river from his saloon but of course only on special occasions. Scott and his wife were no strangers to tragedy. They lost three of their children at very young ages to an assortment of childhood diseases all within one month. Being the pioneers that they were, they and their surviving children remained in New Westminster. Of the tragedies recorded at the Fraser Cemetery, this family endured one of the saddest. In the photograph, there are about fifty people just in the part of the procession that is depicted. Masonic funeral services had members from all the neighbouring lodges attending, and the city came to a temporary standstill to accommodate the sheer size. A richly appointed horse-drawn hearse took Scott to his final resting place in the Masonic section of Fraser Cemetery. Scott was involved in local politics and the day-to-day happenings of the city and was a volunteer member in the New Westminster Volunteer Rifles, a member of the Masonic Lodge, and an official at May Day ceremonies.

~ 11 ~ *This photograph is said to be of Johnny Walsh and Dave Murchie, circa 1916. They were local undertakers. This photograph was carried to France in the First World War.*

Courtesy New Westminster Public Library #1055. JPD Morin, *Columbian* Newspaper Collection.

11

Larger than Life

Every town and every time has its larger-than-life personalities. Just as going through life's experiences forms an individual's character, so do the personalities of a city help in its formation and evolution. Calling some of our town's ancestors "larger than life" is only a departure point to recalling some of the interesting people and the events they shaped, and by no means have they all been included here.

Sometimes the information given within the actual frame of a portrait is all that the future needs, but more often it is not. Sometimes written in the eyes there is a sadness, a confidence, an energy for life, or a curious expression that can reveal a larger-than-life personality. Here are just a few of New Westminster's ancestors and what they, their direct descendents, or an interested researcher has left to be read outside of what is written in these faces.

~ 12 ~ *This is a photograph of Raymond William Stacy Burr partaking in New Westminster's Centennial Celebrations at City Hall in 1956.*

Famous actor Raymond Burr was born on May 21, 1917, in a house on Queens Avenue in New Westminster. He left the province at six years of age when his parents, William Johnston Burr (born 1889) and Minerva Annetta Burr (née Smith, born 1892), divorced. Raymond, his mother, and siblings Geraldine and Edmond moved to California; his father stayed in New Westminster. His father had a long history in this city through connections to the Burr Johnston family and beyond to the early days of the city.

Courtesy New Westminster Public Library #1702. Pacific Newspaper Group Collection. Photographer: Gordon Sedawie.

12

Burr received his first acting job at age twelve when he was in New Westminster on one of his many visits to his father and his father's family. He went on to a great career as the star of the TV dramas *Perry Mason* (which ran from 1957 to 1966) and *Ironside* (1967 to 1975). Burr also appeared in about seventy movies, including Alfred Hitchcock's famous *Rear Window* (1954). His performance as the villain won him an Oscar for best supporting actor. Burr also acted in over five thousand radio shows and more than two hundred plays.

Although he hadn't lived in the city since he was six years old, he frequently visited his family and at times participated in New Westminster and Vancouver civic affairs. He also came back to the city to help in promoting and fundraising. The Raymond Burr Performing Arts Society and the Burr Theatre are named after him, and at the theatre is an active actors' school inspired by him. His efforts in the city are also recognized by May 31 being officially declared Raymond Burr Day.

He died on September 12, 1993, and is buried in the Burr plot of New Westminster's Fraser Cemetery. He has been interred in the family plot along with his sister Geraldine and both his parents. Burr had dual citizenship and said that he always got a thrill out of saying that he was Canadian.

~ 13 ~ *Dr. Ethlyn Trapp, Canadian medical pioneer.*

Dr. Ethlyn Trapp was behind the first radiotherapy cancer treatment research in the country. She was also at the head of the first clinical research project on breast cancer. An honourary degree of Doctor of Science was conferred on her by the University of British Columbia Medical School as its first class graduated in 1954. She specialized in oncology, was made an Honourary Fellow of the Faculty of Radiology of Great Britain, and was the first female president of the Canadian Medical Association. Dr. Trapp was awarded the Medal of Service of the Order of Canada from the Governor General in 1968, and she will be remembered for her valuable work in the area of cancer research. She was the daughter of T.J. Trapp, making New Westminster her hometown. She was born on July 18, 1891, and lived until she was just over the age of eighty-one, dying in Vancouver on July 31, 1972. She is interred in the Fraser Cemetery here in New Westminster, at the Trapp family plot.

Courtesy New Westminster Public Library #0.

13

~ 14 ~ *Henry Edmonds, walking along Columbia Street on his way from the courthouse to his office at the Westminster Building, circa 1950.*

Henry Lovekin Edmonds, KC, was born in New Westminster on November 2, 1870, into the family of Henry Valentine Edmonds and Jane Fortune Edmonds (née Kemp) of 240 First Street, Queens Park. His father came to the province from England in 1862 and went into the real estate and auctioning business. He also was one of the original promoters of the area's interurban line.

Edmonds studied law and became a barrister and solicitor, eventually becoming police chief magistrate. On November 8, 1911, he had appear before him John Bozyk, a newspaper vendor who was arrested in connection with what was thought to be the greatest bank robbery of the century, which took place in New Westminster on September 15, 1911. Edmonds became known as "The Law," said Dorothy Bilton, who worked in his Westminster Block law office, McQuarrie, Edmonds and Selkirk. She said that he was a good-looking man who was always very nice to her. You could call the office and make a consultation appointment with him at LAkeview 2-0621.

Edmonds was a member of the Masonic Lodge. He married Ella Katherine Pringle on July 15, 1908, and they lived at 443 Fifth Street. They had a son, Kemp, and a daughter, who became a local teacher and married fellow teacher Ken Wright. Their son and daughter between them gave Mr. and Mrs. Edmonds six grandchildren. Also known to some as Mickey, Edmonds retired after fifty-seven years of law service in August 1951, just before his eighty-first birthday.

Courtesy author's collection. Dorothy Bilton Collection. #4.DB4.

14

His wife died thirteen years before him in 1938. When he died, his pallbearers consisted of two groups. The honourary pallbearers were T.R. Selkirk, KC; Judge Harry Sullivan; Harry G. Johnston, KC; A.L. MacLennan; J.V.W. Phillips; Charles Callan; Rufus Gilley; and D.H. Collister. The second group was the police pallbearers: Chief Jack Donald, Sergeant S.M. Green, Sergeant Fred Blewett, Deputy Chief Jack Allen, Sergeant William Fraser, and Sergeant Joe Makepeace. Ralph M. Brown and Justice R.S. Woods were the official speakers.

~ 15 ~ *Janet Kathleen Gilley's call to the bar, 1922.*

Janet Gilley was the fifteenth woman to receive a law degree from the University of British Columbia. She was born on August 1, 1898, and grew up in New Westminster within a large family with Walter Ruthven Gilley as her father and Selina Frances Gilley (née Hinch, born April 1, 1868) as her mother. Her father was elected to council in 1899 and 1900 and was the oldest of the Gilley brothers, who started a small logging business soon after arriving. Their company, Mainland Logging Co., grew into two logging camps and a shingle mill, becoming one of New Westminster's largest companies and eventually evolving into a construction supplies company under the name Gilley Brothers. Gilley

Courtesy New Westminster Public Library #3124. Suzanne Spohn Collection.

15

Avenue was so named because their skid road passed over the interurban line.

Janet's family's grand home was built in 1890 and is still a wonderful example of the Victorian Queen Anne style of architecture, with three storeys of Gilley family living space. After the Gilleys purchased the house in 1901 they named it Rostrevor, and they lived in it until 1961.

Janet comes from a long line of strong and resourceful people, and she herself is an excellent example of this lineage. She was a social activist and a suffragette, and her strong beliefs went hand in hand with the thriving law practice that she had for many years. She had an office in the Westminster Trust building at 713 Columbia Street on the second floor facing the street, and she could be reached for a consultation at LAkeview 1-1551.

~ 16 ~ *Leon Mandrake, "Mandrake the Magician."*

Born Leon Mandrake, he went on to become the premier magician of his day as Mandrake the Magician, a truly larger-than-life figure. For many, Mandrake the Magician is known only as a comic book character, and it would surprise some to know he had a true life story beginning in New Westminster. Leon Mandrake's son Lon Mandrake shared the story of his famous father in an interview.

Leon's mother and father were both vaudeville performers working on the road in Washington, and so it was in a small town that, on April 11, 1911, Leon Mandrake was born. Two years later his parents divorced, and Leon and his mother came to New Westminster to live with his aunt, Mildred Wagner. Wagner was a long-time New Westminsterite who worked at the city post office on Columbia Street. Her place of work was a short walk downhill from her home at 307 Carnarvon Street, one of the oldest surviving homes in the downtown area and one of a pair of homes (along with 305 Carnarvon) commissioned by Maria Keary and designed by Samuel Maclure in 1887. Maria Keary was the wife of James Keary, one of the original Royal Engineers, who was

Courtesy Leon Mandrake Collection. #4.LM1.

16

killed at an early age. Maria, now widowed, had the two homes built for rental revenue. Her son, William H. Keary, was a city councillor for many years and mayor of the city from 1902 to 1909.

In New Westminster, Leon Mandrake grew up, attended school, and decided to become a magician. His interest in magic began on his seventh or eighth birthday, when his Aunt Mildred gave him the Mysto Magic Kit. Before long, Leon was using the shed in the back garden to practise his magic. He began to move beyond the lessons of the magic kit, developing his skills and creating his own unique illusions. He learned from watching magicians at the local Edison Theatre's vaudeville shows and studying library books on the craft of magic. The two homes are still standing but are now bordered on both sides by residential high-rises, and unfortunately the back shed where Leon practised with his magic kit has long since been torn down.

Leon went on to act as a hanger-on for the city's visiting circuses, especially the ones at the annual Provincial Exhibition in Queens Park. There, the magicians would occasionally give him lessons and send him off with props. Once, a circus master gave Leon all of the costumes and props left behind by a magician who had left the show. As a child, he learned from many of the era's great magicians, including Howard Thurston, Claude Alexander ("The Man Who Knows"), Doc Verge, Bannister, and the premier magician of the age, Ralph Richards ("The Wizard").

In 1922, at eleven years of age, Mandrake the Magician first appeared on stage in a small part in the Edison Theatre's vaudeville show, where the young lad was the evening's smash hit. Mandrake the Magician became a feature of the annual Provincial Exhibition in 1923, 1924, and 1925. At fourteen years old he officially performed with Moyer's travelling carnival during its visits through the Lower Mainland.

~ 17 ~ *Mandrake at age sixteen. In this portrait of the young magician in 1927, he is at New Westminster's Edison Theatre. In that same year, he left New Westminster after joining the touring show of Ralph Richards, "The Wizard" himself. This was a grand two-hour show. Leon stayed with the show until it was disbanded six months later in Winnipeg, Manitoba.*

Courtesy Leon Mandrake Collection. #4.LM2.

17

Mandrake continued to travel and perform, and he was married twice. His first wife, Narda, to whom he was married from 1939 to 1946, performed with Mandrake the Magician's travelling show. After a divorce, in 1947 he married Velvet, and they were together at home and on stage. Together, they refined the image of the magician and the beautiful assistant. Leon and Velvet were the first magic team to tailor a full two-hour magic show for the nightclubs of the 1940s and 1950s. They also raised four children in between performing and travelling on the road from 1947 to 1958.

It was in 1934 that the comic strip was created in St. Louis by Lee Falk and drawn by cartoonist Phil Davis. According to Lon, Lee Falk had apparently never seen Mandrake the Magician perform, nor had he ever heard of him; he chose the character's name and created the concept completely independently. "Phil Davis, well, he had eventually seen my father, though," said Lon Mandrake, "and drew the cartoon to look just like him." Falk did not continue in ignorance of the actual man. "They ended up with a kind of verbal agreement at that point," Lon said, "and together they participated in a cross-promotion." He continued, "Falk and Davis had said that my father was the best promotion they could have." Mandrake also was able to promote his show through the link to the nationally syndicated cartoon strip.

Mandrake the Magician performed a vast array of magic, including mentalism, changing places, trunk escapes, and even ventriloquism. Edgar Bergen, the puppeteer who made Charlie McCarthy, even made Mandrake's three dummies for his stage performances.

Mandrake the Magician and his troupe were legendary for their publicity stunts upon arriving in towns during their touring years. They would wear their costumes during the day as they went out to eat, shop, and walk around the town. Mandrake would also hypnotize a girl to sleep in a department store window and escape from a box or practise mind reading right out on the street.

~18 ~ *One of Mandrake's most famous stunts was the "Blindfold Drive." This promotional photograph of Mandrake the Magician doing the "Blindfold Drive" was taken in his hometown of New Westminster. The car is from Trapp Motor's Buick and Pontiac. The show he is promoting occurred on February 22, 1958, at the junior high school's large auditorium, with reserved seating tickets available only at Zeller's department store.*

Courtesy Lon Mandrake Collection. #4.LM3.

18

Leon and Velvet Mandrake stopped performing in 1984 and retired to White Rock. Mandrake the Magician passed away on January 27, 1993. For a short while Mandrake's son and daughter-in-law lived at 307 Carnarvon Street, before moving elsewhere in the Lower Mainland on the way to Lon's becoming a respected science teacher and professional magician.

Chapter 5

Arts and Culture: Food for the Soul

The Society of Theatre and Opera

~ 1 ~ *This is the New Westminster Operatic Club's (NWOC) operetta performance of* Merry England, *circa 1917. New Westminster Symphony Orchestra (NWSO) members who supplied the musical accompaniment are in the pit.*

Arts and culture have been major components of life in New Westminster ever since the citizenry felt the need to gather together. Throughout the seasons the community's first citizens were presented with reminders of home through cultural activities they organized and presented. People new to the province attended informal and formal performances and presentations. Giving themselves the pleasure of organizing an event or being a member of the cast was just as fulfilling as being in the audience. The arts served as touchstones from their home countries.

The Royal City's cultural events included lectures, debates, musical and dramatic productions, dances and extravagant balls, and a variety of seasonal celebrations. The early shows that the Royal Engineers presented to

Courtesy New Westminster Public Library #1902. Joe Plaskett Collection. Photographer: Vincent C. Russell.

1

the community at their camp's theatre, some lasting as long as six hours, drew hundreds of people. These events filled the leisure hours with enjoyment and meaning while giving a reason to gather together as a unified community, sharing and being entertained — much as such events do today.

New Westminster can certainly boast its fair share of theatres, from the informal to the fancy, as well as a wide variety of other venues, from a small cramped room to a hall that holds four hundred people. Theatres and performance houses, both temporary and permanent, clustered in places like the sappers' camp or any room altered to fill the need.

When the West End's Twelfth Street Metro Theatre opened on March 23, 1938, movie patrons in the surrounding neighbourhoods relished the fact that they could now go to the movies and spend the money they once spent on travel on more candy at the store. Movie houses cropped up in five locations in New Westminster over the years and became the sort of entertainment that a large majority could go to even weekly. The Metro Theatre, with its stylish art deco lobby, done in pale green trimmed with silver, would have been well worth the price of admission for fifteen cents. New Westminster has a long tradition of arts and cultural events. Over the years, the city has had many theatres open and close, but even today within its modest boundaries, the city can still boast five theatres.

2

Courtesy New Westminster Public Library #154. Morris Vreugde, Bracher Collections.

~ 2 ~ *A few of the notable musicians in this photograph of the New Westminster Symphony Orchestra, February 21, 1916, are first violinist Miss Cave-Brown-Cave, oboist Mr. F.T. Hill, second violinist Master R. Gilley, cellist Mrs. W. Burr, and tuba player Mr. McLeod.*

The New Westminster Symphony Orchestra began in the early days of the First World War and held its first public concert in the Opera House on February 16, 1915. The NWSO lasted for twenty-five years before disbanding. Another orchestra was founded in 1944 and became the New Westminster Civic Orchestra. It was later renamed the New Westminster Symphony Orchestra, and this year is its sixty-first season.

After the Great Fire of 1898, architect Emil Guenther built several buildings in New Westminster, including the still-standing Windsor Hotel and an Opera House at the corner of Lorne and Victoria streets to house the New Westminster Opera Club. A long-time resident of

Courtesy New Westminster Public Library #1028.

3

the city, Dorothy Bilton, remembers that when she was a child her parents would put on "their fancy dress clothes" and attend productions at the Opera House. "It was a big event. They would attend with friends. I can remember that Miss Fillmore would sometimes accompany them." Maria Fillmore was the matron at the Public Hospital for the Insane from 1897 to 1939, and knew Dorothy's parents, Fredrick M. Spooner and Margaret Spooner (née McIntosh). Frederick Spooner worked at the same hospital from 1910 to 1936, becoming chief attendant in 1921.

~ 3 ~ *This photograph was taken at the New Westminster Opera House on December 4, 1912. The opera troupe was giving a performance of* The Brixton Burglary.

~ 4 ~ *In this photograph, taken during the First World War, are two New Westminster Operatic Society members. On the left is Mrs. J.W. Hetherington, on the right is Mrs. H. Mansfield, and this is a promotional shot of them dressed in costume from the production* Serenade.

Courtesy New Westminster Public Library #1040.

4

Courtesy New Westminster Public Library #123.
New Westminster Museum and Archives Collection.
Photographer: Trueman and Caple.

5

izations were represented by a wide variety of performers. A musician, singer, actor, and dancer could find a group in the community in which to learn, perform, and fill the hours with enjoyment. In the city at any point in its history, there has always been an available audience and an available venue of any size. This has given the city a strong identity based upon creative thinking and tradition. This background truly shaped the arts, culture, and festivals that are such a notable part of New Westminster today. "The show must go on" — and this city proves it will be appreciated.

To Read the Music

~ 5 ~ *A group portrait of the New Westminster Hyack Marching Band of 1892.*

The New Westminster Hyack Marching Band was one of the numerous bands and musical groups, amateur and professional, that one could belong to, and these organ-

~ 6 ~ *The Dave McWaters Happy Gang Dance Band playing at the Dreamland Dance Hall at 27 Church Street, circa 1955. Dave McWaters (1895–1983) was the owner and operator of the Dreamland Dance Hall from 1952 to 1958. Currently at this address is Studio 54, which is still a dance hall/nightclub. The musicians are Dave McWaters on drums, Freddie Fisher on the accor-*

Courtesy New Westminster Public Library #2139. Barbara Thompson Collection.

6

dion, and Emma McNaughton on piano. (The saxophone player is not identified.) McWaters also won the 1926 World Roller Skating Championship. He started to play the drums in 1948.

To See into the Frame

~ 7 ~ *This photograph shows an original work of art portraying a section of downtown New Westminster, circa 1865. The artist has taken artistic licence with the scale and form of the buildings. Hyack Hall is the building to the left of centre with the tower and pole, Holy Trinity Anglican Church is on the far right, and the Webster Building is in front of Hyack Hall. The Webster Building was British Columbia's first stone building and housed the Bank of British Columbia and the business of J.A. Webster. The building to the left of the Webster is the Hick's Hotel.*

Courtesy New Westminster Public Library #879.

7

After the Great Fire, New Westminsterites submitted "Applications for Relief" recording their belongings that had perished in the flames. William Turner, residing at the Dupont Block on Columbia Street, who is listed in the directory as "artist, wood engraver and teacher," listed the belongings he lost in the fire as:

> Mahogany box with whole cake colours manufactured by Windsor and Newton; drawing and painting studies; two mahogany boxes containing silver instruments, routeing machine, engraving tools, carving tools, etc.; office table; stool; 27 engraving blocks; miscellaneous and salmon labels etc.; parallels; squares; curves; engraving machine attachments; photograph negatives etc.; and other articles.

Examinations of Wrigley's and Henderson's B.C. Directories show listed parties' professions along with their addresses, tantalizing researchers with the occasional listing of "artist." Such listings represent only a small fraction of the many early artists that produced art in New Westminster for their own pleasure, for public exhibition, and for employment. Many artists struggled in much the same way as today, working hard while pursuing the creative arts to earn their livings. Directory listings like Turner's give an idea of the struggles faced by a pioneer artist. Early citizens of any profession would most often have a number of job listings just to get by, but it is still common today to find people in the creative arts having to hold multiple jobs.

~ 8 ~ *A high school "Painting in the Park" class, taking place underneath the Pattullo Bridge and at the train tracks at the entrance to the Westminster Bridge, circa 1948.*

Courtesy New Westminster Public Library #2338. Ted Clark Collection.

8

Professional and amateur artists and craftspeople of all kinds in the past painstakingly created many of the images, crafts, and designs that are admired today. Through accessing these preserved historic pieces, either through the pieces themselves in the form of visual or performing arts or through all kinds of records, it is easy to admire their passion and conviction. The level of knowledge we have about the past might not have been possible without preserved historical paintings, drawings, photographs, and artifacts.

~ 9 ~ *"Art Exhibit At the Provincial Exhibition at Queens Park," 1906. Entries came from as far away as Manitoba and Washington state.*

Courtesy Vancouver Public Library Collection #1382. Vancouver Public Library #6801. Photographer: Philip Timms.

9

Chapter 6

Ours Is a City of Champions

The Home Team

When the Columbia Detachment of Royal Engineers arrived in 1859 and began clearing the brush around their camp on the future British Columbia Penitentiary property, they also worked with one of the city's first athletic clubs in a "clearing bee." In 1861, the Pioneer Cricket Club and the Columbia Detachment set out to make a cricket pitch on what would become the provincial asylum. The pitch was used for inter-colonial cricket matches between Vancouver Island and British Columbia. Other sports at the time even included horse racing along Columbia Street! The oldest sporting activities have their own institutions as well — formal and informal. Hockey on both grass and ice was popular with men and women, each having very successful and competitive teams. Tennis, badminton, and cycling caught on in the 1880s as recreational and competitive sports. Lawn bowling caught on at this time too, and many teams and clubs were formed. The women's baseball team successfully represented New Westminster and became world champions. Leisure hours were filled with various sports events for simply recreational purposes or for the drive for competition; the desire for sports and appropriate venues was high.

1

Courtesy New Westminster Public Library #2693.
Gordie McDonald Collection.

2

Courtesy New Westminster Public Library #2539.
Mrs. R. Male Collection.
Photographer: Vanderpant Photography Studio.

~1 ~ *The Chislerettes Girls' baseball team from McBride Junior High School, circa 1933. The spares, by last name only, were Angelusy, Angelusy, McDonald, Ingle, Shaw, and Fedewa, and the players were Howden, Robertson, McRayner, Craig, Booth, Ingle, Morrison, McLean, Burrys. The coaches were Mr. Doyle and Mr. Murphy.*

~ 2 ~ *The girls' field hockey team of the Duke of Connaught High School, 1924. According to the donor's information, in the front row (left to right) are: unknown player, Clare Menton, Jean Saint, Helen McIntosh, and Anne Stoddart. The back row (left to right) are: Toots Douglas, Agnes Chapman, Miss*

Carmichael, Rose Bowden, the coach, Mr. McMillan, Pony Eickhoff, Jean Bews, Doreen Turnbull, and Brigit Hulth.

What also put New Westminster on the map as a "City of Champions" was field lacrosse. The Salmonbellies men's lacrosse team was formed in 1889. Vancouver and Victoria had formed teams three years earlier, and they faced New Westminster for the first time in 1890. By 1894 the Salmonbellies began an unrivalled dominance of the sport that would see them win the provincial title that year and up to 1910, with exceptions in 1896 and 1904.

In 1900, the team financed their tour to eastern Canada, and they played six matches in two weeks, never losing, drawing only once, and scoring forty goals against thirteen overall. In 1903 they went back and shut out the world-renowned Montreal Shamrocks. In 1908, the team went east again to national fame by winning its first Minto Cup, and they arrived in New Westminster by streetcar to a hero's welcome. Gilbert John Murray-Kynnynmon Elliott, the fourth Earl of Minto, was Governor General of Canada from 1898 to 1904, and it was he who donated the famous Minto Cup. He created it in 1901 to celebrate Canada's national sport, lacrosse, by giving it to Canada under the power of his office for the top senior lacrosse team in the country. The Salmonbellies defended the cup again in 1909 and won the Mann Cup in 1910. They went on to create a very successful team history by winning more Canadian championships than any other team in any sport. This tradition of excellence continues today.

~ 3 ~ *A B.C. Electric streetcar was assigned to carry the New Westminster Salmonbellies Lacrosse team back to New Westminster with the Minto Cup from the 1908 championship game after they defeated the Montreal Shamrocks. The cup is being held up by team members, just under the door to the back of the streetcar. There is a sign on the side of the streetcar, mostly behind the people, that reads, "New Westminster Lacrosse Team, Champions of the World." The athletes are standing in amongst their families. The team members were Jim Gifford, Len Turnbull, Jack Bryson, Irving Wintemute, Charles Galbraith, Bill Turnbull, Pete Latham, Doughy (or Cliff) Spring, George Rennie,*

3

Courtesy New Westminster Public Library #131. New Westminster Museum and Archives Collection. #1HP0567. Photographer: W.T. Cooksley.

Sandy Gray, Tom Rennie, Tom Gifford, Pat Feeney, and Charles A. Welsh, manager.

~ 4 ~ *The YMCA wrestling class of 1914–15. First row (left to right): W. Bell, D. Trapp, and D. McPhadden. Second row (left to right): S. Trapp, T. Osbourne, R. MacDonald, F. Spencer, and G. Trapp. Third row (left to right): W. Gilchrist, A. Mills, and G. Sovereien.*

~ 5 ~ *The war canoe races on the Fraser River in honour of Indian Days on June 4, 1967. The*

Courtesy New Westminster Public Library #91. New Westminster Museum and Archives Collection. #1HP0397. Photographer: Hurndall.

4

5

Courtesy New Westminster Public Library #1680. Sharon Dibble Collection. Photographer: Bob Dibble.

crowds go all along the shore in the background, and in behind them are teepees and tents with displays. Chief Dan George, who served the Squamish First Nations as their chief from 1951 to 1963, conducted the opening ceremonies at City Hall.

Fans and athletes have always shown great interest in professional and amateur sports in New Westminster. This interest and pride has been alive from the very beginning. The pride that is known to grow within any athlete has been reflected in the many portraits that were taken from our past, and can still be seen today. The community's men, women, and children have shone in many sports arenas over the years. Reflected in the photographs of our sports teams of the past is a great sense of camaraderie, pride, and enthusiasm for the games and team members. In 2004 the sports teams of the city unveiled a Sports Wall of Fame to honour our championship teams of the past and the individual and collective achievements of our "City of Champions."

Watching the Action

~ 6 ~ *In this 1908 crowd scene in the second row, third from the left, is Charles A. Welsh, manager of the New Westminster Salmonbellies Lacrosse team. In 1910 he served as a city councillor. Sitting in the front row, second from the left, is none other than A. Wellesley Gray. He served as a city councillor from 1907 to 1912 and as mayor from 1913 to 1920 and 1927 to 1933.*

Lacrosse was incredibly popular throughout the Lower Mainland during this time, and both the CPR and the B.C. Electric Railway ran lacrosse "specials" carrying fans from as far away as Vancouver to the field at Queens Park. Fifteen to twenty thousand fans attended the bigger games. New Westminster stores closed on Saturday afternoons for lacrosse games. Provincial and national lacrosse finals were often timed to occur in September during the Provincial Exhibition at Queens Park. Box lacrosse developed in the 1930s, played on the wood boards in Queens Park Arena. The teams won such a significant number of both Mann and Minto cups that New Westminster has become the site of Canada's Lacrosse Hall of Fame.

Courtesy New Westminster Public Library #208.

6

Courtesy New Westminster Public Library #2562.

7

~ 7 ~ *Crowds are in the stands in Queens Park during this circa 1912 Minto Cup lacrosse game. The advertisement on the building says, "Ask the Man for a Beaver Cigar made by Fred Lynch."*

The Beaver Cigar Factory first appeared in the 1904 B.C. directory.

~ 8 ~ *A Minto Cup game at Queens Park, 1912 or 1913. This is a wonderful crowd scene taken by professional photographer Samuel J. Ritchie, who was listed in the directory from 1909 to 1914. This photograph was made into a postcard. In 1912 and 1913, Minto Cup games were played in the park.*

~ 9 ~ *This is the newly lit Queens Park Stadium, circa 1948. It is reported that William M. Mott's New Westminster company, Mott Electric, installed these lights. Dan Mott is the grandson of*

Courtesy New Westminster Public Library #3057. White Rock Museum and Archives Collection. Marion Wilson Collection. Photographer: Samuel J. Ritchie.

8

Courtesy New Westminster Public Library #3113. Dan Mott Collection. Jack Lindsay Photographers Ltd.

9

Both 10 and 11 courtesy authors' collection.

10

11

William, the original owner of this photograph. William also served as a city councillor from 1937 to 1941 and then as mayor from 1943 to 1948. In this photo, he was attending a game of baseball.

~ 10 ~ *A women's YMCA ribbon for the Physical Culture Class of 1893–4. Around the YMCA symbol is the credo, "Educational, Devotional, Physical."*

~ 11 ~ *Enamel pin for the New Westminster Lawn Bowling Club, circa 1940s.*

Chapter 7

The Fruits of Our Own Labour

The world of work is all too often left out of any public discourse regarding heritage preservation and historic value. The lives and homes of successful pioneering city entrepreneurs are usually well known and often become the centrepiece of local histories and museums. Their wealth ensures their legacies through the naming of landmarks such as streets, public and private buildings, parks, plazas, squares, and monuments. Much more rare, and frequently undiscovered, are the names, lives, and collective contributions of the ordinary workers, both men and women.

New Westminster and British Columbia both owe their identities to the young men and women who came west to define or redefine themselves. Many wanted to be remembered as the new pioneers and to make their names as well as securing a living. Some wanted to make their fortunes by building industry and becoming the barons of the booming frontier. We imagine these individuals, cut from the mould of Colonel Moody, his Columbia Detachment of Royal Engineers, and the heroic women who came here to join them in a common cause, gazing with determination at the rough wooded bluff and seeing in their minds' eyes a new city surpassing in grandeur the places they had travelled from.

Men came from China dreaming of "Gold Mountain," a place to make a fortune through hard work and good luck. They encountered racial barriers as rigid and hard to scale as the province's many mountains and canyons. The stories of women who bravely challenged themselves by venturing into an adventurous new world were too often lost in the long-standing un-liberated attitude towards them. Life was hardest, though, for those men and women who were already here — the First Nations, driven from their lands, decimated by disease, and detached from their identities.

The history of New Westminster's industrial and working heritage is both complex and undervalued. However, this history alone would be worthy of a future book covering the lives of men and women working with and for the people of the city.

Working the Line

Early West Coast loggers found the techniques they had used back east were of little use: the trees were too large, the ground was too damp, and the rivers were too wild. They had to adapt, devising new techniques and new equipment to harvest B.C.'s forest giants. To avoid the denser wood at the base, and to cut the trees at the narrowest accessible point, the trees were notched and springboards inserted for the men to stand upon. From here they used two-man cross saws, drawing the large cutting teeth forward and back for most of a day facing great risks to fell just a single one of the enormous Douglas firs or cedars.

Moving the mighty trees through the mud and underbrush to get to the mills presented its own special challenges. Loggers employed what they called yarding logs, laid horizontally to form a "Skid Road" where teams of oxen or horses would drag the logs to the mill. This yarding process was referred to as "working the green line," and was used in the late nineteenth century. By the dawn of the new century the animal work teams had mostly been replaced by steam engines called spool donkeys.

Courtesy New Westminster Public Library #51. New Westminster Museum and Archives Collection. #1HP730121.

1

Working the line defined working life for many of the city's citizens, and there were working lines for many of New Westminster's businesses and industries. Shipbuilding was one of the earliest working lines in New Westminster, but there were many others.

~ 1 ~ *"Gilley Ave. near Kingsway," circa 1890. This photo shows the yarding logging process in its twilight years.*

~ 2 ~ *This picture marks the occasion of the end of a shipbuilding line. Taken on July 7, 1910, at Dawe's Shipyard, it shows the blessing and launching of the* Columbia II, *an Anglican missionary hospital boat. The photographer, W.T. Cooksley, shows Mrs. John Antle (wife of the Reverend Mr. J. Antle), who christened the boat. Her husband took command of the boat and sailed it away from the berth of its birth.*

Courtesy New Westminster Public Library #82. New Westminster Museum and Archives Collection. #1HP6403. Photographer: W.T. Cooksley.

2

Courtesy New Westminster Pubic Library #3163. Jozef Podejko Collection.

3

Courtesy New Westminster Public Library #3300. Fay West Collection.

4

~ 3 ~ *At the port of New Westminster, large loading gangs could load at a remarkable rate. This is the* Camilla Gilbert, *the first ore carrier to travel from New Westminster to Belgium on May 16, 1924. The ship is a Norwegian freighter and is moored at the wharf at the foot of Tenth Street. The longshoremen were able to load the* Camilla Gilbert *at the amazing rate of thirty tons of ore an hour.*

~ 4 ~ *Canneries were an early New Westminster industry. Taken by an unknown photographer in July 1930 during their lunch break, this photo shows the women who worked at the Broder Royal City Cannery at 12 Front Street, located near the Fraser River Railway Bridge.*

Other important working lines of the early residents shaped their identities and defined the nature and form of the city's development. New Westminster was the hub of the regional interurban transport network. Its central placement made it the natural location for the B.C. Electric Railway company's streetcar barns and the central interurban hub station. The fact that the car barns were near the Fraser River and just downstream from a large lumber processing mill, Royal City Mills, made it extremely easy to access, at low overhead, a plentiful supply of wood to construct and repair the streetcars.

~ 5 ~ *Shown here in full production line, circa 1946, is Queensborough's Heaps Engineering Company. The company was incorporated in*

Courtesy New Westminster Public Library #2473. Angus T. MacDonald Collection. Photographer: Stride Studios.

5

November 1911, after it had bought out the former Schaake Machine Works on the Queensborough waterfront. Heaps grew into one of the city's largest employers, especially during the two world wars, producing shells, propellers, and other equipment.

Working with People

~ 6 ~ *The interior front office of the Westminster Iron Works building at 66 Tenth Street in April 1920. The proprietor was John Reid, whose company did sawmill repairs, machine work, black-smithing, and even ornamental iron work for businesses and homes. It is likely that the sombre*

Courtesy New Westminster Public Library #2895. Joaquim Ayala Collection.

6

man with the moustache is John Reid, and he is watching his young clerk. On this building's site is now the London Drugs Store.

~ 7 ~ *This formal graduation photograph was taken by Stride Studios of New Westminster. It shows a portion of the Royal Columbian Hospital's School of Nursing in 1928. Seated in the front (left to right) are Isabel Cowie, Esther Paulson, and Marjorie Cunningham. In the back row (left to right) are Edna Edgar and Dorothy Miller.*

7

Courtesy New Westminster Public Library #3224. Esther Paulson Collection.

Courtesy New Westminster Public Library #2548. Donald MacDonald Collection. Photographer: Stride Studios.

8

~ 8 ~ *The interior office and reception of Alfred W. McLeod Ltd, Insurance Loans, Real Estate, and Retails, circa 1947. The company had just relocated from its previous offices at 50 Sixth Street to this location at 713 Columbia Street, in the Westminster Trust Building. McLeod, "The Insurance Man," was a powerful financier in New Westminster during the first half of the twentieth century.*

Courtesy New Westminster Public Library #2984.

9

~ 9 ~ *The main circulation desk of the New Westminster Public Library in 1948, with Ruth Cameron, chief librarian, on the left, and Alma Brundige, circula-*

Courtesy New Westminster Public Library #2983.

10

tion librarian, on the right. This was the interior of the Carnegie Library (1905–1958), formerly located at 705 Carnarvon Street.

~ 10 ~ The circulation desk of the Carnegie Library, this time in December 1956. The innovations of these book cataloguing and checkout machines were already dated by the time this picture was taken. The two librarians at work with their backs to the photographer are (left to right) Pam Williams, library assistant, and Pat Pratt, librarian.

CHAPTER 8

Buildings of Community

It Happens at City Hall

As mentioned earlier, New Westminster has the distinction of being the oldest city in Western Canada. Established on July 17, 1860, the New Westminster Municipal Council allowed for the election of seven aldermen, and all eligible voters had to be male and be property owners. The seven would then elect from amongst themselves one president. The title of the president was not changed to mayor until 1871, and it would be a further four years before voters were allowed to directly vote for their city's mayor. The motto of the new city was "In God We Trust," used before the United States of America chose it also. It wasn't until 1889 that the mayor's position was a paid one, and at that time the payment was set at $250 a year. All civic elections were conducted through the ward system until 1895. This was when the city adopted the at-large voting system for both its council and mayor. All positions were for one term until 1924, when terms became two years, then in 1996 they became three years.

Meetings were held quarterly or at the call of the president. At first the Council rented office space or met in the private residence of the city clerk. The early city clerks had to do most of the city hall's work, and among their duties were property assessment and tax and bill collecting. In 1889, the Council got its first real home, granted by the province in the old agricultural building and grounds on Agnes and Seventh streets. This building, destroyed in the Great Fire of 1898, had an assessed value of $2,653.86.

Courtesy New Westminster Public Library #158.

1

~ 1 ~ *The first City Council meeting after the Great Fire, in 1898. (From the lower left) Mayor Thomas Ovens, with city councillors J.T. Scott, M. Sinclair, R.C. McDonald, R.L. Reid, W.R. Gilley, J. Peck, and J.C. Brown. This Council had a very full agenda. Among its other important decisions it agreed that the city needed a new city hall as soon as possible to encourage civic confi-*

Courtesy New Westminster Public Library #210.
Jozef Podejko Collection. Photographer W. Brown.

2

dence within the city and investor confidence throughout the province.

~ 2 ~ *This postcard photograph, taken in 1918 by Mr. W. Brown, is the next New Westminster City Hall.*

Frederick J. Bauer was the architect of the new city hall, designed after the Great Fire. Bauer was quite productive in rebuilding the post-fire city before his death in 1909. During these ten years he also designed the Blackie Block, the Central Hotel, the Occidental Hotel, and the Schaake Machine Works.

Officially opened on September 27, 1901, on the 500 block of Columbia Street, this city hall was a striking building with great attention paid to its many details. Bauer personally ensured that the mayor and aldermen would each have highly polished oak desks. The first Council meeting in this new building was held October 28, 1901, of which a reporter wrote, "when the aldermen had finished admiring themselves in the polished surface of their respective desks, they came to order." (*Columbian*, October 29, 1901)

Space limitations led to the commissioning and building of the current city hall on Royal Avenue, which officially opened on November 19, 1953. The new city hall recently celebrated its fiftieth anniversary. Despite the nostalgia for the old city hall, the new location, with its fresh, modern style, pleased council and citizens alike when it was officially opened to great pomp and celebration.

Courtesy authors' collection. 8.PC.08

3

~ 3 ~ *Postcard of city hall, circa 1950s.*

A Lifetime of Learning

From the beginning in 1859, citizens showed a concern for the education of their children. One of the very first schools was established at the camp of the Columbian Detachment of Royal Engineers, serving the children of the sappers' families. However, the small number of children within New Westminster as a whole meant that it was not until April 1863 that there were enough pupils for the first public common school. This first school was in a cabin in the garden of the Reverend Mr. R. Jamieson. As one could imagine, the schoolyard provided to the children in the earliest years of the city was a stump-filled, rough and tumble terrain. Other schools followed the growth of the city's neighbourhoods.

4

~ 4 ~ *Sitting second from right in the front row is Edith Louise Johnston (b. 1884). She appears to be about ten to thirteen years old; therefore, this image was taken sometime between 1894 and 1897.*

~5 ~ *This image appeared in the* British Columbian Weekly *of September 3, 1912, with the caption, "New Queensborough School, one of the newer schools in the city of neat design, with basement playground."*

The first Queensborough School had been located above Joseph P. Crane's general store, but by 1912 the growth of Queensborough's population justified the construction of a full-sized school on Ewen Avenue.

Courtesy New Westminster Public Library #1790. Ted Clarke Collection.

5

Courtesy New Westminster Public Library #598.

6

~ 6 ~ *This image shows how the Providence Orphanage appeared fronting on Twelfth Street, 1932.*

By contrast, private schools in New Westminster were religious in origin. One notable example was the Providence Orphanage, established on the upper west side of Twelfth Street in 1900. This imposing four-storey brick building was located on the crest of the Twelfth Street hill, and it was visible from many points throughout the city. The architect of the building was one of the Sisters of Providence of Charity, Mother Joseph of the Sacred Heart (formerly Esther Pariseau, 1823–1902). She called the Providence Orphanage "the last of my children," having already distinguished herself as an architect of note by designing St. Mary's Hospital in New Westminster and the first St. Paul's Hospital in Vancouver. From its fourth-floor laundry area at the back of the building, the Sisters were able to see clearly west to the mouth of the Fraser, east to Langley, and south to Mount Baker in Washington State. The school was closed in 1959, and the building was taken down in 1960.

~ 7 ~ *The interior of the art room of Trapp Technical School in 1931. Trapp Tech, as it was known, was one of New Westminster's secondary schools. When examined with the aid of a loupe, the art on the walls reveals the fashions of the time.*

Courtesy New Westminster Public Library #1791. Ted Clarke Collection.

7

~8 ~ *This 1931 class photo of secondary school students at Duke of Connaught School shows a more sophisticated student body. These students would not be classified as teenagers, but rather as young adults. The expectation for these graduates was immediate entry into the working world. A rare few of them could afford the cost, or had the luxury of time, to attend a post-secondary college or university.*

~ 9 ~ *A graduation pendant for New Westminster Secondary School, circa 1950s.*

Courtesy authors' collection.

8

Courtesy New Westminster Public Library #1064.

Gathering in Faith

Many churches in New Westminster are as old as the city itself, and they have provided a familiar atmosphere for settlers to gather at for over a century. More than just a place of worship, these early churches were often touchstones to those feeling lost in the new world of unfamiliarity and harsh times. In the first few years of the young community, five or six churches were built.

~ 10 ~ *Holy Trinity church, circa 1860. The first established church was Methodist in 1859, with the first sermon by Rev. E. White, but Holy Trinity Anglican Church is much better known and is commonly called New Westminster's oldest church. This remarkable image captures the true feeling of the pioneering churches throughout British Columbia. Holy Trinity's first minister was the Reverend John Sheepshanks. New Westminster's first bishop was Acton Windeyer Sillitoe.*

Courtesy New Westminster Public Library #324.

10

Courtesy New Westminster Public Library #1881. Joe Plaskett Collection.

11

~ 11 ~ This photograph was taken on May 8, 1945, on the occasion of the eightieth anniversary of St. Mary's. St. Mary the Virgin Anglican Church was New Westminster's first Catholic church and is located at 121 East Columbia Street. The church's construction began on January 11, 1865, and was completed by March 20, 1865.

British Columbia's First Public Book Collection

New Westminster has the distinction of having the first public book collection in the province of British Columbia. The library opened its doors in 1865 after a fundraising campaign; it was known as the British Columbia Institute, and membership cost a dollar a year. The old wooden building that housed the library was torn down in 1890, and a striking three-storey brick one was built in 1892. Sadly, it was burnt in the 1898 fire, causing the loss of many rare and irreplaceable maps and books.

After the Great Fire, a temporary library and reading room was opened on April 24, 1899. It was located "on the side of the old drill shed, occupied since the fire by J.E. Philips and the William John Shoe Store," according to the *Daily Columbian* of April 24, 1899. This building housed the library for three years.

~ 12 ~ *Julian Peacock, librarian of the New Westminster Public Library from 1891 to 1898, circa 1884.*

Courtesy New Westminster Public Library #3227.

12

Courtesy New Westminster Public Library #3077.

13

Courtesy New Westminster Public Library #529.

14

~13 & 14 ~ *These two images show the temporary library's exterior and interior. A notice on the wall within the library, and seen in this photo, reads "visitors are cautioned against damaging in any way the newspapers, magazines or other reading matter or removing without authority any material from the reading room. Smoking, chewing, spitting and talking strictly prohibited."*

Courtesy New Westminster Public Library #2986.

15

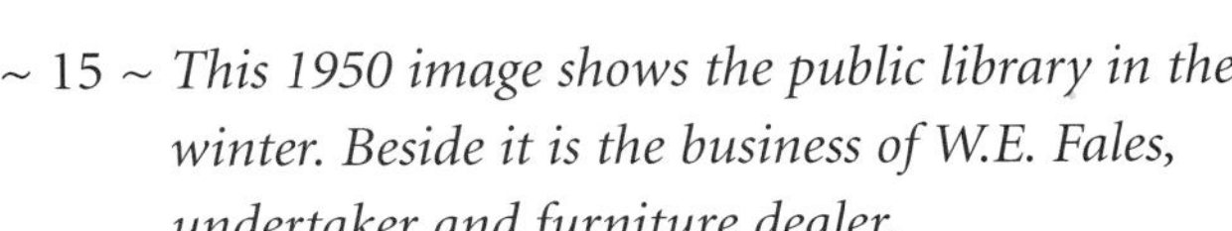

~ 15 ~ *This 1950 image shows the public library in the winter. Beside it is the business of W.E. Fales, undertaker and furniture dealer.*

After 1902, the library shared other spaces within the city. In 1905, the Carnegie Library was built, just off of New Westminster's Market Square. Andrew Carnegie (1835–1919), a true philanthropist, had bequeathed money from his personal fortune to build libraries such as this one all across North America. He had risen from rags to riches through education, and he believed that building these many libraries would provide individuals in poverty the opportunity for education, personal improvement, and success otherwise denied to them. His full-time occupation became granting his own money to communities around the world for the building of free public libraries. New Westminster received a Carnegie grant in 1902.

Courtesy New Westminster Public Library #2982

16

~ 16 ~ *This photo was taken during the opening ceremony for the current public library in New Westminster, at 716 Sixth Avenue, November 19, 1958.*

By the 1950s, the Carnegie Library was in need of repair and was deemed to have outlived its usefulness. The move of the library into the uptown area was a popular one given the growth in the number of residences and stores there. The construction of the Woodwards Centre (now the Royal Centre Mall) right across Sixth Avenue from the new library's site was viewed as another plus for relocation.

Further Serving the Written Word

~ 17 ~ *Cameo portrait of George William Grant, 1900.*

Courtesy New Westminster Public Library #1875.

17

One of the city's surviving gems is its old courthouse, built in 1891. It was designed by noted New Westminster architect George William Grant (1852–1925). Grant also designed many other significant buildings in the city, including the Provincial Exhibition Building in Queens Park (1889), the 1891 city library, and major additions to the Provincial Insane Asylum (Woodlands).

In total, Grant designed and supervised 117 projects between 1888 and 1892 at a total construction value of $919,000. The courthouse building was one of his

Courtesy New Westminster Public Library #69. New Westminster Museum and Archives Collection.

18

better known projects, whose construction costs came in just under $30,000.

~ 18 ~ *Grant's New Westminster Court House in January 1901.*

The courthouse opened on June 2, 1891, and the fine woodwork inside was viewed at the time as outstanding. Of particular note was the Judge Begbie Bench. The courthouse was to suffer two fires within the next seven years. The first, in 1894, was relatively minor. The second was the 1898 Great Fire, which completely burnt the courthouse's interior, including the Begbie Bench. Given the intensity of the fire, it was truly remarkable that so much of the building's outer shell remained; the courthouse was later rebuilt within its former walls. The old courthouse still stands behind today's courthouse, where it serves the dual purpose of

Courtesy New Westminster Public Library #1831. Mr. and Mrs. Johnston Collection.

19

providing storage space and a few offices for court staff and city lawyers.

~ 19 ~ *The Judge Begbie Bench at the New Westminster Court House, 1891.*

Postal service of some form dates back as long as the city and its environs have been settled. The first post office in New Westminster was in the house of Captain William Spalding, district magistrate for New Westminster. He was tasked with the establishment of the city's first post office and was eventually made the postmaster of the colony of British Columbia. A post office was built in Second Empire style in 1883, but was burnt in the 1898 fire. A second post office was quickly built to replace it at the corner of Sixth Street and Columbia in 1900. This post office was torn down in 1958 to make way for the Federal Building.

Courtesy authors' collection. #8.PC9.

20

~ 20 ~ *This photograph of the 1900 post office was sent on August 18, 1915, to Miss S. Lundiver in St. Paul, Minnesota. It reads "Vancouver, B.C. Aug. 13, 1915. Had a short visit with your Mother and she is enjoying herself. Left on train no.14 for Lake Louise and then will be home next Sunday afternoon. How is the little S.D.? Yours truly, Bain Burgh."*

Connecting and Bridging Together

Getting across the river from early New Westminster to South Westminster (later called Surrey) prior to 1904 was done by either ferry or private boat.

This all changed with the building of the remarkable Fraser River Bridge in 1905. Called the "million-dollar bridge," it was a marvel of civil engineering. It featured extremely deep caissons and innovative design ideas developed in response to the engineering challenges presented by the site.

Courtesy New Westminster Public Library #115. New Westminster Museum and Archives Collection.

21

Courtesy New Westminster Public Library #117.

22

Courtesy authors' collection. #8.PC10.

23

~ 21 ~ *This image was taken on July 23, 1905, and shows the engineers who built the bridge ceremonially riding the first train to cross the Fraser River Bridge.*

~ 22 ~ *Opening day for the Fraser River Bridge, July 23, 1905. The waiting spectators are given their first chance to walk right across the Fraser River. They would only have been able to cross the river in this manner during the winters if the river froze over.*

~ 23 ~ *This souvenir postcard, marked February 4, 1907, was sent almost two years after the bridge's opening. It was simply mailed to its recipient, Mrs.*

A.M. Allan of Tacoma, Washington, with no other written message. Its sender likely felt that the image and its embellishments said all that needed to be said.

The opening of the Fraser River Bridge was a major news event — it was celebrated as a commonwealth triumph and a monument for patriotic pride. The Fraser River Bridge served as a toll bridge for a short period of time, and carried trains, trams, cars, and pedestrians on its two levels. It was also able to "swing on a dime" from its middle to allow river passage. The bridge has reached its one hundredth anniversary, but it is now a railway bridge only and is now known as the Fraser Railway Bridge.

~ 24 ~ *This postcard is postmarked December 7, 1940, and was sent to Miss K. Gordon in Ontario. The text reads, "Hear it is a bit cold back there. You can't have everything. Today it is raining cats and dogs and the stores are so crowded with people and dripping wet umbrellas you wouldn't like it. Love from Mrs. Ironside."*

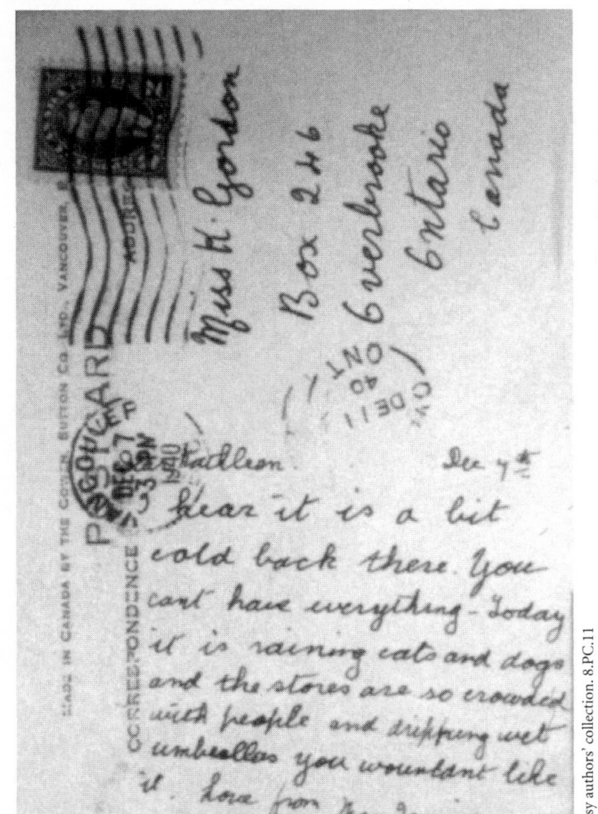

Miss K. Gordon
Box 246
Ontario
Canada

Kathleen Dec 7th
Hear it is a bit cold back there. You cant have everything - Today it is raining cats and dogs and the stores are so crowded with people and dripping wet umbrellas you wouldnt like it. Love from Mrs Ironside.

24

Courtesy authors' collection. 8.PC.11

The Fraser River Bridge was overshadowed only by the construction of the Pattullo Bridge. Built and opened in 1937, during the height of the Great Depression. The Puttullo Bridge's elegant arched design and expensive materials made it a politically symbolic structure, especially for the premier of the day, Thomas Dufferin "Duff" Pattullo, who named the bridge after himself. Duff was a New Deal–style liberal, and he used

Courtesy New Westminster Public Library #3109. Dan Mott Collection. Photographer: Stride Studios.

25

the bridge as a make-work project, which in turn could work for him as well.

~ 25 ~ *In November 1937, just prior to the bridge's official opening, William M. Mott, owner of Mott Electric Co. Ltd., had his portrait taken at the Pattullo Bridge. He is posed with a reel of cable of the type his company provided and installed during the construction of the Pattullo Bridge. In total, the company provided more than thirty-five thousand feet of lead cable and twenty thousand feet of conduit pipe, as well as the lighting.*

By the time the Pattullo Bridge opened on November 15, 1937, it had cost nearly $4 million for

Courtesy authors' collection.

26

four lanes — a million dollars a lane. This metal bridge continues to be the major direct vehicular transport link for New Westminster, and is now showing extensive fatigue from billions of journeys over it.

~ 26 ~ *Souvenir luggage sticker from the opening of the Pattullo. It reads, "Guests of the Royal City, New Westminster, British Columbia."*

Chapter 9

In Case of Emergency Call…

Today calling 911, you will be asked, "Police, fire, or ambulance?" But early residents often had to depend upon volunteers to help them out in the event of an emergency, and getting out the message for help was only the first challenge when these services were established.

Call the Police!

Policing the Royal City and the river was just one of the concerns in the community during the Gold Rush and the early wild days of a new colony. The first inspector of police was Charles Brew, a former inspector with the Irish Constabulary in County Cork who had also served in the Crimean War. However, he resigned his post in 1859 to become chief magistrate. The city had scarcely any recorded crime, as early policing was primarily of the "drunk and disorderly" type, requiring merely a night to sleep it off. Early police officers were volunteers. The first paid officer, Jonathon Morey, a former Royal Engineer sergeant, was hired in 1873.

Courtesy New Westminster Public Library #909.

1

~ 1 ~ *This photograph, taken in 1892, shows all nine members of the City of New Westminster Police Force, including Mayor W.B. Townsend (far left in the front row), seated beside Chief William Hutson (second from the left). 1892 was the only year the police force had that many members until 1910.*

By 1891, the police force had a number of constables and began regular patrols, known as "walking a beat" (either day patrol, from 7:00 a.m. to 6:00 p.m., or night patrol, from 6:00 p.m. to 7:00 a.m.). This was the beginning of a regular city police department.

Putting Out Fires

The first New Westminster fire department was a volunteer brigade organized in the summer of 1861. It called itself Hyack Company, No. 1. (The word *hyack* means "quickly, quickly" in the Chinook trade language.) Fire was a constant risk in the nineteenth century since most of the buildings were constructed of wood and used wood-burning stoves and furnaces. Their first fire engine was dubbed the "Fire King." It had been purchased at the steep cost of $2,600 from San Francisco, along with five hundred feet of hose for an additional $500. The Hyack Company faced its greatest challenge in 1898.

~ 2 ~ *This remarkable image from 1861 shows a horse-drawn firefighting hose wagon at full gallop. To capture this image on film at that time was extremely rare. It is truly going* hyack.

Courtesy New Westminster Public Library #1842. Mr. and Mrs. William Johnson Collection.

2

From 1889 to 1919, horses played an important role in firefighting. Their strength and speed meant a faster response and the arrival of fresher, more energetic firemen at the fire scene. There are stories about horses that were trained to immediately assume their positions when the fire bell rang, ready to be harnessed. Their training was so ingrained that there are also stories of retired horses rushing to their former fire stations long after they were put out to pasture. The last fire horses were driven by Fire Chief C.J. Highsted to the city market in 1919 to be sold at auction.

Courtesy New Westminster Public Library #1685. File #80, Sharon Dibble Collection.

4

~ 3 ~ *The New Westminster Fire Department of 1915 was photographed near the City Market at Lytton Square. Up in the background, observing the photographer at work and watching the impressive fire department, are regular townsfolk. These people are unaware that they add to the impressiveness of the scene. Or did the photographer set them up as part of the image?*

~ 4 ~ *Three firemen riding a fire truck down Eleventh Street's hill, near the intersection with Queen's Avenue and Auckland, 1971. Photographer Bob Dibble, owner of Crofton Studios in Burnaby, rides along facing backwards to record this moment. The men are wearing the very first firefighters' helmets in the city.*

Get to Our Hospitals!

Personal health and safety were of much concern in early New Westminster. Diseases were caused by a lack of sanitation or were carried ashore by travellers and boat traffic. Also, what today would be a minor injury could be fatal in this frontier environment. Smallpox became an epidemic in the area in 1879, and the city responded

Courtesy New Westminster Public Library #105. New Westminster Museum and Archives Collection. #1HP0452. Photographer: H.E. Leash.

3

with isolation and quarantines. One such isolation hospital was located in the Douglas Street Graveyard, on the current site of the secondary school grounds.

The 1862 Royal Columbian Hospital, the first in mainland British Columbia, was a modest one-storey affair at its Agnes and Fourth streets location. The size was inadequate, and the building of a new hospital in Sapperton was used as an enticement to have that community join with the city.

Courtesy authors' collection #9.PC12.

5

~ 5 ~ *Royal Columbian Hospital postcard, 1891.*

The talented partnership of Charles Clow and Samuel Maclure became the design team of the second Royal Columbian. Their striking hospital, with its rural and stately nature, enhanced their reputations, and was much admired when it opened in 1889. Eventually, community needs required that the 1889 hospital be taken down and replaced by a larger and more modern building.

Opening in 1912, the new Royal Columbian Hospital building was designed by S.R.B. Birds and could accommodate 170 patients within its three storeys. Further additions were made during the First World War, and, purely by luck, these were in place for the 1918 influenza pandemic, which struck predominantly healthy twenty- to forty-year-olds and killed 40 million people worldwide.

An earlier hospital had been opened on July 6, 1887, by the Sisters of Providence at Agnes Street, a couple of blocks above Albert Crescent. It was called St. Mary's Hospital and was designed by Mother Joseph, who also later designed the Providence Orphanage. This hospital survived the 1898 fire, which stopped right near its grounds. The *Daily Columbian* newspaper wrote that the Sisters had held a statue or a picture of the Virgin toward the flames, saving the hospital, which was seen by many as a minor miracle.

Courtesy authors' collection #9.PC13.

6

~ 6 ~ *Royal Columbian Hospital, 1912. This image comes from a colour-tinted postcard.*

Courtesy New Westminster Public Library #998. *Columbian* Newspaper Collection.

7

Both of these original hospital buildings, the Royal Columbian and St. Mary's, were eventually torn down and replaced with more modern buildings in similar locations. Just this year, St. Mary's was closed and the site sold to a developer, ending 137 years of service to the community.

~ 7 ~ *St. Mary's Hospital, circa 1954.*

A Group Effort

Sometimes the magnitude of an emergency has the potential to overwhelm the emergency response sys-

Courtesy New Westminster Public Library #3085. Dan Mott Collection. Photographer: Crofton Studios.Columbian Newspaper Collection.

8

tem. At such times, all must pitch in and work together. One such instance for New Westminster was the 1948 spring flood. It was not the worst flood in living memory for the Fraser Valley (that occurred in 1894), but it was the second worst, and it was the most expensive. In the three weeks from May 27 to June 10, 1948, the Fraser rose by three feet as a heat wave caused the heavier than normal snow pack to melt and pour down the Fraser in a massive pulse that threatened to breach the dykes constructed in the years since 1894. Within New Westminster, Queensborough was at the greatest risk.

The flooding began to be noticeable by May, up the Fraser Valley at a place called Bonaparte Creek, near Cache Creek. As the flood hit the valley, wide areas of fertile flat land came to resemble shallow inland lakes.

~ 8 *Filling sand bags for the Queensborough dykes at the CPA plant, May–June 1948.*

~ 9 *Laying sandbags at the Queensborough dykes, May–June 1948.*

Courtesy New Westminster Public Library #3085, #3092. Dan Mott Collection. Photographer: Crofton Studios.Columbian Newspaper Ccollection.

9

To meet the challenge, all had to pitch in. Approximately 1 million sand bags were filled at the CPA plant, then carried to and placed along the dykes over a three-week period, eventually winning the war against the waters in Queensborough.

It was reported that in 1894's great flood, once the waters had subsided there weren't any dead salmon found by the retreating waters along Columbia Street. However, according to one written source, a woman living down by the Fraser Mills had caught a live salmon under her bed.

Chapter 10

The Great Fire

The Fire

"The Day Before the Fire of '98"

I'd sailed to all the ports of call from Boston to
Bombay,
Always yearning for a place to settle down;
then I found the Royal City, and knew that I would
stay;
it seemed to me the perfect frontier town.

For it had a river ambience — a flavour all its own,
It faced south on a wooded, sun-lit knoll;
Downtown were sights and sounds and smells, like
none I'd ever known,
And that became my favourite place to stroll.

I'd walk along the waterfront to watch the paddle
streamers
Loading passengers and firewood and freight,
I'd mingle with the miners, gamblers, showgirls,
drunks and dreamers,
Who were headed for the "Trail of Ninety-Eight."

On Columbia were clopping horses, clanging
streetcar bells,
Shouts and barking dogs and squeaking wheels,
A mix of baking bread, saloon, and livery stable
smells,
And characters like Irving, Edmonds, Peale.

We'd had a vintage summer, as townsfolk will
remember,
And were getting set to host our big fall fair;
I recall that when I strolled downtown that 10th
day of September,
The birds were still, and smoke hung in the air.

A sailing man, I should have seen these omens as a
warning,
But didn't guess at fate's destructive scheme;
For the rivertown I'd come to love had vanished by
next morning —
Had vanished ... like a half-remembered dream.

The fire had burnt to ashes the toil of forty years,
But there wasn't time for sadness or self-pity;
It was time to prove our townsfolk had the stuff of
pioneers —
Time to build a bigger, better Royal City.

— Don Benson,
New Westminster poet laureate

September 1898 was part of one of those very dry, hot summers in New Westminster, the kind that, if it were this year, would result in the inconvenience of watering restrictions and brown lawns. Something much more akin to 2003's interior forest fires was what awaited the city in this, its most tragic year.

September 11, 1898, the city ended up with its downtown centre in rubble and ash, its citizens wandering in shocked and dazed disbelief at the changed condition of their once prosperous streets. The city had been reduced to blackened and smouldering shells in one night, and the damage was devastating — but it could have been much worse.

The fire began at about 11:00 p.m. on the night of September 10, 1898. The night was hot and dry, and the wind was blowing inward from the Fraser River. It is certain that the fire began near or at the Brackman and Kerr wharf at the waterfront's eastern end. It was likely a huge pile of hay on their dock (about two hundred tons) that went up first. Then the unexpected happened: the ignited dockside burnt through the mooring ropes of three sternwheeler steamers, the *Edgar*, the *Gladys*, and the *Bon Accord*. The flaming ships ignited the warehouses and docks as they bumped and bashed their way along like Viking funeral ships. These new fires amplified the flames already spreading along the waterfront.

Courtesy New Westminster Public Library #1438 / Vancouver City Archives.

1

~ 1 ~ *Front Street from Begbie, September 10, 1898.*

As the wind picked up, it further fuelled the firestorm. Flames jumped to Columbia Street, spreading quickly along the north side, up and along the downtown area. The many covered wooden culverts of former stream courses underneath Columbia Street made the fire spread even faster. These had been built to make the street more level. However, the culverts were full of scrap wood, old brush, and rubbish that fed the fire into buildings' basements while they were also being burnt from above. This process was terrible in its effectiveness. Curious onlookers quickly rushed home and began rescuing their household belongings, carrying them further and further uptown. Buildings literally exploded in the uncontrollable heat. The local Hyack fire brigade lost their station quickly and fought the flames to marginal effect with hand pumping machines and an unfortunately lowered water pressure.

The emergency response failed in part because the alderman who was sent up the hill with the key to open the fourteen-inch fire gate connecting to the twenty-two-inch main found that he couldn't operate the complicated system. In his confusion he left the key beside the valve and began helping nearby residents move furniture instead. Remarkably, a message was sent to the Vancouver Fire Department, and within seventy-five minutes after the fire had started, Chief Carlisle arrived with reinforcements and two hose reels that could pump from the river. Carlisle is credited with saving the Burr Block and protecting the eastern slope. To the west, the fire was brought to a halt near 10th Street. By daybreak, the wind reversed its course, and the fire burnt itself out. The smoking, sizzling, and smells lingered for months. Amazingly, no loss of life was recorded, but the loss in personal and business property was substantial. The city had suffered a blow much greater than its loss of capital status thirty years before.

~ 2 ~ *The view of New Westminster from across the Fraser River the morning after the Great Fire, showing the burnt-out shells of what was once the bustling heart of the downtown. From this perspective it can be seen that the fire's advance had been stopped before cresting the hilltop, which is at approximately Royal Avenue. The wide street coming down the hill near the photo's left side is Eighth Street. The fire's western-most edge is off the left of the picture. The right side of the picture shows the burnt-out Begbie Block beside the visibly undamaged Burr Block.*

Courtesy New Westminster Public Library #3140. Spohn Collection.

2

~ 3 ~ *This image is taken from the roof of the Burr Block looking directly west into the heart of the Great Fire's burn zone. This was Chief Carlisle's rooftop vantage point. This photograph could*

Courtesy New Westminster Public Library #238. Photographer: S.J. Thompson.

3

very well be mistaken for any city bombed during one of history's world wars. The arch near the image's centre is all that remains of the YMCA building. Directly behind it were City Hall, the city library, Hyack Hall, and the post office.

~ 4 ~ *In the morning after the devastation, people walk bewilderedly along the remains of a once proud Columbia Street.*

Courtesy authors' collection.

5

~ 5 ~ *A fork and spoon, burnt, melted, and blackened by fire. They were uncovered at a dig by the authors in 2004 at the 700 block of Agnes Street, near the western perimeter of the 1898 Great Fire zone. This area was used as a dumping ground for the refuse from the fire.*

Courtesy New Westminster Public Library #321.

4

Courtesy New Westminster Public Library #25. New Westminster Museum and Archives Collection #1HP0318. Photographer: S.J. Thompson.

6

~ 6 ~ *All that remained of the courthouse. The rebuilding of the courthouse within the remaining shell would have seemed a remote possibility on this morning.*

Courtesy New Westminster Public Library #275.

7

~ 7 ~ *Going through the rubble and burnt remains, people lay out books that had somehow been saved from the fire. These could be records from the courthouse, which had had many of its documents kept from disaster in a large safe.*

~ 8 ~ *One person to experience a lucky escape was the Reverend Alfred Shildrick, the fifth rector of Holy Trinity Church (from 1898 to 1910). He had become the church rector on April 22, 1898. He became somewhat famous for having the presence of mind to grab a wheelbarrow and pile it high with the church's records, lectern, and candlesticks, then to wheel this burden and himself to safety ahead of the flames. The church itself was burnt to a shell, with only its outer stone walls surviving.*

Courtesy New Westminster Public Library #1643. Lucy Chambers Collection. Photographer: Easthope of New Westminster.

8

Courtesy New Westminster Public Library #268.

9

~ 9 ~ *Within several weeks after the Great Fire, it became a novelty to stroll through the burn zone, rather than a horror. These men are standing by the bells of Holy Trinity Anglican Church. The man at the far left is Reverend Alfred Shildrick. The other two are not identified. A group of women stand together on Church Street, making these bells a strange and sad reminder of the street's namesake. The Reverend Mr. Shildrick is almost certainly thinking of his near escape with a few precious items, and the overwhelming loss of the church of which he'd been rector for only five months.*

The rest of that September was a turning point in the formation of New Westminster's character. Some

Courtesy New Westminster Public Library #2433. Lougheed Collection.

10

felt they could not stay and decided to move on, but others doubled their efforts and advanced the civic pride with resilience. It was not long before makeshift accommodations for businesses established themselves.

~ 10 ~ *Lost in the fire was the original City Market, built in 1892. It had been an early victim of the blaze, being near the waterfront wharves. The open-air market shown here has the feel of a garage sale rather than an official and vibrant marketplace.*

~ 11 ~ *Reichenbach Meats was the first business back on Columbia Street, but another early business was T.J. Trapp and Co. shown here one week after the Great Fire. They have built a small lean-to and painted a business sign for the front out of building paper. (Left to right) Tom Hunter, Jack*

Courtesy New Westminster Public Library #24. New Westminster Museum and Archives Collection. #1HP0341.

11

Poindester, George Blakeley, T.J. Trapp, and Robert Bulf. Behind them are the remains of the courthouse. The horse wagon on the left had been inside the Trapp store the night of the fire, containing twenty cases of dynamite. According to accounts, T.J. Trapp got the wagon out on the night of the fire and "had it run across the Lulu Island Bridge by a gang of chinamen, while [he] got the rest of the powder out of the store and backed it up the hill."

12

Courtesy New Westminster Public Library #222. *Columbian* Newspaper Collection.

~ 12 ~ *This picture of the corner of McKenzie and Agnes streets captures a later stage of the come-back of the downtown after the fire. All of these wooden-framed business buildings had been well-established within fine brick, wood, and stone just several weeks before. They now look like a newly built Wild West town, not a city established fifty years earlier.*

Just One Year Later

Although it was a personal and emotional tragedy for many citizens, and the memory of the fire's events and aftermath stayed with them the rest of their lives, most people remained in the city or nearby. New Westminster had built itself into a great city out of the wilderness — why not do it all over again, and this time do it even better?

~ 13 ~ *By shooting from on top of the Burr Block, this unknown photographer was most likely recreating S.J. Thompson's famous image to highlight the progress made by the city in just a year. The domed building with the roof skylight in the centre is the Bank of Montreal, designed by architect Francis Rattenbury. At the time of this picture it was not yet opened. The street activity shows a city that has regained its momentum and optimism.*

Courtesy New Westminster Public Library #1650. Chambers Collection.

13

Within a year, New Westminster citizens could well celebrate their success, and the newspapers in New Westminster, Victoria, and Vancouver recognized the anniversary with special editions, all sharing images of the Royal City as a phoenix rising out from the ashes of the 1898 Great Fire.

Chapter 11

"The Robbery of the Century"

THE BRITISH COLUMBIAN

4 P.M. EDITION

NEW WESTMINSTER, SATURDAY, NOVEMBER 4, 1911.

DAILY 4 AND 6 P.M.

ONDUCTOR KILLED ON RUNAWAY TRAIN

ive Freight Cars And Electric Shunter Take Wild Dash Down Steep Grade on Twelfth—Train Left Track on Curve at Royal Avenue And Piled Up in Ruins—Motorman in Hospital—Brakemen Escape Luckily.

OUTLOOK IS BRIGHT

PUSHING GOOD ROADS

JOHN BOZYK IS THE ALLEGED BURGLAR

One Armed Man Whose Strange Experience With Dyna mite Attracted Attention of Authorities Last Winte Is Prisoner in City Lock-up—Was First Caught i Chinatown, Vancouver—Had Thousands of Dollars.

~ 1 ~ *This is the Bank of Montreal at 511 Columbia Street at the corner of Church Street, circa 1935. The bank manager at the time was George Brymner, who, on his retirement, became the second owner of the Melrose estate in the West End. Construction on this building began in the year after the Great Fire destroyed the previous bank. The building was torn down in 1946 and replaced with the current building, done in the International style, with its exterior facade displaying a sculptured mural. This photograph was taken by the donor's father, who worked as an accountant for the bank from 1933 to 1938.*

Courtesy New Westminster Public Library #3240. Eveline Burman Collection. Photographer: Joseph Burman

1

In what was billed as the greatest bank robbery that ever occurred on the North American continent — "the robbery of the century" — New Westminster's Bank of Montreal made front-page news on September 15, 1911, spectacularly contrasting the positive headlines of its grand opening a dozen years before. The news went international thanks to the amount of loot stolen and the boldness and intrigue of the caper.

In total, the thieves made off with an astonishing swag that included $258,000 in bundled bills and 150 pounds of gold (worth an additional $20,000). The style in which the crime was executed surpassed the panache of "Grey Fox" Billy Miner's train robberies at Mission (1904) and Kamloops (1906) combined, and newspapers suspected that it was remaining members of Miner's gang who committed the robbery.

The total number of thieves is unknown. Sources tend to say there were five members, given the logistics and speed of the robbery. However, a Chinese janitor named Hong (at the time menial workers were referred to by last names only) had come in at 4:00 a.m. to start the fires and clean up. Instead, he was met at the door at gunpoint, gagged, taken down to the bank's basement, and hog-tied to a chair. Hong stated he saw only three masked men. Investigators suspected there were more.

They had entered the bank by digging their way into the vault and using nitroglycerine with such skill that it did not shake the Lavery Block adjacent to the bank or disturb the block's residents, asleep in the building's second-floor apartments. In its account of the crime, the *British Columbian* marvelled that the break-in had not aroused the police, since their station was only seventy feet from the bank, directly behind the Lavery Block.

How long it had taken them to get into the bank is not known, but their escape was rapid. The gang must have carried suitcases crammed full, because thousands of dollars' worth of bills and gold were left strewn across the floor. They left by about 5:00 a.m. By 5:30 a.m., Hong worked his hands free and ran to the police station to sound the alarm. The large amount of money was in the bank for that week's scheduled paydays for the salmon fishermen, the Fraser Mills, and other large businesses up the valley.

The *British Columbian* concluded, "From the professional burglar's standpoint it was the neatest, cleanest, best-planned job and the biggest cash haul ever pulled off in the Western Hemisphere and will go down in the annals of crime as a classic."

Later that day a high-powered roadster (a McLaughlin-Buick valued at $3,000) owned by T.J. Trapp was reported stolen from his garage on Cunningham Street. The car had been rolled down Royal Avenue in an attempt to jumpstart it, but the theft of the getaway car failed due to a missing sparkplug. It was found abandoned at the bottom of the hill at Royal Avenue's steepest point.

Investigators believed that since about $150,000 of the bills stolen were new, they might appear and be easily identified. It was also possible that money might still be found in or near New Westminster.

The first break in the case came when some of the loot was found stashed under an old boardwalk at Fourth and Carnarvon streets, only a few blocks from the bank. City workers who were repairing the street made the discovery and quickly notified the police. Chief of Police George T. Bradshaw arrived to personally take charge of $23,080 of the missing swag.

The second break occurred on October 31, 1911. Vancouver police arrested suspect John Bozyk and turned him over to the New Westminster detachment on November 3, 1911. He had become the prime suspect for a number of reasons. First, he had been found with $4,700 of the stolen money (some of which he had spent in Vancouver on costly personal items and a handgun, some in his pocket, the rest at his well-furnished Vancouver hotel room). Second, he was missing an eye and one arm from an old dynamite explosion that was later found in public record. Bozyk, a resident of New Westminster at the time, claimed he had been walking along the railway tracks near the waterfront in Sapperton when he picked up an old tobacco tin on the rails below East Columbia Street. According to Bozyk it was a complete surprise when the dynamite-filled tin exploded in his hand, causing his disfigurement. Bozyk became known locally as "that odd young Russian." He sold copies of the *British Columbian* at the BCER station and unsuccessfully attempted to sue the city for negligence. The police suspected he had made or transported a bomb for criminal purposes. To cap it all off, Bozyk had not been seen in town since the night of the robbery.

The true story emerged during Bozyk's arraignment before Police Magistrate Henry Lovekin Edmonds, son of former mayor H.V. Edmonds. An eleven-year-old paperboy named George Lavery, son of the owner of the Lavery Block, testified that he'd skipped school and walked by the ravine near Carnarvon Street, where he saw something under the footbridge. It turned out to be a bundle of bills amounting to $5,000. Young Lavery had put $500 in his pocket, leaving the rest. John Bozyk soon came upon him, took the money from him, obtained the rest from the ravine, and went to Vancouver. Bozyk was found guilty on the sole charge of possession of stolen money.

It was not until January 1912 that two of the men accused of having been leaders in the robbery were arrested in the United States: John McNamara in New York (in possession of only $1,000) and Charles Dean in Los Angeles (in possession of a large amount of currency). They both fought hard against extradition for over a year. Chief Bradshaw and two agents from Pinkerton's smuggled Charles Dean over the border into Canada and back to New Westminster on August 10, 1912, to face charges. After facing two trials, he was acquitted of all charges in October 1913. He quickly returned to the United States, and was eventually murdered.

John McNamara, also known as "Australian Mac" and "Big John," was sent back to New Westminster to face charges — not of masterminding the robbery, which he very likely was a part of, but for attempting to steal T.J. Trapp's car. He was found guilty and sentenced to nine years in the B.C. Penitentiary.

After being arrested in Toronto in possession of over $9,000 traced to the Bank of Montreal, Walter Davis was acquitted in New Westminster on lack of evidence, but was re-arrested and pleaded guilty, serving six months in Toronto. Arrested in Detroit earlier that same year, William McCorkill (alias Martin Powell and Chas. Butcher) was found in possession of Canadian currency amounting to $4,000. The balance of the loot was never recovered.

Courtesy New Westminster Public Library #3242. Eveline Burman Collection. Photographer: Joseph Burman.

2

~ 2 ~ *Shown in the centre of the photograph are the two lockable tellers' cages, circa 1935. The farthest cages over were for the coin teller and the head teller.*

Chapter 12

Ever on the Move

In the early days of New Westminster, the journey was as important as the destination. A slower pace of life was reflected in the way people went from point A to point B. However, the Victorians equated movement with progress. The pace steadily increased over the years with more innovations in the technology of transportation. Now it seems many of us would like a somewhat slower journey as a means to get away from a world where everything is on the move.

~ 1 ~ *This image of Columbia Street, looking east from the western side of Albert Crescent, circa 1911, includes aspects of most forms of early travel in New Westminster: on foot, by horse, on rail, and on rubber.*

On Foot

Early New Westminster citizens were forced to contend with uneven roads and trails. When they walked they often did so through mud or, if more fortunate, on wooden sidewalks. Rarely did they relish long walks on unlit pathways. Columbia Street and other

1

Courtesy New Westminster Public Library #2398. Edward Greame Collection.

Courtesy New Westminster Public Library #880. Columbian Collection.

2

areas were transected by gullies, canyons, and streams. Early on, the sappers graded the streets and built culverts over the obviously treacherous spots. The nicer neighbourhoods could afford smoother sidewalks and treed, flowery boulevards. But journeying on foot required preparation for the elements, and watching where your feet fell. Dorothy Bilton recalls the uneven boards on wooden sidewalks that she and her brother ran on. She remembers lots of scraped and painful knees as a result.

~ 2 ~ *This postcard image was taken circa 1910 and shows "Lovers' Walk," actually First Street, on the Queens Park side of the street. The little boy and girl are standing beside this lovely promenade, behind the wooden fence of Queens Park.*

By Horse

In early times, to travel any real distance at any real speed meant travelling by horse. The streets of the early city saw a variety of traps, wagons, stagecoaches, and even single riders on horseback.

~ 3 ~ *Central Livery Feed and Sale Stable, shown here circa 1910, was located on Eighth Street on its western side, and the image is looking downhill toward Columbia Street. Behind and downhill from the building is the Central Hotel, facing Columbia Street and flying a flag from its rooftop. Taken at the transition to automobile transportation, the image marks the end of the horse as primary transportation. The Central Livery Feed and Sale Stable became the Dunsmuir Hotel after it was fully converted to housing humans, not horses.*

Courtesy New Westminster Public Library #139. *Columbian* Newspaper Collection.

3

Liveries and feed stables were successful businesses, as was the re-shoeing of horses and the repair of damaged axles and wheels.

Horse travel was uncomfortable by today's standards, especially since even the best carriages and coaches had solid wooden wheels and leather shock absorbers.

Rarely would a stagecoach travel at night, for even with lanterns visibility was lost in the dark. Major roads from New Westminster, like the trail to Vancouver or the North Road to Port Moody, had coach houses at strategic points with food, lodging, and stables at the back for travellers planning or forced to stay overnight during a trip that today would be an hour's drive.

On Rails

One of the items granted to British Columbia upon entering into Confederation in 1871 was a trans-Canadian railway. As the largest and most profitable port city on the West Coast, New Westminster had every expectation that it would become the western terminus of the Canadian Pacific Railway and would reap the benefits that naturally went along with such status. It was this optimistic outlook that softened the blow for many citizens regarding the city's loss of capital status. The train took a long time in coming, and when it did it passed far north of New Westminster, not along the Fraser River's shore. Instead it passed by Port Moody to Gastown and then to Granville, planting the seed that would continue the growth of Vancouver. It was only strong lobbying and special agreements of sale that enticed the CPR to extend a branch line south into New Westminster in December 1887, after the company had received $75,000 and free right-of-way.

~ 4 ~ *New Westminster's landmark CPR station at the foot of Eighth and Front streets, circa 1905. The station had been rebuilt in 1899 after the Great Fire in the Château style using local brick and stone, upon the orders of William Van Horne. It was designed by the official hotel architect, at a cost to the company of $35,000. This was seen by the city as a vote confidence from the company.*

Courtesy New Westminster Public Library #1129.

4

On Valentine's Day 1891, the U.S. Great Northern Railway officially opened a line into New Westminster. The city became a rail hub after the construction of the 1904 Fraser River Bridge and the establishment of the Canadian National Railway's regular service along the Fraser River, which arrived on October 15, 1915.

~ 5 ~ *Print taken from an original postcard. Taken circa 1918, just before mounting the Fraser River Railway Bridge, this image shows a Great Northern train leaving New Westminster and heading south to Seattle. Having just passed below the sites of the B.C. Penitentiary and the Provincial Hospital for the Insane, it is cornering around the Royal City Cannery on the image's lower right side.*

Courtesy New Westminster Public Library #3150. Jozef Podejko Collection.

5

~ 6 ~ *Railway accidents occasionally occurred, and the aftermath was usually quite spectacular. This image comes from a negative entitled "Brunette Saw Mill 1905," and this train has fallen through the wooden bridge crossing the Brunette River before reaching the sawmill. What is particularly unusual is the apparent ease of the collected sightseers. The crowd includes men, women, small children, and even dogs and a horse. All seem unconcerned about the threat posed to them*

Courtesy New Westminster Public Library #79. New Westminster Museum and Archives Collection.

6

should the engine's weight have compromised the safety of the wooden wharf they are on. There are even several boys clambering on top of the engine's "cow catcher" front grill.

~ 7 ~ *This image was taken in 1912 and shows a street-car heading east along Columbia Street as it approaches Albert Crescent, where Columbia intersects with Elliot Street, at the lower western corner of the neighbourhood. This streetcar was run by the BCER, the second streetcar company to operate within New Westminster.*

Courtesy New Westminster Public Library #142. Marjorie and Edward Greame Collection.

7

The first streetcars in New Westminster began with the formation of the New Westminster Street Railway and Vancouver Electric Railway and Light Company, commonly known as the Westminster and Vancouver Tramway Company (W&VTC), incorporated in 1890. Bringing rails all the way from England, they started construction in November of a twelve-mile track that would leave the CPR station and loop through New Westminster along Royal Avenue.

To build it they had to overcome a substantial grade (sometimes as high as 11 percent), a technical as well as a financial challenge. When they connected this line directly to Vancouver in 1890, it became the longest track in Canada. Between 1891 and 1892, they began and finished a rail network within the city, spurring further growth and civic pride. The W&VTC soon went bankrupt in the depression of the early 1890s and was taken over by a newly formed company, the British Columbia Electric Railway Company Limited, incorporated on April 3, 1897. The BCER also purchased and consolidated the streetcar lines of Vancouver and Victoria.

The BCER located its new interurban station for the region adjacent to the CPR station, and it took over the building and repair of its streetcars and larger interurban cars in its own car barns in February 1903. The city streetcars ran with two operators up until the 1920s, but were downsized to a single operator by the 1930s. At its height, the BCER was running more streetcars than San Francisco, and it had the distinction of the longest line of streetcar track in Canada. On September 26, 1911, the BCER opened expanded car barns at the western foot of Twelfth Street, along with an expanded interurban depot as the hub at the previous site, located at 760 Columbia Street.

Prior to the 1912 royal visit of the Duke of Connaught, the BCER designed and built a BCER interurban car called the "Duke of Connaught" at the Twelfth Street car barn. The duke used this car to travel from Vancouver through Burnaby along Kingsway, then through New Westminster down Twelfth Street, arriving at the downtown station in style. After the

Courtesy New Westminster Public Library #2320. Graham McDonnell Collection.

8

visit the car was renamed car #1304 and ran along the Fraser Valley line all the way to Chilliwack from New Westminster. The car caught fire in October 1945 while it was travelling along the Vedder Mountain rail line, and the motorman only noticed the flames as the car entered Cloverdale. The fire burnt the car right down to its waistline. However, after being rebuilt, car #1304 ran the BCER lines for four more years, from 1946 to 1950. It was the very last car to run the Fraser Valley line on a run and return trip from September 30 to October 1, 1950.

~ 8 ~ *The "Duke of Connaught" car, 1912.*

Located at 760 Columbia Street, the interurban depot was built in 1911 to act as the BCER transit hub and transfer point, extending the company's transportation network right up the Fraser Valley. The

Courtesy New Westminster Public Library #3171. Jozef Podejko Collection.

9

design and construction of this depot was a substantial investment by the BCER. It cost approximately $100,000, and they needed to sell many tickets to cover the expense. The building itself was designed by Maclure and Fox in 1909 and was similar to the Indiana Traction Company's station in Indianapolis. It was both structurally sound and aesthetically appealing, and it was transected diagonally by parallel lines of track, allowing quick embarking and disembarking of the BCER's passengers. From here, passengers could hop on another car right into Vancouver or travel on by interurban to Richmond. During the 1920s and 1930s, the high cost of automobiles made the streetcars and interurbans of the BCER the primary means of transportation for most people within the Lower Mainland and New Westminster. Increasingly, the BCER's passengers were living further up the Fraser Valley and travelling further on their interurban lines. The last streetcar ran its last trip within New Westminster in 1936. The interurbans continued elsewhere for another twenty years, when it appeared everyone had shifted from wanting to needing their own vehicles.

~ 9 ~ *This photo from an original postcard, taken in 1947, shows the BCER interurban depot at a time when city streetcars were being gradually phased out in favour of buses.*

On Rubber

The first motorcars in New Westminster were viewed as novelties of the rich or eccentric. They seemed more bother than they were worth: they were noisy, messy, and frequently broke down. The city agreed and passed an ordinance saying the motorcars must not exceed 10 miles per hour and must have a man walking in front waving a flag.

Courtesy New Westminster Public Library #2092. Odin Collection.

10

~ 10 ~ *This image from 1914 is of George Odin in the driver's seat, chauffeuring his client, W.S. Collister, parked out front of the home of his in-laws, William Johnston and Elizabeth Burr Johnston, at 212 Queens Avenue. This beautiful car is a 1913 Peerless. George Odin apparently drove the Collisters on a family vacation all the way to Florida and back.*

By the 1910s motorcars had become more common and were symbols of prestige and success. Who wouldn't want a car if they could afford one, advertising said, and most citizens agreed. This was especially true after the move was made from solid to inflatable rubber tires. Even the transit buses seemed to have more style than the clattering streetcars. The shift was made, and soon the car became a form of personal expression as well as a means whereby its owner could travel in comfort and style.

~ 11, 12,& 13 ~ *Accidents will happen. This sequence of photos shows a Chevrolet being towed from a ditch in 1925, probably in Queensborough, by Odin and Mayers of New Westminster, at 401 Columbia Street. The same George Odin who had chauffeured the Collisters ran this business. The vehicle is a wrecker built by Cadillac, and this car was likely being taken back to their shop for repairs. A year later the Odin and Mayers shop moved up the hill to 816 Carnarvon Street.*

Courtesy New Westminster Public Library #2075. Odin Collection.

11

Courtesy New Westminster Public Library #2076. Odin Collection.

12

Courtesy New Westminster Public Library #2077. Odin Collection.

13

14

~ 14 ~ *Like George Odin, John A. Baxter was one of New Westminster's pioneer auto dealers. His auto repair shop was located on Columbia Street in the 1920s, near Odin and Mayers. This photograph provides a rare interior view of a New Westminster auto garage. Baxter's Motors Ltd. eventually moved up to 845 Carnarvon Street and became again a close competitor for Odin and Mayers.*

Chapter 13

A Storekeeper's Intimate Knowledge

Going to the shops was always about much more than merely getting the goods. The local general store, here and all over the country, provided an informal place for people to gather as well as shop. Some stores set hours to the pulse of the community by opening as early as 6:00 a.m. and/or staying open as late as 11:00 p.m., and they would often close while an event took place so that they and their employees could attend. It all depended on what was happening in the area. Even opening simply to offer a warm place for people to congregate in winter was not unusual. Stores often had stools at a counter or by a warm stove, and customers would sit and chat with the proprietor and other customers. This developed not just to make more sales but also to provide the community with a needed public amenity. Shops of all kinds seem to have a deep connection to a neighbourhood, its people, and the streetscape in general. It wasn't until 1867 that the merchants decided that on November 18 they would all start setting shop closing hours of 7:30 p.m. every night except Saturday, when they would not close until 9:00 p.m.

Many people remember the businesses in their neighbourhoods and the people who ran them. Patrons often showed their loyalty to a certain café by eating there every time they went out for a meal. In the early to mid-twentieth century some people developed fixed routines whereby they would shop only on certain days of the week. For example, Monday was laundry day, Tuesday was ironing, and Wednesday the house was cleaned. On Friday the weekly shopping was done. For some, going for lunch and meeting friends was also on the list for that day. Even if you were a woman who worked outside of the house, you might still have tried to stick to a routine. A woman who worked at a legal office on Columbia Street from the 1930s to the late 1970s reported that she did her shopping on Fridays as much as she could, and her laundry on Mondays, and if she went out for lunch, she always went to the Royal City Café. It was easier to keep such schedules when times were more predictable and the pace of life was more leisurely. However, many people still follow this schedule, either from family tradition or from many years of a familiar routine.

Going to Market

~ 1 ~ *This is the 1908 public market. Rattenbury's Bank of Montreal Building can clearly be seen with its turrets. Set back in the centre is Holy Trinity Church. A streetcar headed west has made a stop to drop off and receive market passengers.*

Public markets served the same purposes as markets do today, supplying not only a place where ordinary people

Courtesy New Westminster Public Library #136. New Westminster Museum and Archives Collection. #1HP0153

1

could buy, sell, and exchange goods and services with no retail middleman but also a place to gather. Some merchants who had shops elsewhere in the city had stands in the market too. The first official public market in New Westminster was located in Lytton Square, right on the waterfront at an open area on Front Street. On November 4, 1892, the city sponsored and opened its own market building, the first of many, all located at Lytton Square. When the 1898 fire burnt the building, the location of the market moved slightly east near the foot of what would later become Church Street, still below Columbia Street.

~ 2 ~ *This image was taken on April 30, 1926, when the city officially opened its three-storey public market in the art deco style, designed by John Young McCarter and George Colvill Nairne — the partnership who also designed the famous Marine Building in Vancouver. The front entrance on Columbia Street had an open appeal for the public, while the less inviting back way on Front Street served mainly as a service entrance.*

~ 3 ~ *Rear entrance from Front Street to the public market, circa 1940s. This building would in time become a variety of department stores, beginning with Spencer's, then Eaton's, and currently the Army and Navy Store.*

~ 4 ~ *The interior of the public market in 1932.*

Courtesy New Westminster Public Library #185.

3

Courtesy New Westminster Public Library #133.
New Westminster Museum and Archives Collection. #1HP3736.

2

Courtesy New Westminster Public Library #1470.
Vivian Sinclair Collection. Photographer: Stride Studios.

4

Money in the Bank

The Gold Rush of 1859 meant that assayed gold was used as an early form of currency. However, the colonial government and early merchants felt that wealth was being lost, since miners were forced to travel with their gold all the way to San Francisco. The image of a miner entering a saloon and ordering drinks with a bag of gold dust fresh from a claim is a myth, because to determine the gold's value, it had to be assayed for quality at a professional assay office. Once a miner went to San Francisco with his gold, there was no point in travelling all the way back to British Columbia to spend it.

~ 5 ~ *Bank of British Columbia, circa 1862.*

Courtesy New Westminster Public Library #256.

5

The Royal Engineers set up an assay building for the colonial government in New Westminster in May 1860, but their staff was soon reduced, and the building closed in 1867. Calls for the establishment of a British Columbian mint resulted in Governor Douglas establishing one very briefly at New Westminster in the summer of 1862. Only a few very rare gold and silver coins were struck before the whole enterprise was shut down. Governor Douglas, who had decided that he did not want this much power located in New Westminster, put a stop to production in 1862, as this was, after all, the location of Victoria's rival for provincial capital. The Bank of British Columbia, which opened in 1862, was closed seven years later due to a lack of coins.

The former Bank of Montreal is one of four banks commissioned by the company to be located in New Westminster, one dating right after the 1898 fire. Francis Rattenbury, the architect of the Legislature Buildings of British Columbia, designed the central branch that was built at 511 Columbia at Church Street. This fine building boasted pressed brick, fine stone (quarried from Gabriola Island), and imported terra cotta. It incorporated a Middle Eastern influence with Moorish minarets on its three street-side corners and a centre dome, constructed with a layer of leaded glass protecting the beautiful stained glass skylight that was visible only from the bank's interior. When the bank opened on October 4, 1899, the *Daily Columbian* newspaper reported it as a proud moment for all involved, and especially for the company, trumpeting its beautifully detailed design inside and out.

~ 6 ~ *This monumental structure is the Canadian Imperial Bank of Commerce, circa 1918, located at 544 Columbia Street and designed by architects Frank Darling and Lawrence Pearson of Toronto. Darling and Pearson are best known as the partnership that designed the Parliament Building in Ottawa. This design speaks of immovable finan-*

Courtesy New Westminster Public Library #1018. Jozef Podejko Collection. Photographer: W. Brown

6

cial security (although many people still preferred to hide their money somewhere in their house or, if they had one, in their house's safe) and would have appeared as a true temple of commerce, befitting the term "Imperial." The building was purchased by the city in 2004, and a public process has begun to decide its use.

Shopping Lists and the Golden Mile

By 1898, New Westminster already had a reputation as a goods centre that was profitable for both merchants and purchasers. This reputation travelled the Fraser Valley far and wide. The *B.C. Directories* and the *Provincial Exhibition Prize List* both refer to the plentiful supply and choice of New Westminster's mercantile operations. Both publications are filled with an abundance of local advertisements that show not only the variety of shops available in the city but also the large numbers of competing businesses to choose from.

~ 7 ~ A receipt dated April 29, 1899, from W.E. Fales, Furniture Dealer, Upholsterer, etc., 716-718 Columbia Street. The purchase was for sixteen yards of linoleum and one small stand: total cost $12.20.

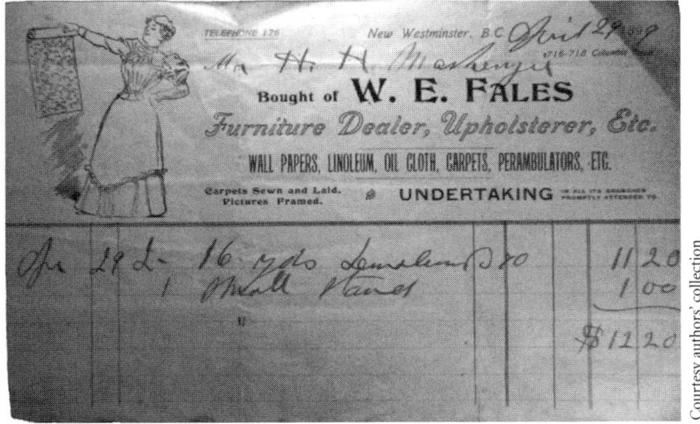

TELEPHONE 176 New Westminster, B.C.

716-718 Columbia Street

Bought of **W. E. FALES**

Furniture Dealer, Upholsterer, Etc.

WALL PAPERS, LINOLEUM, OIL CLOTH, CARPETS, PERAMBULATORS, ETC.

Carpets Sewn and Laid. Pictures Framed.

UNDERTAKING

16 yds Linoleum @ 70	11 20
1 Small Stand	1 00
	$12 20

Courtesy authors' collection

7

Courtesy New Westminster Public Library #59. New Westminster Museum and Archives Collection. Photographer: Thompson and Bovill. #IHP0320.

8

~ 8 ~ This 1889 butcher shop was located on Front Street. The Reichenbach family had sold meat in the city for generations, and in 1903 they were listed as running a meat processing facility and

slaughterhouse on Edmonds Street, just at the boundary of Burnaby. In the doorway stands employee Pete Batt, and inside behind the counter stands owner Joe Reichenbach. His partner, Steve Manahan, is in the window looking out, and posing on either side of the building are neighbourhood brothers Skinny (left) and Johnny (right) Eickhoff. Both boys appear very happy to be there and balance the composition of the photograph. Reichenbach's Meats was the very first business to rebuild on Columbia Street after the 1898 Fire.

~ 9 ~ *McQuarrie and Mitchell Milliners, located first at 627, then at 623 Columbia Street, in 1917. Standing out front on the left is one of the employees, Katie Campbell, and beside her is a woman known only as Clare. Campbell started at the store earning $6 a week, later moving to $10 a week. She was employed there from 1913 until her marriage in 1918, and one of her duties was making hats for the city's May Queens. In the notebook she kept, she wrote the cost of hats at 70 cents, $1.10, and $1.50, with the cost of pins being 50 cents. The donor of this photograph was Katie's daughter.*

~ 10 ~ *In the interior of the shop in 1914 are (left to right) Katie Campbell and Ethel Morrow. On the far right side are the owners, Bessie Mitchell and Miss McQuarrie. The two women in the back of the store look like employees, but there is currently no information on their names. Notice the bare light bulbs hanging down from the ceiling. There were no wall switches, and lights had pull-chains within reach.*

Courtesy New Westminster Public Library #2377. Mary Bovee Collection.

9

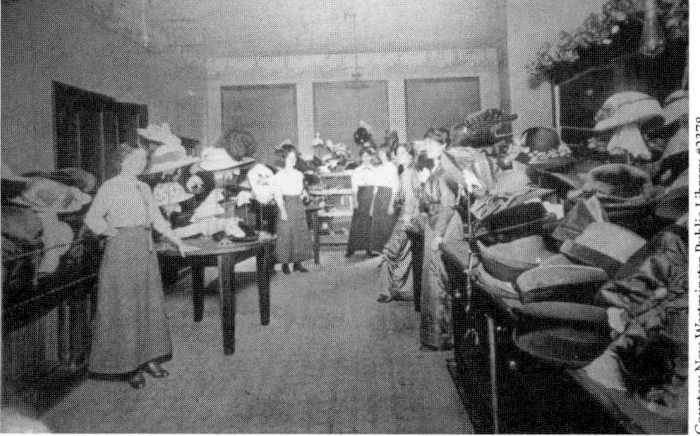

Courtesy New Westminster Public Library #2378. Mary Bovee Collection.

10

By the time the 1930s and '40s were well on their way, the Columbia Street area was known for the strong and varied productivity of its industries and for the value of its commercial ventures. Columbia Street was known for a time as the "Golden Mile." People came to the area from near and far either to start a business with the knowledge that it would be a success or to shop with the excitement of quality and choice.

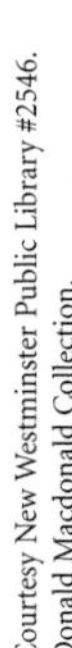
Courtesy New Westminster Public Library #2546. Donald Macdonald Collection.

11

12

Courtesy authors' collection. #13.GK1.

~ 11 ~ *This is Alfred W. McLeod Ltd. in 1946 — "The Insurance Man," as the sign in the window says. The business was located at 50 Sixth Street, on the corner of Carnarvon, from 1920 to 1946. Shortly after this picture was taken, McLeod's moved to the Westminster Trust Building at 713 Columbia Street. The business handled insurance, loans, real estate, rentals, land developing, and mortgages.*

~ 12 ~ *Kandid Kamera Snaps at 624 Columbia Street had a "roaming photographer" who approached people walking along the area's streets and, after snapping their picture, asked them if they would like to purchase the photograph. The deals were finalized on the spot, and today many people have photographs of relatives and friends walking along bustling streets of the past. This "snap," taken along the 600 block of Columbia Street in the summer of 1951, across the street from Kandid Kamera, is of Alexander and Augusta Freund. On Mrs. Freund's right is menswear shop Gregory-Price Ltd. at 649 Columbia Street, whose telephone number was LAkeview 1-5981. In the background on the right is the low-rise building at 502, which at this time housed the T. Eaton Company. The streetlight hanging in the upper right is at Sixth Street. The Freunds resided in the Okanagan Valley, and they came to the Lower Mainland to visit family and shop the Golden Mile.*

~ 13 ~ *A "Please Drop In" invitation to the grand opening of the New Westminster store Wosk's at 782 Columbia Street, formerly in the B.C. Electric Railway's New Westminster Interurban Depot. Invitation date is February 4, 1955.*

Courtesy authors' collection.

13

Rested and Refreshed

~ 14 ~ *The Queensborough Hotel, 1912.*

Courtesy New Westminster Public Library #877.

14

As inns and halfway houses became a thing of the past, hotels cropped up, bringing to New Westminster travellers the modern comforts and high quality one would expect in a city of this size at the beginning of the century. Most of the hotels were in the downtown area, but on the corner of Mercer Street and Ewen Avenue along the streetcar line in Queensborough, there was the Queensborough Hotel. In 1912 the hotel was built and opened for business. Mr. and Mrs. Harold Fairweather spent $3,500 to have the hotel built, and they envisioned long-term boarders from the island's industries along with a flow of travellers. The hotel had rooms for 125 people and could seat this same number in the dinning room at one time. Unfortunately, their dreams of becoming the hotel right across the street from the British Columbian Lumber Mill, which would have been the largest mill ever built in Queensborough, ended in

1913. The recession began quickly, putting an end to the mill before it even began. The outbreak of war and the retooling of industry had the Fairweathers running the hotel with only two hired staff, while Mr. Fairweather worked at the Poplar Island Shipyards. Mrs. Fairweather saw to boating lunches over to the few remaining boarders working on the island. In 1921, the Fairweathers decided to disassemble the hotel and ship it to the new town of Oliver. They made a decent living there as the new settlement grew, then four years later they sold the hotel. Today it remains on Oliver's main street.

~ 15 ~ *Russell Hotel, 1912. Photo taken from postcard.*

Courtesy New Westminster Public Library #3168. Jozef Podejko Collection.

15

The Russell Hotel at 740 Carnarvon Street was another of New Westminster's great hotels. It was built on the former site of the Ewen home that burnt down in the fire of 1898. The hotel was built in 1908 for businessman Elijah J. Fader. Fader, whose family name is attached to a street in Sapperton, commissioned the partnership of architects William Tinniswood Dalton and Sydney Morgan Eveleigh. They designed a hotel for Fader with eighty rooms and a restaurant and met his very high standards, as stated in their contract. Fader had wanted the Russell to have all the modern city comforts, and he envisioned it as not only a place for travellers but also a well-frequented site for social and business occasions of the city's residents.

~16 ~ *The Retreat, circa 1865. A stone's throw away from the saloon to the right is the Anglican Church of St. Mary the Virgin, which is still at this location at the intersection of East Columbia Street and Brunette Avenue.*

Courtesy New Westminster Public Library #286.

16

The first saloon in Sapperton was called The Retreat. Many other saloons appeared quickly thereafter around the early New Westminster. The Retreat served Sapperton's locals, travellers, and remaining members of the Columbia Detachment who resided at the old sappers' campsite.

~ 17 ~ *Standing in front of the Mouse's Ear are the proprietors, Mr. and Mrs. John H. Moor. The year is 1953, and reflected in the glass above the Sweet Caporal Cigarette advertisement in the window on the right is the woman taking the photograph, looking into her "Brownie" camera. Also reflected is the building across the street, the Mandeville Block, built in 1911 in the height of a real estate boom that started in 1909 and ended 1912. It is still there, although its original fine Clayburn bricks were stuccoed over in 1987 and then painted pink. The awning can just be made out, as well as the laneway across.*

Courtesy Moor collection.

17

Restaurants also began to grow in the city. Fish and chips, steak and chops, hamburgers, Pepsi, and an eight-cent coffee were a few of the items on the menu at Mouse's Ear Fish and Chips. Customers could go right in, hang up their coats at the end of a booth, and sit down in one of the bolt-upright, white-painted tongue and grove benches. The Mouse's Ear Café, formerly called the Devon Café, was located at 610 Twelfth Street. The Mouse's Ear building is covered in Bottle Dash or Rock Dash stucco.

Changing Needs and Changing Faces

~ 18 ~ *This interior of the William Rae Globe House Dry Goods and Millinery at 625 Columbia Street, circa 1890s, is within the Brine Block. Sitting at the left is George Brine, standing in the background is William Rae, behind the counter is Alfred Brine, and the woman is Jessie Rae. Jessie was married to William and was George and Alfred's sister.*

Courtesy New Westminster Public Library #1071.

18

~ 19 ~ *George William Grant designed the Brine Block just after the 1898 fire. The photograph, circa 1900, has the following businesses housed in the store fronts: (ground floor, left to right) the Canadian Pacific Telegraph Company, the Globe House Dry Goods and Millinery, and the MacKenzie Brothers dry goods and crockery;*

Courtesy New Westminster Public Library #968.

19

Courtesy New Westminster Public Library #61.
New Westminster Museum and Archives Collection. #1HP0134.

20

(upper floor, left to right) A E. White Insurance and Loan, A.G. MacFarlane and Co. Brokers.

~ 20 ~ *The three shops on the ground floor of the Brine Block made way for T.H. Smith Dry Goods, which converted the space to one store in 1905 and stayed there until 1935. In this photo, circa 1920, the upper floor has also been converted into the Westminster Modern Business School. The woman in the fifth window from the left looks like her attention to typing would never be challenged by the goings-on outside. The patrons below are eagerly lining up out front, awaiting the opening of the doors for the "Friday S Day" sale. Shops encouraged customers to keep Friday as shopping day by having big sales on Fridays. In this case, there is also a play on words (or letters), with Smith's using the "S" in the campaign to promote their name and represent the sale. The majority of the crowd are women, and a woman in the left quadrant is one of the few holding a baby. It appears that only a couple of women in the doorway notice that they are all being photographed. The men, on the other hand, who are probably less eager than the women for the sale to begin, are mostly looking at the photographer.*

~ 21 ~ *The Holmes Block was constructed on the north-eastern corner of Columbia and MacKenzie streets, to the right of the Brine Block. Dr. D.*

Courtesy New Westminster Public Library #183.
Photographer: Wadds Bros.

21

Holmes, a dentist, shared the upstairs in this two-storey brick business block. He had the building commissioned and completed by 1901, and this photo was taken shortly after its opening. In the windows are three men looking out at the photographer — it might be Dr. Holmes himself with his colleagues or patients. The ground floor had two retail businesses. The corner half was W.S. Collister and Company, selling both dry goods and clothing, including millinery. The second store was the jewellery store of T. Gifford, whose advertising spills out of the store and as far as the curb's edge. On Gifford's window is written "Spectacles" and "Diamonds." Leaning on the front of the building is a sidewalk advertisement of a watch, indicating that Gifford's also sold and repaired watches. It is interesting to note that Gifford's placed a business sign at the curb-side gutter for further advertising impact. He could have commissioned this photograph, taken by Wadds Bros. of Vancouver and Nelson. The brickwork and detailing on the roofline make this an attractive business building, with wooden sidewalks still in place (those remained until building owners worked with the city to pay for new concrete sidewalks). This program began in 1906. Note Chamberlin Jewellers on the right, a tenant of the Brine Block at this time.

~ 22 ~ *Here is the same building on March 4, 1977. The building has changed beyond recognition to satisfy the department store Fields. The Holmes Block is still there, but masked behind the facade of Fields, with its boisterous lettering.*

22

Courtesy New Westminster Public Library #1112. Hynek Collection.

Chapter 14

A Cause for Celebration

Many of the traditions, festivals, organizations, and societies of the city of New Westminster have been a part of its social fabric for a hundred years. Some can be traced right back to the Royal Engineers and British Columbia's colonial past before Confederation. Many families in the city have watched, participated in, or led these traditions for three or more generations, and therefore view them as being part of who they are. Participation has become a way of honouring ancestors and establishing a deep footing within the community.

In a recent unpublished paper, Dr. Gerald Thomson states, "The May Queens of 1874–1900 reflected the evolution of New Westminster's social structure from the British Colonial period to that of a west coast city within the Canadian federation." Canadian elites actively fashioned the collective identity of the new Canadian cities by fostering specific cultural traditions within celebrations that romanticized selected aspects of England's past. By acting as leaders of these celebrations and actively promoting and financing them, the elites increased their social status within the community (as well as their wealth, through the business contacts they made). This was particularly true of New Westminster, Thomson believes, because it was a specifically planned creation of the Royal Engineers that could be tailor-made in the style of "Olde and Merrie England" from its very beginning.

Honourary Hyacks

Begun initially as a volunteer fire department in 1861, the Hyacks also acted as an honourary society from the very beginning. A great many of the original Hyacks were men from the Columbia Detachment of Royal Engineers who chose to stay in the city when the detachment was disbanded in 1863. Upon the arrival of their first fire engine, the Fire King, from San Francisco in that same year, the Hyack Fire Brigade marched their prize to Hyack Hall, with the Hyack Band in the lead. They continued marching through the main streets with the Fire King, visiting prominent homes along the way to the sapper camp while accepting refreshments, before capping off the day's excitement and pride by attending an evening to mark the arrival of the Fire King at the Colonial Hotel.

~ 1 ~ *This image shows the Hyacks at the May Day Parade. The May Queen and her suite are in the carriage at the photo's left. The building with the elaborate porch railing the Hyacks are gathered in front of is the Hyack Fire Hall, located on Columbia Street facing the river and close to the Church Street intersection. In the middle of the Hyacks is the Fire King, decorated for its part in the parade. The mansard-roofed building visible behind the May Queen's carriage is the post office, constructed in 1892. Since all the buildings here were burnt to the ground in 1898, this undated image would have been taken roughly between 1893 and 1897.*

With the introduction of a fire department on payroll, the volunteer Hyacks continued as a symbolic organization. Later a group developed under the title The Ancient and Honourable Hyack Anvil Battery.

The firing of salutes, by gun or cannon, has a long history within military ceremony. The Anvil Battery's

Courtesy New Westminster Public Library #109. New Westminster Museum and Archives Collection. #1HP0086.

1

first firings began after the government decided not to further support the firing of a twenty-one-cannon salute to the queen in the city. This was because the cannons were no longer suitable for firing as their age made them unsafe, and a death had occurred. A local blacksmith named Thomas Ovens had heard of an English method of firing salutes using two anvils. One anvil was placed on top of the other with a charge of gunpowder in between. The charge was then ignited by a hot iron, held at a distance on a pole that followed a trail of gunpowder acting as a fuse for the blast, sending the upper anvil flying.

~ 2 ~ *This image from May 24, 1912, records that year's traditional salute on Queen Victoria's birthday. The Hyacks are standing on Eighth Street facing its intersection with Columbia Street. Ovens' Blacksmith shop is on the right on Eighth Street but is outside the image. The Livery Stable on the*

Courtesy New Westminster Public Library #67. New Westminster Museum and Archives Collection. Photographer: likely W.T. Cooksley.

2

left side is the Central Livery Feed and Sale Stable. Thomas Ovens is the fourth man from the right.

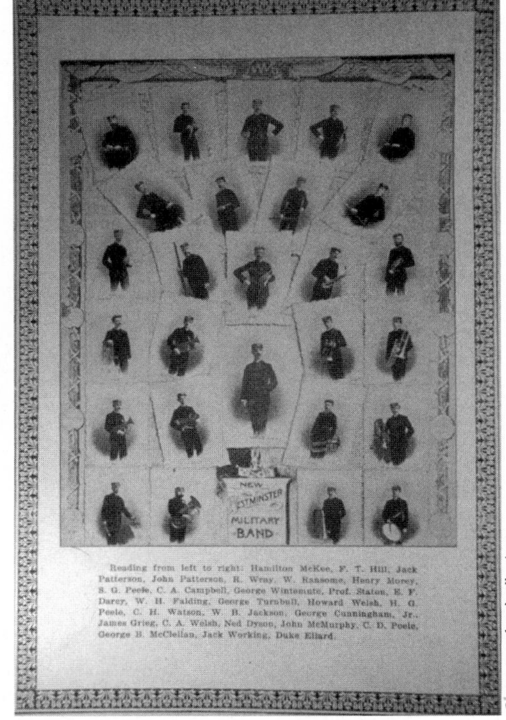

Courtesy authors' collection.

3

~ 3 ~ *The New Westminster Military Band (Hyacks) on a page in the* May Day Golden Jubilee Official Souvenir and Programme, *1920.*

~ 4 ~ *The location of the salute has changed over time. It had always been fired on Victoria Day, but now it is part of an annual week-long Hyack Festival occurring in Queens Park. This picture from the* Columbian *of 1954 shows Jack Allen "touching off" the Hyack salute.*

Courtesy New Westminster Public Library #290. *Columbian* newspaper Collection.

4

In 1958, the official Hyack Anvil Battery uniform was introduced. It was black pants with a tunic of scarlet and blue. It was similar in style to the original Hyack Fire Brigade uniform, but was stylized with an anvil on the cap as a symbolic icon. Fourteen men make up the Hyacks, and membership requires that a potential brigade member have a New Westminster ancestor.

May Day, Heyday

~ 5 ~ *This portrait is of the 1901 May Queen, Aldyen Irene Hendry, shown here at the age of sixteen. Her father was John Hendry, a pioneer British Columbian and owner of the Hastings Saw Mill in Vancouver. Aldyen attended St. Ann's Academy in New Westminster, Annie Wright's Seminary in Oregon, and finished school in Germany. In her twenties, while on vacation in England, she was presented at court. She met and married Eric Werge Hamber in London on May 14, 1912. In 1936, Hamber became the lieutenant-governor of British Columbia, and he later became the chancellor of the University of British Columbia. In 1937 the Hambers represented British Columbia at the coronation of King George VI in London. The Hambers were the only Canadians who were private guests when Queen Elizabeth married in 1947. Before her death on October 3, 1988, Aldyen was thought to be the oldest living New Westminster May Queen.*

Courtesy New Westminster Public Library #2428. D.W. McPhee Collection.

5

May Day is based on the fertility and pagan rites of spring dating back to pre-Christian England. New Westminster's 135-year-old May Day ritual represents a blending of aspects of the original May Days with traditions that were established by the former Royal Engineers at the very first May Day, held on May 4, 1870. The Hyack Fire Brigade travelled from Hyack Hall on Columbia Street up to the cricket field near the former Royal Engineer Camp. They carried with them the first May Queen, Helen McColl, and her suite on top of the Fire King, decorated as the first May Queen float. At the cricket field, the first maypole dance occurred, and after the oldest bachelor crowned the queen, a banquet luncheon occurred. Among the many attending was a baby named John Joseph (J.J.) Johnston, who later became a city councillor, mayor, and a key May Day organizer. He was nicknamed "Mr. May Day," as he participated in every May Day until his passing in 1966.

According to Thomson, May Queens from 1870 to 1908 were selected from the daughters of high society. Also, it appears some effort was usually made to award the crown to a girl whose father had passed away that year.

The site used for May Day was changed several times before it found a permanent home in Queens Park. For a while it continued to be held near the former Government House (built on what had been the camp for the Royal Engineers). They were forced to move the fete from this area by the provincial secretary because he felt it was disturbing the inmates of the prison. Bishop Acton Sillitoe allowed the fete to be held on the church grounds up on Saint Mary's mount, above Saint Mary the Virgin Anglican Church, but only until 1889. Then the event arrived, for its first time, at Queens Park, near the new upscale neighbourhood up the hill from Albert Crescent, which was beginning its social decline.

Courtesy New Westminster Public Library #3010. White Rock Museum and Archives Collection #1993-98-85. Marion Wilson Collection.

6

~ 6 ~ *John James Cambridge is in the front. Seated to the right of him is 1907's May Queen, Anne Tidy, with her maids of honour, Dorothy Reichenbach (left) and Bella Hood (right), behind. Seated to the left is the newly elected 1908 May Queen, Kathleen Dashwood-Jones, with maids of honour Naomi Rolph (left) and Ruby Fletcher (right).*

In 1908, schoolchildren for the first time elected a candidate from their school for the May Queen, with the actual queen chosen at random by a draw held with great pomp and ceremony at City Hall. Those candidates who did not get chosen as May Queen became the members of Royal Suite for that year. The change was a positive one, increasing the participation and excitement amongst the schoolchildren about the event. May Day then became a school holiday, so that all students could attend and participate.

J.J. Cambridge was for a long time the master of ceremonies for the annual May Day, but 1908 was his first year in that role. He had the difficult job of filling the shoes of the previous MC, Colonel J.T. Scott, who had died earlier that same year. Scott had been MC for the event for many years and was incredibly popular for his great involvement in all aspects of the city's social life. His funeral procession is shown in Chapter 4.

It wasn't until 1915 that all schools participated in the maypole dancing, as we know it today. That was the year that an elementary schoolteacher from England, Beatrice Cave-Browne-Cave, adapted a May Day folk dance suite from English folk dancer Cecil Sharp. Sharp's style of dance was part of a revival of early rural English folk dancing. Cave-Brown-Cave designed the complex

Courtesy New Westminster Public Library #3188. Jozef Podejko Collection.

7

maypole dancing forms that are now the standard and that each school strives to perfect in competition during the May Day celebrations. These celebrations are remembered long after students have danced around their last pole.

~ 7 ~ *This photograph, from an original postcard, was taken at the 1908 May Day in Queens Park and shows the enthusiasm generated for the event that year.*

~ 8 ~ *New Westminster-based photographer F.L. Hacking captured this remarkable image from the May Day*

Courtesy New Westminster Public Library #3042. White Rock Museum and Archives Collection.

8

of 1908. The May Queen and her suite are seated under the ribbons of the maypole, with the ribbons held by members of the Queens Park crowd.

~ 9 ~ *Homer Leash worked in New Westminster as a photographer and took this 1917 May Day photo of May Queen Louise Frances Cunningham being crowned by outgoing 1916 May Queen Evelyn Dawe. This image, taken during the final years of the First World War, also clearly shows the deep connection between the Royal City of New Westminster and England.*

Courtesy New Westminster Public Library #3288. West Collection.

9

~ 10 ~ *"Maypole Dancing Expresses the Very Spirit of May Day," is the centre spread of the 1920* May Day Golden Jubilee Official Souvenir and Programme. *It also features portraits of Lillooet Green, 1920 May Queen, and Millicent Meeham, 1920 Maid of Honour.*

MAYPOLE DANCING EXPRESSES THE VERY SPIRIT OF MAY DAY

Courtesy authors' collection.

10

~ 11 ~ *This is a souvenir postcard from the 1928 May Day, with students parading within the Queens Park oval in front of the buildings of the Provincial Exhibition. Stride Studios in New Westminster took the picture. The next day, when these students returned to their classes, each pupil was given a copy of this photograph, courtesy of the City of New Westminster and the May Day Organizing*

Courtesy Eileen Bradford (née Thompson) Collection.

11

Committee. This would be one of the last such May Day events to occur with these buildings as backdrops, as they would be burnt to the ground in a little over one hour on the evening of July 14, 1929.

The sixty-fifth annual May Day Celebration, which was held in the midst of the Great Depression, was made particularly festive to lift the community's spirits.

~ 12 ~ *Flower girls for the sixty-fifth annual May Day celebration on May 11, 1934, stand at the base of the steps up to the seating platform for the May Queen, the Royal Suite, the mayor and council, and other dignitaries.*

~ 13 ~ *This photo is of the May Day procession in 1934. Mayor Fred J. Hume escorts 1934 May Queen Kathleen Finlayson, preceded by the dancing*

ourtesy New Westminster Public Library #3221. Eva West Gassner Collection Photographer: Stride Studios.

12

Courtesy New Westminster Public Library #3219.
Eva West Gassner Collection. Photographer: Stride Studios.

13

flower girls. One of these girls is Eva Gassner, who donated these two images to the New Westminster Library. The gentleman whose head appears directly behind Mayor Hume and Queen Kathleen is none other than J.J. Johnston, known as "Mr. May Day."

~ 14 ~ *This is a portrait of Ruth Sayer (later Kelly), who was a maid of honour on May Day 1943 and who donated this photograph. She was the daughter of Mr. and Mrs. Stanley Sayer, 1213 Seventh Avenue, New Westminster. The May Queen was June Marie Brown; the other maid of honour was Patricia Logan. A unique aspect of this May Day was that the May Queen rode to Queens Park in an armoured truck of a reconnaissance unit, appropriate as this May Day took place during the Second World War. May Day 1944 featured the more traditional horse and carriage.*

Courtesy New Westminster Public Library #3264. Ruth Kelly Collection. Photographer: Stride Studios.

14

Everybody Loves a Parade

May Day has always meant a parade. Parades in New Westminster are like any romantic would have them be. Floats are designed to outshine each other, but collectively they create a procession of wonder, beauty, humour, and surprise. The crowds line up along Sixth Street and are close enough to call out to friends, family, and neighbours passing by in procession. Finally, as the parade reaches its end, the crowd can join in to follow and feel a part of a unified community.

Courtesy New Westminster Public Library #881.

15

~ 15 ~ *May Day parade along Columbia Street, 1912. The Fraser River Bridge, built in 1905, is visible at the left of the image.*

~ 16 ~ *Taken just out front of the Queens Park Provincial Exhibition's Industrial Building in 1913, this May Queen car float includes (front row, left to right) Charles Miller, Hugh Miller, and Janet Gilley; (middle row, left to right) Venna Gilley, Hazel Gilley, and Jean Gilley; (back row, left to right) Beatrice Gilley, Grace Gilley, Mildred Oliver, and Marjorie Gilley. The car, since it was built before 1922, is designed to drive on the British side of the road, rather than the American. In 1922, Janet Gilley was called to the bar and became B.C.'s fifteenth female lawyer.*

~ 17 & 18 ~ *These two images show different perspectives on the same May Day parade, the sixty-eighth annual May Day celebration on May 13, 1938. The first is the view from the crowd on the northern side of Columbia Street, looking westward. The awning at far left belongs to the Edison Theatre and has a man standing on it for a balcony-style seat to watch the passing parade. The second image shows the crowd lined along Columbia Street, as those within the floats and ceremonial cars would have seen them. The sheer pleasure of the event can be read on the faces of these women*

Courtesy New Westminster Public Library #898.

16

Courtesy New Westminster Public Library #2181. Norlund Collection. Photographer: Stride Studios.

17

Courtesy New Westminster Public Library #3222. Eva West Gassner Collection. Photographer: Stride Studios.

18

Courtesy New Westminster Public Library #3247. Albert Fox Collection. Photographer Alice Fox.

19

standing in front of the 600 block of Columbia Street. Behind them are the Sally Shop (clothing for women) at 642 and the Chong Hee Market.

~ 19 ~ *This image by photographer Alice Fox (née Ringstad) of Stride Studios was taken in 1955, and could be a May Day parade. The view here is looking east along Columbia Street from Lorne Street.*

Courtesy Connie Smart Collection. #14.CS1. Photographer: Stride Studios.

20

Alice took the picture of this remarkable float dress from the window of Stride Studios itself.

~ 20 ~ *This image shows the judging of car floats within the oval of Queens Park by the 1955 May Queen, her suite, and honourary judges. The Rose Shop, located on Twelfth Street beside Ann Govier's Beauty Salon, designed this car float entry. The owners of the Rose Shop were Mary Simpson and Harry Walker. They eventually married, and it is due to the kindness of their daughter Connie Smart that this image was included.*

~ 21 ~ *The 1958 May Day Parade, taken by Crofton Studio.*

Excursions

A chance to get away from town on a day trip excursion or holiday was surprisingly popular with groups

Courtesy New Westminster Public Library #363.

21

in New Westminster. River excursions by paddleboat as a "citizens' picnic" or with a group were well subscribed, and not to be missed. The Sons of Scotland hosted an annual Canada Day excursion to Langley, where highland games and dancing occurred.

~ 22 ~ *This is a citizens' picnic sailing to Victoria from New Westminster aboard the SS* Princess May *on July 30, 1908. The photographer was W.T. Cooksley of New Westminster.*

~ 23 ~ *Sunday school excursions, like this image of St. Paul's Reformed Episcopal Church in 1908, travelled to places like Stanley Park, Canada Place, Deep Cove, Belcarra Park, Ambleside, Lighthouse Park, and Lonsdale Quay. According to historians, they would also "pitch a tent on Burrard Inlet" at what is now New Brighton Park.*

Many New Westminster citizens owned beach cabins on Crescent Beach, Ambleside, and White Rock,

Courtesy New Westminster Public Library #967.

22

Courtesy New Westminster Public Library #3125. Photographer: Bullen Photo. Suzanne Spohn Collection.

23

where they vacationed each summer. Many still do. Getting away from it all sometimes meant going away with "them all," as the familiar faces transplanted themselves together to other surroundings.

~ 24 ~ *The gathering of the delegates of the Grand Lodge of B.C. of the Independent Order of Oddfellows (IOOF) on June 11, 1902. At the opening session of the Grand Lodge, Mayor*

Courtesy New Westminster Public Library #2890.

24

Keary accompanied the delegates, shown here on a sightseeing tour of the city in special BCER tramcars. They travelled right through New Westminster to Sapperton and back to the IOOF hall to complete their opening ceremonies.

The late nineteenth and early twentieth centuries saw an enormous interest in clubs, societies, associations, organizations, committees, and ceremonial lodges. To modern eyes, the number of possibilities might seem ridiculously large for such a small city. When did they ever have the time, and how could they survive the pace of so much socializing and community volunteerism? The answer is that the citizens had a great need to be around other people, to find common cause, and to share in moments that made common memories. A newcomer to the city could make immediate networks of friends, find work, and get established in New Westminster by joining an organization, party, society, or lodge or by already being a member of one whence they came. Many, like the Knights of Pythias, were Grand Lodges that no longer exist. Others still stand as amongst the first or the oldest established in the province. The Kiwanis Club of New Westminster had its eighty-fifth anniversary in 2004. Its motto is "I Serve."

Courtesy New Westminster Public Library #2367. Geoff Meugens Collection.

25

Courtesy New Westminster Public Library #2368. Geoff Meugens Collection.

26

Courtesy authors' collection #14.PC14.

28

Courtesy New Westminster Public Library #2369. Geoff Meugens Collection.

27

Courtesy New Westminster Public Library #2182. Esther Paulson Collection.

29

~ 25, 26 & 27 ~ *These three images show a sequence of summer holiday fun in 1909 at Bedwell Bay in the North Arm Inlet of the Fraser River. The older woman is the mother of the three younger women. Their family name is Crake, and the three daughters are Edith, Ethel, and Helena. All three are school-teachers in New Westminster, and all resided at 230 Third Avenue.*

~ 28 ~ *Blending both natural and man-made beauty, gardens and parks were a way to get away without going far. Their tranquility provided, as it still does, a place for early citizens to relax and reflect and be at peace. This postcard, circa 1910, is titled "Rose Gardens, Queens Park, New Westminster, B.C." and shows both the stately homes of First Street and the Queens Park caretaker's home at the far right. The caretaker is likely one of the three men shown tending this rose garden.*

~ 29 ~ *The neighbourhood of Queens Park also featured smaller public gardens, like the one pic-*

Courtesy authors' collection. 14.PC.15

30

tured on this print taken from a postcard titled "Lawns, Queens Park, New Westminster, B.C.," sent on August 26, 1913. This image captures the sense of tranquility and playful exploration parks can provide even in the middle of a city.

~ 30 ~ *This postcard is of Moody Park looking toward the west, circa early 1920s, and shows two interesting features, a West Coast Native totem and the Arts and Craft–style building with the red sloped roof. This pole was carved in 1920 by Andrew Brown, a well-known and experienced carver, and was forty feet high. During the Depression, Brown was reduced to poverty and returned to Prince Rupert, where he sold miniature totem poles at the docks to tourists for a few dollars apiece. The now-altered building known as Century House is a seniors' centre and head office for the city's Parks and Recreation Department. It was formerly the Moody Park Clubhouse, opened on August 23, 1938. It was built at a cost of $8,000 and belonged to the New*

Courtesy authors' collection. 14.PC.16

31

Westminster Kiwanis Club. In these early years, this building boasted a spacious community room, locker rooms, showers for children using the Moody Square playgrounds, and accommodation for the resident Moody Park caretaker.

~ 31 ~ *This later postcard of Moody Park from the 1950s shows Century House and its crescent driveway from the other entrance, looking south. The totem pole is missing, and it can no longer be found in Moody Park.*

Parks were a place to picnic and to celebrate. The idea of getting married in the park also developed around this period. New Westminster's Horticultural Association is still the city's largest association, and the city has always taken pride in its many parks.

Also in the 1930s, during the Great Depression, unemployed men worked for the relief money the city doled out by building many of the newer parks of the city. One example is Hume Park. The growing neighbourhoods required aesthetic amenities as well as practical ones. This phenomenon was repeated in the 1950s post-war economic and development boom in new neighbourhoods such as Victory Heights and Honeymoon Heights (which was essentially the infill development of the West End). Many long-time residents of the city have strong attachments to parks that continue to enrich their lives.

Chapter 15

The Great Fair

1

Courtesy authors' collection.

~ 1 ~ *A panoramic view in front of the Provincial Exhibition Building circa 1922. It shows the judging of entries in the children's livestock division.*

~ 2 ~ *"Dominion Exhibition Is Now Open." This* Columbian *front page from September 27, 1905, shows a detailed map of the Exhibition during its heyday.*

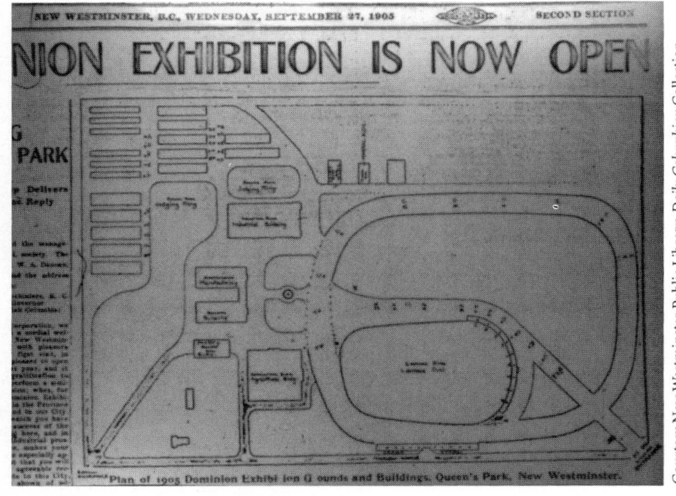
NEW WESTMINSTER, B.C., WEDNESDAY, SEPTEMBER 27, 1905 SECOND SECTION

NION EXHIBITION IS NOW OPEN

PARK

Plan of 1905 Dominion Exhibition Grounds and Buildings, Queen's Park, New Westminster.

2

Courtesy New Westminster Public Library. *Daily Columbian* Collection.

Before Vancouver's Pacific National Exhibition (PNE), the city of New Westminster hosted the annual Provincial Exhibition at Queens Park. Beginning in 1889, the exhibition ran without interruption until 1929. The event was hosted and organized by the Royal Agricultural and Industrial Society of British Columbia; it was an extension of the city's natural hub status for the transport of goods produced in the Fraser Valley and a celebration of that abundance. It was a truly provincial event that lasted more than a week and involved communities, small and large businesses, schools, circuses, and a carnival midway called the Sockeye Run.

Accounts exist of the annual treks to Queens Park from the railway station of a menagerie of large and small livestock arriving from across the province, which would be herded up the city streets and then through the upscale neighbourhood to the stock stalls within the exhibition area. En route, these beasts on occasion trampled or grazed upon the fine gardens of the stately homes and left hoofprints, bare branches, and other, more pungent, reminders of their passage. Circuses and other carnivals also informally paraded more exotic animals and attractions to the park via the same route. Many of the Queens Parks residents chose to go out of town during fair times and wait the whole thing out in more pleasing surroundings.

~ 3 ~ *This image taken in 1906 shows a very interesting carnival midway attraction. The woman seated on the cargo box is fortune teller Mrs. Cook, who used the six budgies standing above the slate to tell the future. This was one of the Sockeye Run's many fascinating attractions.*

The scope of the New Westminster event surpassed Vancouver's PNE and arose from a desire by the Royal Agricultural and Industrial Society of British Columbia

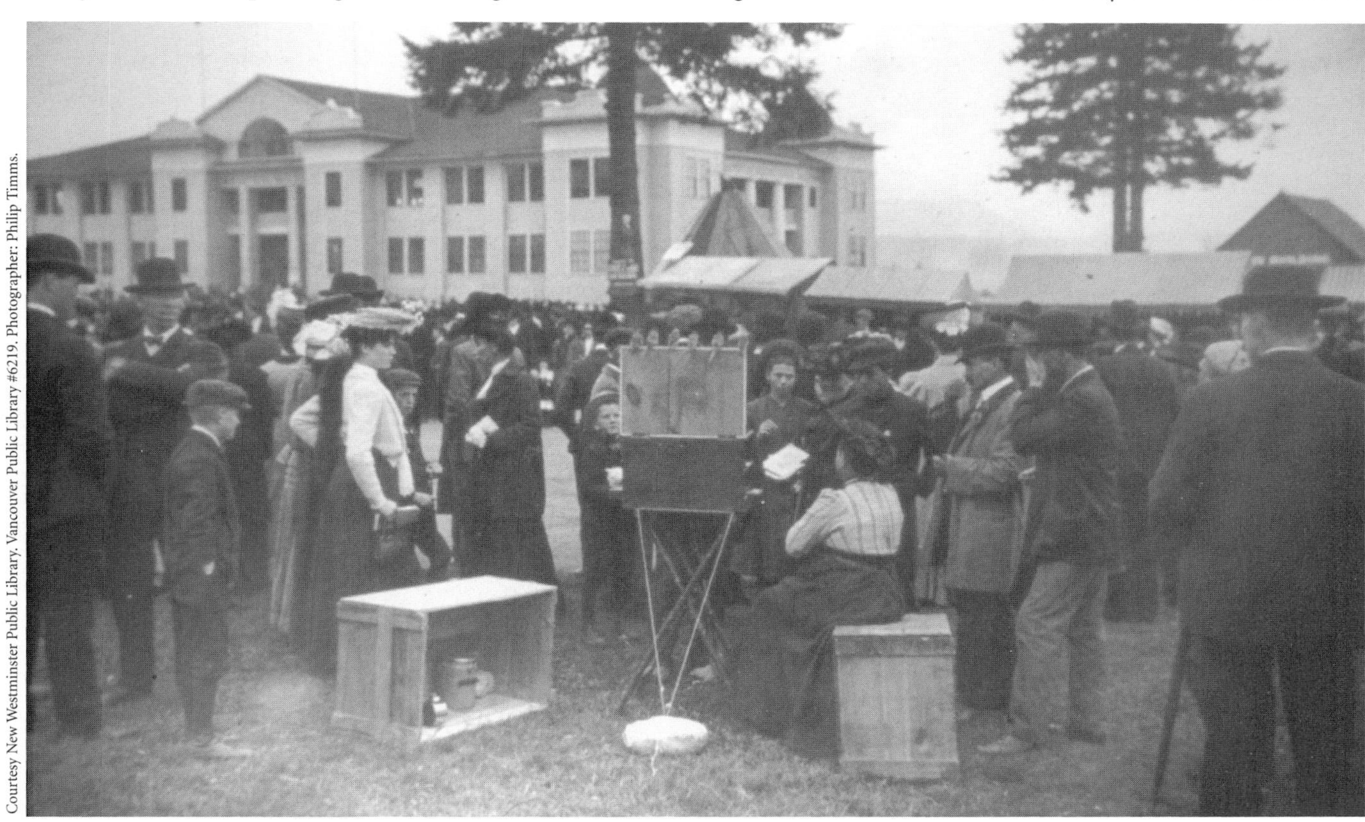

Courtesy New Westminster Public Library. Vancouver Public Library #6219. Photographer: Philip Timms.

3

Courtesy New Westminster Public Library #2359.
Geoff Meugens Collection.

4

to replicate, within Queens Park, the style of the great exhibitions of Europe.

~ 4 ~ *The exhibition included many unusual attractions, but this image shows one of the more peculiar. In 1909, aeronaut Harry Ginter piloted this dirigible twice daily over the fair. The* Columbian *of October 11, 1909, described it as being made of Japanese silk, fifty-six feet long and sixteen feet wide, encasing six thousand cubic feet of inert gas once fully inflated. Ginter piloted the airship while standing, using rods and levers to control both the speed of the engine powering the propeller in front and the directional heading of the tail fin rudder behind. All that can be made out from the advertising banner on the dirigible's side is "Motor Boats Built by Hinton Electric Co. Ltd. At Victoria … Boats-Launches-Cruisers."*

New Westminster's exhibition grew to be an enormous success and included thousands of prizes and competitions. The 1919 prize list is by no means atypical, running over 134 pages. There was judging for all kinds and breeds of livestock, including horses, cattle, sheep, swine, poultry, rabbits, and pigeons, as well as a variety of food items.

~ 5 ~ *This 1909 image taken by photographer P. Timms on the second floor of the Exhibition Building shows the entries and prizewinners in the apples*

Courtesy New Westminster Public Library #1384.
Vancouver Public Library #6897.

5

Courtesy authors' collection. 15.PC.17

6

category. The awards within the produce section included a vast array of other fruits and vegetables, a variety of dairy produce, eggs, breads, and honey. Each of these contests was run by its own division: A (cattle); B (horses); C (sheep and goats); D (swine); E (poultry); F (dairy produce); G (potatoes and vegetables); H (field produce and B.C.-grown seed); and I (fruit).

~ 6 ~ *Entitled "Exhibition Buildings, New Westminster, B.C.," this unused hand-tinted postcard, circa 1900, shows both the Industrial Building and the Women's Building.*

The Industrial Building showcased a full industrial exhibition component, Division J (manufacturers and industrial). It included engines; wood and iron working machinery; carriage fixtures; agricultural implements; dairy machinery; boats; hardware tools; cutlery; refrigerators; shoes and boots; harnesses and saddles; glass and earthenware; bookbinding and printing; wearing apparel of all kinds; mathematical and surgical equipment; and stoves and ranges.

Division K was for fine arts, awarding prizes in professional and amateur categories for painting and drawing, watercolours, and craftwork. And for children under sixteen years, there were competitions in the domestic sciences (for example, the best bottled rhubarb) and school exhibits. Classes won $3.00 for first prize in categories like "best collection of insects injurious to orchard or grain crops," and "best collection of weeds properly mounted and named." Within the Women's Building, the Women's Institute housed exhibits and juried contests in all of the domestic arts, including cooking, floral arrangement, laundry, dairy, and gardening.

One of the more unusual contests by today's standards was the "Better Babies Contest." According to Gerald Thomson, New Westminster's Local Council of Women held this contest from 1920 to 1929, taking it over from the Vancouver Council of Women, who had run it in Vancouver since 1913. Six nurses and twelve assistants ran the contest under the direction of Dr. J.G. McKay. Under the guise of educational value and health, all aspects of the submitted babies were measured and marked according to scored qualities worth two, three, or four points each, for a total possible score of one hundred. Often as many as two hundred babies were entered, and the event was one of the most popular to watch.

Like any fair, there were also games of skill and chance, food to eat, events and entertainment, and souvenirs to buy. And the Provincial Exhibition was a major tourist attraction. As mentioned earlier, sporting matches, especially lacrosse, were very popular to watch. There was even a rodeo event.

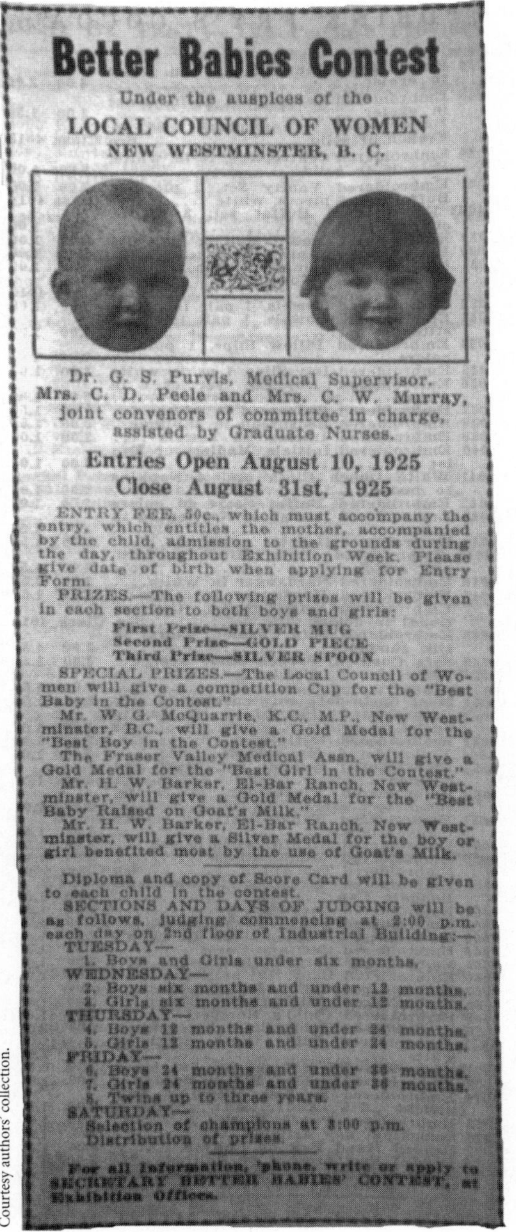

Better Babies Contest

Under the auspices of the

LOCAL COUNCIL OF WOMEN

NEW WESTMINSTER, B. C.

Dr. G. S. Purvis, Medical Supervisor.
Mrs. C. D. Peele and Mrs. C. W. Murray, joint convenors of committee in charge, assisted by Graduate Nurses.

Entries Open August 10, 1925
Close August 31st, 1925

ENTRY FEE, 50c., which must accompany the entry, which entitles the mother, accompanied by the child, admission to the grounds during the day, throughout Exhibition Week. Please give date of birth when applying for Entry Form.

PRIZES.—The following prizes will be given in each section to both boys and girls:

First Prize—SILVER MUG
Second Prize—GOLD PIECE
Third Prize—SILVER SPOON

SPECIAL PRIZES.—The Local Council of Women will give a competition Cup for the "Best Baby in the Contest."

Mr. W. G. McQuarrie, K.C., M.P., New Westminster, B.C., will give a Gold Medal for the "Best Boy in the Contest."

The Fraser Valley Medical Assn. will give a Gold Medal for the "Best Girl in the Contest."

Mr. H. W. Barker, El-Bar Ranch, New Westminster, will give a Gold Medal for the "Best Baby Raised on Goat's Milk."

Mr. H. W. Barker, El-Bar Ranch, New Westminster, will give a Silver Medal for the boy or girl benefited most by the use of Goat's Milk.

Diploma and copy of Score Card will be given to each child in the contest.

SECTIONS AND DAYS OF JUDGING will be as follows, judging commencing at 2:00 p.m. each day on 2nd floor of Industrial Building:—

TUESDAY—
1. Boys and Girls under six months.

WEDNESDAY—
2. Boys six months and under 12 months.
3. Girls six months and under 12 months.

THURSDAY—
4. Boys 12 months and under 24 months.
5. Girls 12 months and under 24 months.

FRIDAY—
6. Boys 24 months and under 36 months.
7. Girls 24 months and under 36 months.
8. Twins up to three years.

SATURDAY—
Selection of champions at 3:00 p.m.
Distribution of prizes.

For all information, 'phone, write or apply to SECRETARY BETTER BABIES' CONTEST, at Exhibition Offices.

Courtesy authors' collection.

7

~ 7 ~ *An advertisement for the Better Babies Contest, 1925. Provincial Exhibition Prize Book. Entries opened on August 10, 1925, and officially closed on August 31, 1925.*

~ 8 ~ *This postcard image shows the central area of the Provincial Exhibition grounds and their proximity to the B.C. Electric Streetcar line on First Street. The postcard was sent through the post and reads, "Oct. 8,1907. There was a fair*

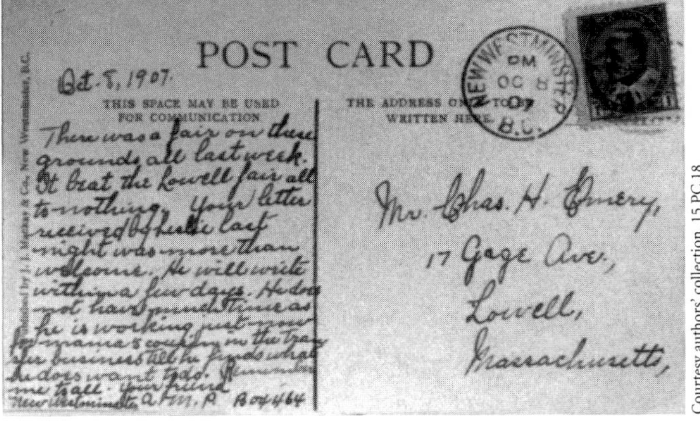

Courtesy authors' collection. 15.PC.18

8

on these grounds all last week. It beat the Lowell fair all to nothing. Your letter received by Leslie last night was more than welcome. He will write within a few days. He does not have much time as he's working just now for mama's couping in the transfer business till he finds what he does want to do. Remember me to all. Your friend, New Westminster, A.M.P. P004464." It is addressed to Chas. H. Emery of Lowell, Massachusetts.

The B.C. Electric Railway ran "specials" right into Queens Park, and there was even a place to camp overnight in the "Gyro" car campsite.

~ 9 ~ *This postcard image shows the "Gyro" Auto Tourist Camp in Queens Park, although it was taken after 1929, the fair's last year. The postcard was sent through the post and reads, "Aprl 20-36. Dear Mr. & Mrs. Bozer, Still enjoying the lovely weather. It has rained several times but has been very welcome. Have driven miles around the sea shore with many people I know. Vancouver is a wonderfull large City. Going to visit this week. Hope you are both well. With best wishes. Sincerely, H. Hoe."*

The newspaper printed special exhibition editions that covered the events and listed the names of all prizewinners. The edition went on for pages, and sold out quickly.

The buildings that stood within Queens Park and were used for the fair (and also for May Day events)

9

Courtesy authors' collection.15.PC.1 9

were striking, with the oldest being the most central and distinctive. Noted New Westminster architect George William Grant built the Provincial Exhibition Building in 1889. Its doubled four squared chateau-style entranceways converged to a central six-storey tower. The building was visible from throughout Queens Park, especially when each of the towers flew flags during the exhibition.

10

Courtesy New Westminster Public Library #129.

~ 10 ~ *"Public School Exercises." Taken on June 26, 1911, this photograph was "possibly in preparation for Dominion Day, July 1, 1911."*

~ 11 ~ *This image of the Women's Building, taken circa 1908, shows the beauty of its nighttime illumination. Other buildings were illuminated as well, beautifying the evening events during the fair and those hosted on the site throughout the year.*

11

Courtesy New Westminster Public Library #3149.
Jozef Podejko Collection. Photographer: F.L. Hacking.

New Westminster's Provincial Exhibition years were a glorious, golden time, and a symbolic triumph over the adversities of the past. Then, on the hot summer night of July 14, 1929, the whole exhibition site and all the fair's buildings went up in flames (except for one small fishery building that had been recently moved from the site), spectacularly burning down nearly everything that had been so well visited, and so well loved, by so many — all in one hour and ten minutes.

The account of the evening's horrific events from July 15, 1929, describes the blaze as beginning at about 5:50 p.m. in the Agricultural Building. "Quickly, the flames leaped the narrow spaces between the structures and the Women's and Manufacturers' buildings next

New Westminster Public Library #71. New Westminster Museum and Archives #1HP356.

12

caught fire, followed by the Arena, Poultry and Industrial buildings."

Fighting this fire, just as in the 1898 Great Fire, was made worse by the lack of water pressure. Only the arrival of a pumper engine from Vancouver prevented the fire from spreading to the forested area of Queens Park, the "Gyro" car camp, and the homes of First Street. Dorothy Bilton remembers being called to the window to see a very large fire, its location not known until the next morning.

Only a few of the exhibition's outbuildings were saved, as well as the old Dufferin stagecoach, ridden in by Lord Dufferin during his visit to the Royal City in 1876. A crew of volunteers pushed it to safety just outside of Queens Park on McBride Boulevard. According to that day's *British Columbian*:

> The totem pole which was brought from Northern British Columbia some years ago and placed in position alongside the Agricultural building was one the interesting relics to fall into the flames. The tall flag pole in the centre of the green spot in front of the Women's building caught fire, but remained in position after the main blaze had subsided, until workmen cut it down as a safety measure.

The city asked Alfred W. McLeod to assess the value of the property lost to the city, which he estimated at approximately $100,000. He would have been an early witness, and could have been a victim of the fire, residing only one block from First Street and Queens Park. Sadly, "The Insurance Man" reported that the Royal Agricultural and Industrial Society of British Columbia had carried no insurance on its property.

Grim events seemed to have once again ravaged the citizens of New Westminster just thirty-one years after its Great Fire of 1898, still in the living memories of many of its citizens. It should have been the end, but there was to be one last hurrah, done in true New Westminster style and opened by one of the greatest leaders of the twentieth century, Winston Churchill.

Chapter 16

Guests of Renown

As the first city in Western Canada, the former capital of first the mainland colony of British Columbia and briefly the combined colonies of Vancouver Island and British Columbia, and the site of the province's annual Provincial Exhibition, the Royal City of New Westminster has served as host to an astonishing number of guests of renown. Eminent guests have come and gone, staying in New Westminster for days or less than an hour, and all have had an impact on this community.

~ 1 ~ *Winston Churchill, September 3, 1929.*

Courtesy New Westminster Public Library #2149. Bob Robertson Collection. Photographer: Stride Studio.

1

The Royal Agricultural and Industrial Society and the City of New Westminster wanted the Diamond Jubilee (sixtieth) Provincial Exhibition to be the most memorable ever. Instead of diamonds, they were faced with carbon in the form of ashes. They were also to have had at the exhibition the finest orator and master of the English language of his time. Even in 1929, Churchill's "wilderness years," when he was generally considered to be a spent political force, his eloquence and power to hold a crowd were legendary.

Would Churchill still come if a makeshift exhibition could be pulled together? Would the Royal Agricultural and Industrial Society decide to cancel given the enormity of the loss just months from the exhibition's opening day? Churchill was indomitable in his commitment that he would be there and that he would speak in Queens Park on September 3, 1929.

An exhibition under tents was quickly arranged, and in the same manner that New Westminster had quickly rebuilt itself, stronger and more united, in the aftermath of the Great Fire of 1898, the city seemed sworn to make tangible Churchill's belief that they'd all come through with a great sixtieth-anniversary Provincial Exhibition. The *British Columbian* of September 2, 1929, under the banner headline "Provincial Exhibition Opened by Rt. Hon. Winston Churchill; Tremendous Crowd is Present," reported that Churchill "responded to the stimulus of the greatest gathering he has ever addressed in the new world, and delivered a speech worthy of his reputation."

Churchill, as a skilled historian, would have known of the Great Fire of 1898, and as an inspired politician, he would have been able to assess the impact of the 1929 Provincial Exhibition as clearly as he would have been able to see the remains of burnt-out relics around him. Reading the mood of the crowd to perfection, Churchill opened by noting, "You are a people tested by fire … you have come through the fire and I admire the courage and resources of those in charge, which have been such that not even the heavy blow you have sustained has been able to mar the success of your undertaking." The speech went on to thunderous applause. Churchill then said that he saw in this "the perseverance and dogged courage that does not know defeat, typical of the British race." He added, "Sixty years is a long time in the history of a young nation and a sixty years they have been, so fateful for Canada, for the British Empire, and the World."

Churchill, in 1929, with the next great war a decade away, had taken the crowd's charcoal and, through harnessing collective will, had forged from it a diamond, just as he would accomplish time and again.

~ 2 ~ *Duke of Connaught, September 21, 1912.*

Courtesy New Westminster Public Library #36. Ted Clark Collection.

2

The third son of Queen Victoria, His Royal Highness Arthur William Patrick Albert, the first Duke of Connaught, was also Governor General of Canada from 1911 to 1916. The city named by Queen Victoria went all out to welcome her son in a manner befitting New Westminster's status as British Columbia's Royal City. The Duke of Connaught arrived to a massive crowd of devoted subjects, and the 104th Regiment, dressed in scarlet uniforms, paraded while its band played the national anthem. There were greetings by citizens from all points of the Lower Mainland, civic leaders, a body of Sikhs of the British Regiment in India, the Fraser Valley Native bands, boy scouts, soldiers, and veterans, to mention just a few. One of the most interesting elements was an elaborate archway constructed on Columbia and Fourth streets representing the wealth of the province's natural resources. It included at least six men on top of the arch's four support pillars in costume (precariously standing more than three storeys above the hard ground). The decoration of natural resources included cedar boughs and freshly caught salmon. Contemporary accounts state that the fish did not stay fresh very long in the heat of the Indian summer, adding an unanticipated ripe aroma to the display.

~ 3 ~ *Lord Tweedsmuir, August 27, 1936. C.E. Stride of Stride Studios captured the official photograph as Lord Tweedsmuir said his goodbyes to New Westminster on August 27, 1936, his first of two visits. Lord Tweedsmuir is sitting in the front row, fourth from left. Sitting beside him to his right are Mayor Fred J. Hume (1934–1942), Councillor Frederick H. "Toby" Jackson (1936–1948), and, on the end of the front row on the right, city clerk George Brine.*

Governor General of Canada from 1935 to 1940, John Buchan, Lord Tweedsmuir, was a talented writer before becoming Governor General. He penned what became known as the Buchan Version of the famous "The Maple

Courtesy New Westminster Public Library #1975.

3

Leaf Forever," which was viewed by many as the unofficial anthem of Canada until "O Canada" in 1964. The city's regiment regarded his song as important long before this. Buchan is best known as the author of the book *39 Steps* (1915), made into an even more famous film of the same name by Alfred Hitchcock in 1935.

~ 4 ~ *King George VI, Queen Elizabeth, and Prime Minister William L. Mackenzie King, May 31, 1939.*

Courtesy New Westminster Public Library #1607. Jim Clawson Collection. Photographer: Jabe Auton.

4

In 1939, the reigning king and queen embarked on the first Royal Tour of Canada, which lasted for a full month. The royal couple started in Quebec, travelled west to Vancouver, and then returned to depart from Halifax. Many saw this as a visit on the eve of war, whipping up patriotism. It was a smashing success and had a profound and lasting impact on the country as a whole. On May 29, 1939, more than sixty thousand people lined the procession route out of Vancouver. Two days later, the royal couple travelled a well-publicized route into New Westminster, entering at 3:00 p.m. from the north onto Twelfth Street, having just journeyed past the crowds of Burnaby citizens thronging both sides of Kingsway. However, they spent only forty minutes in New Westminster. The royal procession's drive from the edge of New Westminster to Queens Park took twelve minutes, turning left at Eighth Avenue, right again onto Eighth Street, left on Sixth Avenue, right down Second Street, then left into Queens Park through the elaborate wrought iron gate at Third Avenue at exactly 3:12 p.m.

Although Queens Park contained a massive crowd of eleven thousand children, with twenty-seven hundred of them performing their May Day dances, including twenty-four decorated poles, the car did not stop. They circled the track and then travelled back out of the park eight minutes later. This was the longest time they spent in one spot during their whole visit to New Westminster. They went south one block on First Street and turned right to travel west on Queens Avenue as far as Eighth Street, then turned left. Turning left again, the royal procession ran the length of Columbia Street and arrived at the railway platform just below the penitentiary at 3:33 p.m.

~ 5 ~ *May 29, 1939. Before the royal procession drove by McBride Boulevard, crossing Columbia Street at the southwest corner of the Provincial Asylum for the Insane, the former chief attendant (now chief superintendent at the Colquitz hospital in Saanich) and his daughter, Dorothy Bilton, stood waiting. At the right moment, Spooner captured a perfect fleeting moment with his camera.*

5

Courtesy **authors' collection #16.DBS.** Dorothy Bilton Collection. Photographer: Frederick M. Spooner.

The platform had been used to receive and transport prisoners in the past, but it had been decorated with a red carpet and bunting for the seven minutes of formal ceremonies commemorating this historic royal visit (one minute less than the circle driven in Queens Park).

~ 6 ~ *The map of the route through New Westminster for the official procession of the royal visit of King George VI and Queen Elizabeth to New Westminster, May 31, 1939.*

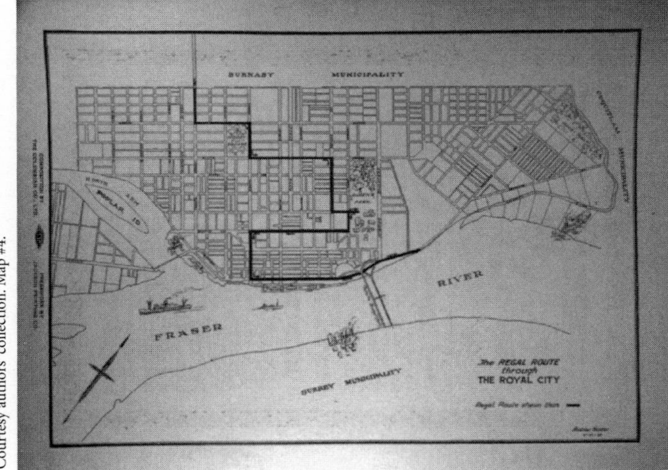

Courtesy authors' collection. Map #4.

6

The royal procession contained four cars. The first car held the king, the queen, and an equerry in waiting; the second held Prime Minister Mackenzie King, the lord- and lady-in-waiting to the king and queen, and the Prime Minister's principal secretary; the third held Ian Mackenzie, a member of the federal Cabinet from B.C., another lady-in-waiting, and the lord chamberlain to the queen; and fourth held the king's private secretary, the royal couple's medical officer, their chief press liaison officer, and the equerry. At 3:40 p.m. they left the city, travelling up the Fraser Valley line in their royal train of blue and silver. (In later years this train became the Royal Hudson excursion train from North Vancouver to Squamish.) The *Columbian* reported the events that followed shortly after the train's departure:

> The thousands of spectators descended upon the downtown section like an invading army in search of food and refreshment. Within minutes of the departure of the Royal train, every café, lunch counter and teashop was filled to the doors and long lines of customers were waiting for service. Thousands had eaten very sketchily since morning. Café operators reported the invasion as the most amazing they had ever seen.
>
> The final stage was the trek for buses and trams. Scores of extra trains and buses were in service but it was nearly six o'clock before the crowds thinned out and Columbia Street assumed its normal evening appearance. The only signs of its greatest day in modern history were the flags and bunting fluttering from buildings and light standards.

~ 7 ~ *The cover of the official souvenir programme for the royal visit of King George VI and Queen Elizabeth to New Westminster.*

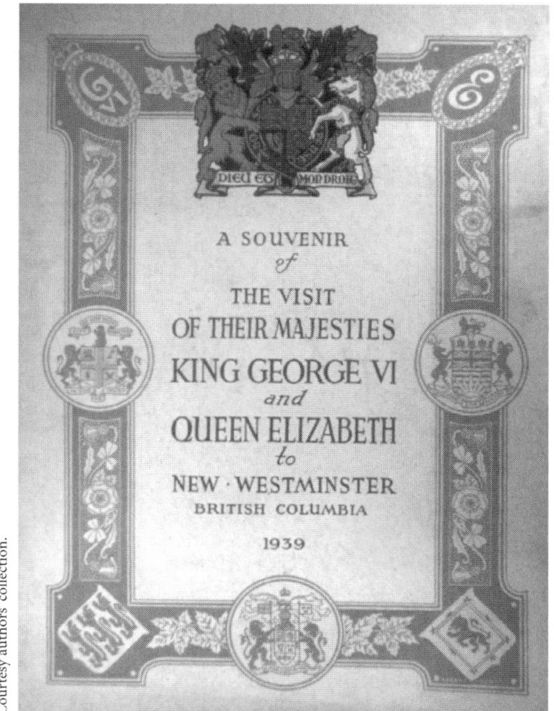
A SOUVENIR
of
THE VISIT
OF THEIR MAJESTIES
KING GEORGE VI
and
QUEEN ELIZABETH
to
NEW · WESTMINSTER
BRITISH COLUMBIA
1939

Courtesy authors' collection.

7

Courtesy New Westminster Public Library #2387. Ted Clark Collection.

9

Courtesy authors' collection.

8

~ 8 ~ *Souvenir buttons and ribbons from the 1939 royal visit.*

~ 9 ~ *While he was national leader of the Liberal party and Opposition leader, Lester Pearson attended a Liberal party coffee reception on September 27, 1958, that included several hundred people. The*

Columbian *reported that he was disappointed at not being able to meet the students of Lester Pearson High School because, "I had such a good time with them before." On this day he had a photo session with some of the school's cheerleaders. Two photos were donated to the library by a private citizen. This is one, showing him relaxing and playfully posing with cheerleader Leona Smud, holding the school mascot.*

~ 10 ~ *Pierre Trudeau was honourary parade marshal for the May 11, 1968, May Day. "Trudeau-mania" was at its peak, and there was concern he would be mobbed, so some details of his itinerary had been kept secret and he was travelling with heightened security. What the public did know was that the parade would depart from its traditional scheduled point on Columbia Street, where he met and greeted many adoring*

Courtesy New Westminster Public Library #2681. Craig Hodge Collection. *Columbian* Newspaper Collection. Photographer: Craig Hodge.

10

citizens. This photo shows Trudeau visiting New Westminster again in 1974 at the waterfront area between Front Street and the river, near what is now the parking entrance to the Westminster Quay.

Courtesy New Westminster Public Library #3099. Dan Mott Collection. Photographer: On-The-Spot Photographers.

11

~ 11 ~ *When CKNW opened a new broadcast tower in 1946 in Queensborough, designed to amplify the station's range, they arranged for a photo op by the tower including the mayor, Bill Mott, Tex Ritter, and radio DJ Dave Armstrong. Tex Ritter was the father of recently deceased television actor John Ritter and was a Hollywood actor and country western singer.*

CKNW Radio began in New Westminster in 1946, using the Windsor Hotel as their first broadcast studio. The hotel was one of the first buildings hurried to completion after the Great Fire; it was finished in 1899. Ironically, it is one of the few that were made out of wood during the reconstruction period, and it stands today looking very like it did 104 years ago. The radio station had its studio on the second floor for six years and broadcast live — even having speakers outside the building broadcasting right out on the street.

CKNW eventually moved from the Windsor Hotel and out of New Westminster entirely to downtown Vancouver. There, until just last year, they reigned as the "top dog" station, claiming the largest share of listeners in the Lower Mainland, with a blend of talk radio and current affair call-ins. CKNW is now second to JACK Radio's successful mix of unusual and eclectic rock music selections it calls "playing what we want" — much like the young upstart CKNW was when it began. In the station's bandwidth name, the "C" stands for "Canadian," and the "NW" stands for "New Westminster."

~ 12 ~ *Dan George (Teswahno) was chief of the Tsleil Waututh (Burrard Band) of the Squamish First Nation from 1951 to 1963. Born in 1899, he took*

Courtesy New Westminster Public Library #1688. Sharon Dibble Collection. Photographer: Bob Dibble.

12

up his new career as an actor for television, stage, and film at sixty years of age. Appearing on the stairs in front of New Westminster's City Hall on June 4, 1967, as part of the city's Canadian Centennial celebration and to launch the second annual Indian Days event, Chief Dan George was already a celebrity in Canada and an inspirational leader and spokesperson for First Nations. He received an Academy Award nomination for his role in Little Big Man *in 1970, and he earned success as a writer of prose and poetry through* My Heart Soars *(1974) and* My Spirit Soars *(1982), printed after his death in 1981.*

13

Courtesy New Westminster Public Library #1687. Sharon Dibble Collection. Photographer: Bob Dibble.

~ 13 ~ *Premier Bill Bennett visited the New Westminster Library on September 8, 1978, to present a provincial grant toward the renovation and expansion of the current library, which had been built in 1958. The grant was for $400,000, and along with an additional $1 million from other sources, it allowed the library to expand a further 17,800 square feet and add a third-floor addition, including more room for the reference department. On the right is Mayor Muni Evers (1969–1982). On the far left is chief librarian (now retired) Alan Woodland.*

Chapter 17

The Change of Roles in Wartime

New Westminster has a rich and varied military history dating back almost a century and a half. Since its very creation, the city has taken pride in its military traditions. The historic wooden Armoury building has served many functions since its construction in 1895. As well as a drill hall and armoury, the building has been and is still used as a banquet and dance hall for important civic occasions. After the 1898 Great Fire, the site was also used as the centre for distribution of relief to those civilians burnt out of house and home. The sight of uniformed soldiers and officers has been commonplace within New Westminster — during times of peace as well as in times of war.

In Formation

The regimental family tree within the city is deeply rooted. The antecedents to the current regiment are the New Westminster Volunteer Rifles (1863), the Seymour Battery of Garrison Artillery (1874), the Duke of Connaught's Own Rifles (1899), the Duke of Connaught's Own Rifles, 6th Battery (1902), the 104th Westminster Fusiliers of Canada (1910), the 47th Battalion Canadian Expeditionary Force (1915), the 131st Battalion Canadian Expeditionary Force (1916), the Westminster Regiment (1936), and the Royal Westminster Regiment (1966).

Courtesy New Westminster Public Library #98.

1

After the disbanding of the Columbian Detachment of the Royal Engineers in 1863, many of the former detachment that stayed on created the New Westminster Volunteer Rifles. The Volunteer Rifles were the source of several traditions, such as sporting and competitive shooting, the formation of the home guard, and the eventual creation of the Seymour Battery of Garrison Artillery in 1874.

~ 1 ~ *This photograph shows the Seymour Battery soldiers standing proud circa 1882, despite the uniforms that they had to pay for themselves. They fired cannon volleys into the Fraser River, where cannonballs now sit on the river floor. These cannons have been refurbished to sit in front of City Hall.*

The city's armament consisted of two brass, muzzle-loading, twenty-four-pound field guns. These two cannons were surplus items from the Crimean War and were brought to New Westminster in 1867. The citizen-trained gunners practised weekly as well as ceremonially firing their cannons at all official salutes. The Home Guards were volunteer citizens. The Seymour Artillery Company, formed in 1866, was made up of five former Royal Engineers and thirty-five citizens. Each of the volunteer members paid a fifty-cent fee for drill instructions, and the three groups numbered 180 members in total. Later in 1866, after New Westminster Rifles, No. 1 was formed, they and the Seymour Artillery Company helped lay the foundation for the militia in British Columbia. It is believed that the gun placement called "The Battery" was in the Albert Crescent area at Prospect Park's southeastern corner.

~ 2 ~ *The members of the Seymour Battery of Garrison Artillery, now absorbed into the 5th B.C. Battalion of Garrison Artillery, are posed formally circa 1892. This is a studio portrait, and the backdrop appears in other group pictures of that time. Their white, spiked pith helmets were part of the uniform from 1878 to 1886. It is thought that the photo was taken for the farewell of Captain Tinley, who left the group upon his promotion to the rank of major.*

Courtesy New Westminster Public Library #14. Photographer: S.J. Thompson and Bovill.

2

~ 3 ~ *Ceremonial parades such as this one circa 1894 were a common aspect of military life in the city, and still are today. This parade on Columbia Street, headed west, with the Columbian Building*

Courtesy New Westminster Public Library #1.

3

Courtesy New Westminster Public Library #3020. Bob Collum Collection. Photographer: J.C. Cornish

4

prominent in the background, might include the 5th B.C. Brigade of Garrison Artillery. The parade's significance is undetermined. Cedar being plentiful and ready at hand, it was frequently used to decorate streets, homes, and buildings at this time. In this image, cut cedar trees are also being used to add some colour to this event, along with the draping cedar garlands.

~ 4 ~ *In 1899 the regiment was renamed the Duke of Connaught's Own Rifles, and in 1902, it became the Duke of Connaught's Own Rifles, 6th Battery. Eleven of the "Connaughts" stand proudly in front of the Armoury's doors in 1908. The reason that photographer J.C. Cornish captured this particular moment, and the names of these gentlemen, can only be guessed at. A blend of seasoned officers and young recruits (except one) all sport shoulder sashes. At the centre, one man stands out in particular, due to both his height and his medals of decoration. The finely moustached officer at the image's far right stands at ease in true regimental manner. The regiment proudly welcomed the Duke of Connaught to the Royal City in 1912, but under a different name: the 104th Westminster Fusiliers (formed in 1910).*

Military training builds character, and this was a common Edwardian-era refrain, particularly for its youth. The early twentieth century saw a proliferation of boy scout–style youth battalions. Schools such as Trapp Tech even had their own Boys Battalions. There was also the New Westminster Home Guard, formed during the First World War. Such local home guard units were organized across Canada, and unlike the Home Guards of the United Kingdom, they were never called to actively defend their cities from attack.

~ 5 ~ *During the First World War, soldiers of the 131st Battalion, Canadian Expeditionary Force*

Courtesy New Westminster Public Library #174.

5

(CEF), such as these from New Westminster, engaged in training at camps in Vernon. As can be seen on the faces of the men in this photograph, the dangers of warfare seemed impossibly distant, and the thought of conflict merely an adventure to enjoy with your comrades. The soldier fourth from the left is J. Louis Sangster, who survived the war to be elected city councillor for seventeen years and mayor for two years in a political career spanning the years 1931–1960.

6

Courtesy authors' collection.

~ 6 ~ *Shoulder badge for the 131st Battalion of New Westminster in the First World War.*

Floating Steel

A small, heavily wooded island is visible within the Fraser's North Channel. It is south of the West End neighbourhood at the upstream end of Queensborough, and it is covered in rich green second growth. It would be quite reasonable to assume that not much has happened on Poplar Island. For a brief time it was the site of one of three New Westminster Native reserves established in 1860. When the First Nations left this location, it was used for a while as a small cemetery. At the beginning of the First World War, a shipbuilding plant was built on the island's upriver end. This operation ran from 1914 to 1919, and a small wooden footbridge was built for some workers to cross the North Arm to Poplar Island near the foot of Third Avenue. Others were ferried across in a small boat from Queensborough.

The plant was called the Poplar Island Shipyard, and four ships were built there for the Imperial Munitions Board. Each weighed in at 2,800 tons. These ships were

Courtesy New Westminster Public Library #100. New Westminster Museum and Archives Collection. #1HP6404.

7

named the *War Ewen*, *War Comox*, *War Edensaw*, and *War Kitimat*. Great excitement surrounded the launches of the Poplar Island boats. Once launched, momentum carried the ships forward until they bumped into the then wooden Queensborough Bridge.

What is particularly interesting about these warships is that they were built with wooden hulls. This design allowed them to steal past the enemy mines, whose magnets drew them to metal hulls, where they detonated on impact. These wooden-hulled ships carried steel guns and shells to Great Britain, greatly helping the war effort. By 1919, the Poplar Island Shipyard's purpose had been served. The wooden bridge to Queensborough was not removed until 1935, and over time the island has returned to a wild state.

Other New Westminster shipbuilding facilities were also turned to the war effort. The Dawe shipyard was located in Queensborough adjacent to Poplar Island. Samuel Dawe, who originally hailed from Newfoundland, founded Dawe's in the summer of 1908. Dawe was born on May 23, 1860. He moved to Vancouver in 1890 with his wife, Emma, and they eventually settled in New Westminster to raise their five children. Dawe's Shipyard was also called New Westminster Marine Railway Co. Ltd., and it provided many with steady employment throughout the First World War. In the post-war years, it had become so profitable that it was able to greatly expand its operations in 1925 by building an additional large land-based workshop. However, the company did not survive the Depression, and it was taken over by the Star Shipyard, a long-time rival, during the 1930s.

~ 7 ~ *The* Samson III *and the* Skeena *at their docks, circa 1915. The* Samson III *is in the image's centre, and the* Skeena *is located at an angle to the left. The* Skeena *was the last sternwheeler to run on the Fraser River. She was eventually sold off, becoming first a floating boarding house and then a barge before being scuttled.*

In the Factory

As the waterfront factories adjusted and retooled for the war effort, so too did the general citizenry of New Westminster. Edward Heaps had arrived in British Columbia in 1888 and had begun in the lumber industry, making sashes and doors at his first factory in Vancouver's False Creek. He was quickly able to expand his business; within ten years there was both a Heaps Timber and a Heaps Brick Company. He acquired a Queensborough-based engineering company by purchasing the Schaake Machine Works on New Westminster's front street, clearing his land on Queensborough, and moving Schaake's machinery and assets across the river to the company's new home — worth nearly a quarter-million dollars in 1912. Heaps even hired Henry Schaake himself to manage the plant for him.

The company had suffered during the depression years of 1912 to 1914, but was able to turn red ink into black when in 1915 it was given a very lucrative contract producing shell casings for the Munitions Board. After the war, Heaps Engineering altered its business direction into doing repair and construction of sawmill and logging equipment. The company suffered through

Courtesy New Westminster Public Library #2472. J. MacDonald Collection. Photographer: Stride Studio.

8

the Great Depression until it was acquired by the city for non-payment of taxes. It languished on the city's books until Mayor Fred Hume saw an opportunity with the beginning of the Second World War to put the facilities at the disposal of federal departments needing war materials. Heaps Engineering employed three shifts of men and women, several hundred employees in total, and the book value of the asset to the city quadrupled from $250,000 to $1 million. Over seven hundred employees worked for the war effort at Heaps during the height of its war contributing years.

~ 8 ~ *The production floor of Heaps, producing both shell lathes and munitions casings. Ironically, the shell casings shown in this image were shipped to Hong Kong, only to be seized by the Japanese after the fall of Hong Kong in 1941.*

In addition to shell casings, the company also produced other machinery, such as cargo winches. After the Second World War, the Heaps Company again fell on hard times, and it was closed in 1955.

Also during the Second World War, the Pacific Veneer Company Ltd., at the foot of Braid Street in Sapperton, produced veneer for military aircrafts used by the Royal Air Force. The veneer was then put to use by de Havilland, so they could produce fast, light, twin-engined aircraft known as Mosquitoes. These planes were entered in service in the beginning of the war as light bombers, and later took on the roles of reconnaissance planes, night fighters, fighter-bombers, and even escort fighters. There were many women employed in this plant during this war.

~ 9 ~ *Women working at the Pacific Veneer Company, circa 1943.*

Courtesy New Westminster Public Library #3177. Jozef Podejko Collection.Photographer: Leonard Frank.

9

Doing Your Bit

In addition to those in uniform, the regular citizens of the city also rallied to the call of war. They retooled their workplaces and their lives to help do their bit to support their boys at the front and bring them home victorious. One method of doing this was selling Saving Stamps. The additional fundraising events around them were a powerful contribution by those on the home front in support of the war effort. The "Miss Canada Sales Campaign" became active all across Canada to aid the victory effort. New Westminster began its own campaign in approximately mid-August 1942. Citizens also rallied around the soldiers, providing them with places to relax and holding contests to support the war effort.

Courtesy New Westminster Public Library #3289. Faye West Collection.Photographer: Stride Studios.

10

Courtesy New Westminster Public Library #2653. Amy Hutchenson Collection.

11

~ 10 ~ *This photograph that was in the* British Columbian *is publicizing the "Selling Saving Stamps for Victory Dance," sponsored by the Kiwanis Club, as well as the volunteer girls' efforts in doing their part for victory. The girls were dressed in Miss Canada costumes to promote and sell the Savings Stamps. (Standing, left to right) H.W. Mansfield, Rae McLean, Betty Hopkins, Inez Davis, Linda Barwood, Norma Sangster, and Mrs. R.J. Smyth, president of the Kiwanis Club. (Seated, left to right) Marion Broder, Althea Bell, Nora Barwood, Margaret Holt, and Audrey Sangster. August 28, 1942.*

~ 11 ~ *A group of women volunteers and two soldiers relax circa 1943, sitting upon the steps of Galbraith House, then known as Westminster House. Hugh Galbraith built the house in 1894, and the family lost it to the city for unpaid taxes in 1940. The city allowed the Soroptomist Club to turn the home into the Westminster House, a gathering point and hostel for service men and women. Amy Hutcheson, who is in the photograph, is the picture's donor. (Front row, left to right) Hilda Smith, unknown, Doris Mawhinney (a relative of the owner of a 1925 Provincial Exhibition Prize List book that is in the authors' collection), and Jean Fulton. (Back row, left to right) Amy Hutcheson, unknown, Isabelle Harbard, unknown, and Helen McIntosh.*

~ 12 ~ *The origins of this 1917 contest to choose "the most patriotic girl," and any other pertinent information on this interesting photograph, are a mystery. (Left to right) W. Eilers, Mayor Gray, Mrs. Foster, Miss Stewart ("the most patriotic girl"), E.W. Wry, Bessie Flynn, Stan Gilchrist, and J.E. Brown.*

In Remembrance

There are many ways in which to remember an event or a person. There are collectively organized events and

12

Courtesy New Westminster Public Library #2892. Johnson (Sivewright) Collection. Photographer: Canadian Photo Co.

traditions in which the community unites in recalling sacrifices and victories, especially around the profundity of war. However, it is the personal memories that are the deepest and most lasting. Dorothy Bilton has allowed us to share her family's story and some of their memories of the war years.

~ 13 ~ *Marvin Spooner is twelve years old in the mid-1920s, in this photograph taken beside 914 Thirteenth Street, the Spooner family home. He looks proud and smart in his youth patrol cadet's uniform. He is standing at the home's northern side with his back to the street.*

~ 14 ~ *Mrs. Bilton stands by the front steps of her and her husband's house at 912 Thirteenth Street in March 1940. She lived right beside the Spooner family home to the south, where Dorothy and Marvin spent their later childhood years. Dorothy is playfully wearing her brother Marvin's infantry uniform, and this is close to his departing for service in the Second World War. Dorothy remembers wanting to have a picture taken of herself in the uniform. Marvin Duncan Spooner's attestation date was July 3, 1940. He went on to serve for the full duration of the war.*

Courtesy authors' collection. Dorothy Bilton Collection. #17.DB6.

13

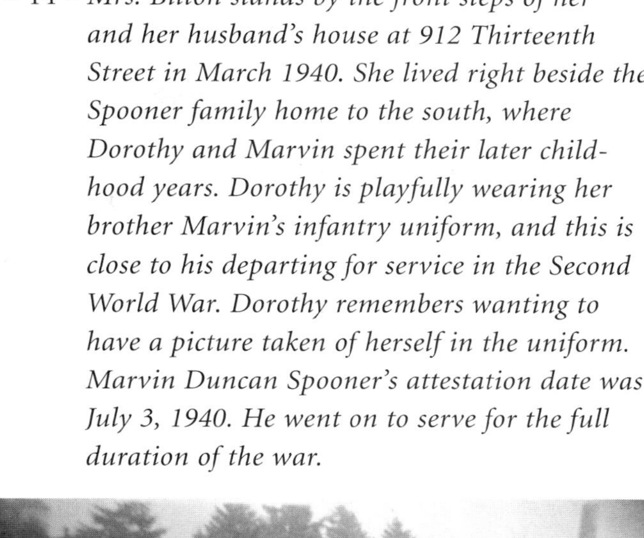

Courtesy authors' collection. Dorothy Bilton Collection. #17.DB7.

14

~ 15 ~ *This is Marvin Spooner's active service pay book from the Canadian 3rd Infantry Division, from 1940 to 1945. These pay books were carried with each solider and were presented to the company pay master to receive payment and to record the amount received.*

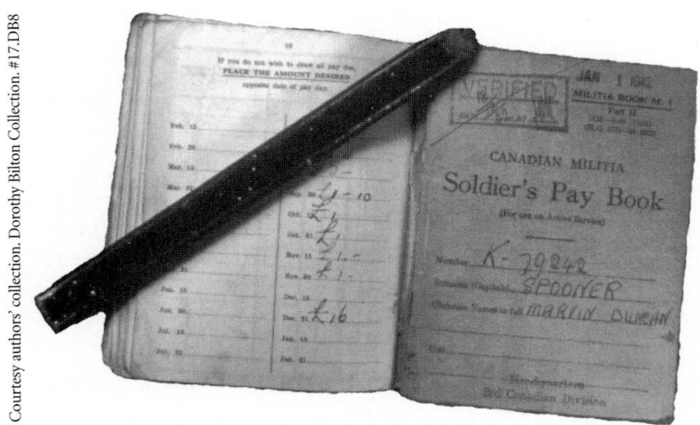

Courtesy authors' collection. Dorothy Bilton Collection. #17.DB8

15

~ 16 ~ *This picture, taken in 1942, was sent home to Marvin's family in New Westminster when he was in Europe. He participated in the western advance right into Berlin. Photographs like this were all that his family regularly saw of him during his five years of duty. He was twenty-seven years old when he left, and did not return until he was thirty-two. Marvin later moved to Kelowna in B.C.'s Okanagan region, where until recently he ran an orchard he planted after the war. He passed away in October 2004.*

Courtesy authors' collection. Dorothy Bilton Collection. #17.DB9.

16

~ 17 ~ *Dorothy Bilton and Ann Govier on the roof of the Douglas Block on VE Day, May 5, 1945. Dorothy is on the left and Ann is on the right as they marked this historic moment with an image they both could share. VE Day was jubilantly celebrated in all the Allied countries. Hitler and the Nazis had been defeated at long last. "I called my friend Ann Govier at her apartment," said Dorothy, "which was just above her store on the corner of the Douglas Block." The Douglas Block was a two-storey building with commercial spaces on the main and residential suites up top. Ann's shop, the Ann Govier Beauty Salon at 730 Twelfth Street, was at its corner. This was one of the first beauty salons set up in New Westminster and was locally famous, particularly for those selected to become May Queen. "We've got to get our picture taken today," they both said. Dorothy says they agreed to meet at Ann's apartment, and they climbed to the roof, where residents would*

Courtesy authors' collection.Dorothy Bilton Collection. #17.DB10.

17

sometimes go to relax. Later the two would share the same last name, as Ann Govier married Dorothy's brother-in-law, Don.

~ 18 ~ *On Armistice Day, November 11, 1922, the city unveiled a First World War memorial in Leopold Park. It has a base of British Columbia grey granite quarried from the mountains of Vancouver's North Shore. Children play amongst the floral tributes left that day. The monument, now moved to its current placement in front of City Hall, is the centre of the city's annual act of remembrance.*

Courtesy New Westminster Public Library #3141. Jozef Podejko Collection.

18

This poem won the City Poetry Prize during Heritage Week 2003 in New Westminster, in honour of military heritage. Amongst the judges was New Westminster's poet laureate, Don Benson. The winning poet, Wendy Faith Tarasoff, reported that her inspiration for the poem comes from the photograph called "Wait For Me, Daddy," by professional photographer Claude Dettloff (see page 228). The photograph was taken in New Westminster, and when Wendy wrote her award-winning poem, "We Stand," she was about only eight blocks and sixty-four years away from the moment that the photograph began its journey to her.

"We Stand"

Three hearts abreast in footfalls pass …
Three abreast, uniformed in courage,
colours upright in flight on high,
They marched Oh, Canada
Fathers, brothers, sons

woman and child
wheeled their shoulders
in support upon
a war they did nay court
A distant whistle blows
a father loses last human touch
whilst we gather here what thought
the unknown man, a soldier,
pounded by bullet-thunder,
covered in tears, in mud and in rain
to
the
bone
What sacrifice was made …
Want to go home …
A moment-please-for poppies die,
whose rifles were at the ready aye,
whose planes flew not on standby
Oh Canada, our home
Three red hearts abreast
In footfalls pass … aye,
We stand for thee.

…

— Wendy Faith Tarasoff

Chapter 18

Changing Streetscapes

Looking at historical photographs of streetscapes can invite the romantic notion of what it would be like to walk into the past. The difference between seeing what you see every day and seeing what is lost in time can be captivating. Photographs of streets with regular, daily events taking place are fascinating. Historical photographs can be the next best thing to actually being there, especially when mixed with curiosity and a bit of imagination. Which picture captures interest is usually up to individual taste, but experiencing the streets of a different time through a photograph can be a tantalizing and fascinating form of research and just plain enjoyment.

~ 1 ~ *The photographer was standing at the corner of what would become Douglas and Columbia streets looking east. Much of Columbia Street had a corduroy road surface (logs half-buried to prevent getting stuck in the mud). The planks that join Columbia at a right angle from the left would become Douglas Street. This image is appealing partly because so much of it is unknown, including the year it was taken and by whom. We can assume it was taken before the fall of 1865, because that is when Holy Trinity Church burnt down. The pale building*

Courtesy New Westminster Public Library #271.

1

on the extreme left is the Customs House, which was built in 1859. The taller gabled wooden building at the back centre of the cluster is the first Holy Trinity Church, built in 1860, where the Rev. Mr. Sheepshanks was minister. Beyond that, the majority of the buildings are unidentifiable. How interesting it would be to stop and talk to people and enter the ramshackle clusters of buildings, and how amazing it is to think that this is a photograph of the first incorporated city in the whole of Western Canada.

~ 2 ~ *This picture was taken from a point overlooking the corner of Church and Columbia streets in 1889. The photographer's name is W. Bovill. (The "W" stood for either William or Wheatley, who were both photographers, and also brothers. One or both had been in partnership with photographer S.J. Thompson from 1886 to 1889.) He had been in partnership with photographer S.J. Thompson from 1888 to 1889. The picture looks northeast and might very well have been taken*

New Westminster Public Library #680.

2

from the roof of the new home of the Daily *and* Weekly Columbian, *the Powell Block, built in 1889. Its architect was James Kennedy, whose sons were co-publishers of the newspaper. The building was completed at a total cost of $30,000. This image, from the paper's photo collection, was taken shortly after the building opened and appeared in an issue of the paper. The building was five floors high facing Lytton Square, and three floors facing Columbia. There is so much activity going on, it seems to be bursting from the frame. The first thing to catch the eye is the white building with its second-floor balcony. The sign hanging from the side reads, "B.C. Monumental Works," and the balcony is filled with firewood. The man on the right with the crumbled rock about him is carving gravestones. It is amusing that a doctor's surgery is one door over on the left. The next white building on the left has lumber stacked and piled in front of it. The wooden sign above says "Farmer's Home." This building was previously a Temperance Hall. (Ironic, since the Queen's Hotel and Saloon had been close by.) The smoke that seems to be erupting from the chimney behind the hotel and the Farmer's Home is probably from a woodstove, but in the long time needed to make the exposure, the plume's drift created this effect.*

~ 3 ~ *This is part of New Westminster's former Chinatown in 1890. The city's Chinatown was one of the first, and was the largest in British Columbia. The number of residents peaked at about a thousand before beginning a gradual*

Courtesy New Westminster Public Library #1012. Josef Podejko Collection.

3

decline due to social pressures within the city and especially due to the growth and consolidation of Vancouver's burgeoning downtown Chinatown between the 1920s and 1940s. The road that cuts across the image is McInnes Street. Below McInnes, none of the buildings are identifiable. The unknown photographer took this picture from a rooftop with his or her back close to Tenth Street. The foreground appears to be mixed business, modest housing, and industrial. It looks like the set of an old western movie town, but is instead remnants of an authentic one. There is lumber neatly stacked in the lower right, so it is not unused. This whole area would be destroyed in the 1898 Great Fire. Above McInnes Street and running perpendicular is a broad street that heads up the hill to the horizon. This is Royal Avenue, beginning at about the 900 block. Near the horizon and left of Royal is Eighth Street. The two-storey building on the corner of McInnes and Carnarvon with the four white posts and a balcony is importer Ying Tai and Co., general merchants and local contractors. Carnarvon runs up and to the right to meet the horizon near Sixth Street. By 1899, Ying Tai and

Co. had moved down to the corner of McInnes and Columbia, briefly joining with the post-fire building boom along Columbia Street. In the summer of 2005, an area at the intersection of Agnes and McInnes (between Royal and Carnarvon) was rezoned for the construction of condominium towers. During excavation for a residential parking area and foundation, the authors of this book took part in the discovery of pieces of china, rice pots, soya sauce jugs, and medicine bottles.

~ 4 ~ *Photographer Paul Okamura placed his camera tripod on the south hillside of Columbia and Fourth streets and shot this image in the summer before the 1898 fire. He most likely took the shot for the novelty of the miniature circus coming toward him. The building at the right edge is the Burr Block, the only building in this picture to survive the 1898 Great Fire. To the left of the Burr Block is the beautiful Begbie Block. The building on the far left of the photo, where the wooden boardwalk seems headed, is the office of the* Daily Columbian*, the same building whose rooftop Bovill took his photo from in 1889. The dramatic building with the conical tower is the YMCA at the corner of Church and Columbia. Further along Columbia's north side of the 500 block are some of the city's most important buildings, including the post office, the library, and the Hyack Fire Hall. The Hyack Hall is the white, peaked-roofed building directly above the streetcar coming east.*

~ 5 ~ *What a treat it would be to travel up and down Columbia Street in 1904. The streets are filled with all the vibrancy and optimism of a city on the move. At the beginning of the century, Prime Minister Wilfrid Laurier stated that the twentieth century belonged to Canada. This image, taken four years later, seems to show that New Westminster still shared Laurier's grand vision. Imagine what a walk would provide in the way of snippets of conversations, smells, and sounds. In*

Courtesy New Westminster Public Library #241. Okamura Collection.

4

Courtesy New Westminster Public Library #827.

5

particular, what did the old streetcars sound like? Dorothy Bilton recalled that in her early youth in Sapperton during the late 1910s, she could tell the difference between the streetcars' individual sounds. The one coming east from McBride Boulevard into Sapperton via East Columbia brought her father home, and the other one turned instead westward into downtown. At this portion of Columbia, Lorne Street is visible to the left, as it is the roadway where the building signs read, "Drugs, H. Ryall." Just above that is T.J. Trapp's Hardware, making great use of its corner with what is almost a collage of competing advertisements. A child is skipping past Ryall's Drugs, coming toward the vast awning of the Geo. Adams Grocery. Could that be him arranging the produce in front for maximum effect and street appeal?

~ 6 ~ *Columbia and Sixth streets, looking west, 1904. What would it be like to travel along Columbia in the deep snow in a horse-drawn sleigh, to journey all the way to the city's distant horizon and back again? For a while the horse and sleigh, and more than likely bells as well, would be the only sounds.*

Courtesy New Westminster Public Library #816.

6

~ 7 ~ *Columbia and Church streets, looking west, 1911. Wet from the rain, both the blocks of sidewalk and the Hassam road paving glisten under the "modern streetlights." Columbia's sidewalks appear to ripple as the texture within catches light from different angles. The sidewalk appears ready for a night game of hopscotch, and the 1901 City Hall building has an illuminated sign that appears to be floating in the night sky. There are not many nighttime photographs around, and, as is seen here, this is a shame.*

Courtesy New Westminster Public Library #1035.

7

~ 8 ~ *This image was probably taken from the top of the smokestack of the B.C. Penitentiary's boiler house. The dated caption is characteristic of many images taken for the institution. In the foreground is the lengthy perimeter fence. Running along the fence is Cumberland Street, which meets Richmond Street at the photograph's left. Travelling down the hill into Sapperton in 1932, you would soon reach the elaborate Arts and Crafts–style home with the winged roofline and quarried stone front stairway railings. This building, no longer there, was the home of the Bourne family. When one of the daughters, Beatrice, was married in 1939, Mr. Bourne built the newlyweds a Mission Revival–style home to the right of his own. It was decorated with full art deco features inside and out. The house seen here was demolished in the 1960s. If one were to keep walking, one would end up at the upper end of Sapperton's business and shopping district on East Columbia Street. This would be worth the trip as images of early Sapperton are rare — especially from this time period, which some would view as quaint, and not old enough to qualify as historic. Walking the Richmond Street route would take you past Fraser Cemetery and what was then the top portion of the Sapperton neighbourhood. Turning right down the hill on any street connecting with Richmond would bring you past a treasure trove of early Sapperton homes. There is a glimmer of what this walk might have been like while walking some of Sapperton's quiet residential streets now. But in 1932, what would be*

Courtesy New Westminster Public Library #626.

8

found down streets such as Alberta, Simpson, Hospital, Keary, and Sherbrooke?

~ 9 ~ *This 1944 image was taken by Amy Hutcheson from the top of the Brackman and Kerr building right on the waterfront, and is looking back north at Front and Mackenzie streets. It shows a time when Front Street was just as vibrant as Columbia Street, many years before it was placed in the shadow of the present large multi-storied parkade that now prevents the sun from shining on these storefronts. The many two-storey brick buildings contain stores, offices, and businesses, and from this elevation the scene invites the viewer to come back down to ground level and explore its varied, box-like landscape. Two unknown women stand in conversation at the corner.*

~ 10 ~ *This view facing east was taken from the Westminster Trust Building. This is New Westminster's Columbia Street in 1945, when it continued to be a regional shopping mecca. The Trapp Building in the far right looks to be open for business. This was Trapp's store and warehouse, with his former business right across the street (sold in the late 1920s). The ornate windows of the building's five storeys showed off his merchandise. Beside the Trapp Block is the Best Hotel. It had previously been the Savoy Hotel, with another hotel, the Holbrook House, behind it (in the same building but operated separately). The building goes back to 1899, but by 1945 only the Best Hotel existed, since the Holbrook Block on the Front Street section had been taken down. Beside the Best Hotel is the Edison Theatre, which was still playing vaudeville, as it had since 1910. Within two years of this photograph, the Edison's owner and impresario, Frank Kerr, passed away, and the theatre was leased to Famous Players. At the corner of McKenzie is the Sally Shop, and across McKenzie is Copp the Shoe Man (later to become Copp's Shoes). The traffic appears light by today's standards, but this is probably a normal business day caught on film.*

Courtesy New Westminster Public Library #165. Hutcheson Collection.

9

Courtesy New Westminster Public Library #2424. *Columbian* Newspaper Collection.

10

Chapter 19

Built Glories Lost

Heritage preservation is like a field of battle where the lines are clear. This conflict is the subject of headlines, petitions, letters, and rallies. Each building fought for or against does not have the same degree of value. Save the building in what manner, for what purpose, and of what period? Sadly, the "heartless developer" often truly believes that his actions are creating a public value by rejuvenating a stagnating area, when a possible solution might be to rejuvenate what is there already.

Two other issues exist as well. First, often a stunningly beautiful heritage building has been taken down in the past, and now another fine heritage building stands in its place, representing a heritage paradox of loss and gain. Second, it is often the homeowner's personal style that has altered a building over a lifetime of successive ownerships and usages that have diluted or removed the heritage features of value. Homes and buildings are like living entities that grow and change over the years, a natural and valuable aspect of their heritage itself.

Other significant built glories lost have been covered earlier in this work. These include the Providence Orphanage, the Provincial Exhibition buildings, and the Carnegie Library. This chapter provides some examples of each type of built glories lost, some well known, others that might surprise even the long-time resident.

Courtesy New Westminster Public Library #1637. John Boyd Wilson Collection.

1

Melrose, 1621 Sixth Avenue

~ 1 ~ *Taken in 1914, this image shows the J.B. Wilson family in front of their home, the Melrose. The Wilson children in this photograph are (left to right) Violet, Ann, and John Boyd Wilson, Jr.*

Begun in 1910, the Melrose estate covered two full city blocks, stretching along Sixth Avenue between Sixteenth and Eighteenth streets and north to Nanaimo Street's south side. The property formed a large rectangle bounded on all four sides with a cut granite wall about four feet high. Melrose itself rose from the centre of the estate and was accessible either by a ring road in front or by a series of ornate stone balustrades. The home was built in the very grand Classical Revival style for lumberman James Boyd Wilson and his wife, as a family residence. Wilson had made a fortune in the real estate business and speculation during the 1910 land boom in the Lower Mainland.

The home took a year to build, and Wilson spared no expense, spending as much on the shapely grounds and rock walls as he did on the home and its interior. The home's centrepiece was a stained glass masterpiece for the central dome, seventeen feet in diameter. Charles Bloomfield's Standard Glass Company created the beautiful centrepiece. The Wilson family had at least four children during their period of ownership, three daughters, Violet, Ann, and Melrose, and one son, John Boyd, Jr.

Accounts differ as to whether the home was named after the youngest daughter or after John Boyd Wilson, Sr.'s sister, also named Melrose. Before 1918, something went wrong with Wilson's finances, and the Bank of Montreal foreclosed on all of Wilson's properties, including the Melrose. The family had to move out, leaving after just seven years in the stately home. George D. Brymner, manager of the Bank of Montreal on Columbia Street since 1888, purchased the home. Brymner was the manager of the bank during the great robbery of September 14, 1911. The home was purchased upon his retirement in 1918. George and Annie Brymner owned the home for almost twenty years. George passed away in 1924, and Annie joined him in 1937. The home was turned into the Melrose Park Private Hospital in 1942, because a private buyer could not be found for such a large estate during the Depression. The Melrose lasted as a medium care retirement nursing hospital until December 16, 1977. All that remains of the estate is one stretch of the surrounding stone wall on Sixth Avenue, and the stained glass dome, saved and moved to the Vancouver Museum's collection of locally made art glass. The Melrose was demolished in 1980 to make way for twenty single-family dwellings.

St. Ann's Academy, 1878 Albert Crescent

~ 2 ~ *This postcard, dated November 19, 1911, was mailed from 432 13th Street to Marnie Cocheleen*

Courtesy authors' collection. #19.PC20.

2

in Chicago, Illinois. It reads, "Dear Marnie, hello girlie how are you? Are you married yet? Don't forget to send me a note will you? Where are you working now? I am working every day + feeling fine. Lillie is the same. I should have wrote long ago but seems I could never get to it. Well how have you been keeping? All's well here. Will write later. Best regards from all. Yours ever, E.E.B."

Fronting on Agnes Street with a striking view of the river across Prospect Park, St. Ann's Academy was a real jewel in the Royal City's crown. Built and run by the Sisters of the Order of St. Ann as a girls' school and convent, it opened its doors in 1877 in front of the much smaller old building, built in 1865. Designed in the Second Empire style (by architects William Turnbull and Thomas McKay), its most distinctive feature was its ornate central tower, which contained a clock that chimed hourly. The tower bell could be heard throughout the city, and the overall building was a river landmark clearly visible from the water. St. Ann's continued as a girls' school until 1968, becoming a high school in 1958.

Courtesy New Westminster Public Library #1004. *Columbian* Newspaper Collection.

3

The tower suffered a fire in the upper portion in 1944, started by a student (we wonder if it was due to secret smoking hidden from the nuns?). It gutted the top two floors of the tower. It was never refurbished, and it sat as an empty shell until 1968. Its demolition day was dramatically recorded on October 17, 1968. St. Ann's was replaced by twin apartment towers.

~ 3 ~ Columbian *newspaper photographer Basil King took this photo on October 17, 1968. Its original caption read, "End of the line for historic St. Ann's Academy in New Westminster is the wrecking bar in the hands of workmen now tearing the ancient building apart. Demolition contractors Lloyd Kadin and Jeff Cayer survey the outer structure for demolition next week. Stripping of furnishings, doors, and windows is now complete. Antique hunters prowl the scene looking for an array of old but good furnishings and fixtures still available."*

~ 4 ~ *October 17, 1968. Photographer Randy Glover of the* Columbian *dramatically records the end of the line for St. Ann's.*

Columbian College, "College Court"

~ 5 ~ *This image taken in 1920 by Universal Photographers of New Westminster shows the Columbian College when it still stood at "College Court," a cul-de-sac off of First Street and below Third Avenue. Before it was made into a college it had been the stately home Bloom Grove, originally commissioned as a private residence for Henry Valentine Edmonds and his wife, Jane Fortune (née Kemp), when he was a city*

4

Courtesy New Westminster Public Library #1049.
Columbian Newspaper Collection.

5

Courtesy New Westminster Public Library #17.
New Westminster Museum and Archives Collection. #1HP0315.
Photographer: Universal Photographers.

councillor in 1882 (he became mayor in 1883). He came to the city from Ireland in 1862 and made his fortune in real estate development, insurance, and a wide range of investments, one of which was the New Westminster Street Railway and Vancouver Electric Railway and Light Company. The home was designed and built by architect George William Grant in 1889.

In 1893, the Methodist Church of New Westminster purchased the large private home and converted it into a fully recognized and incorporated college, the Columbian Methodist College. At first the college offered degrees in theology, which it could grant outright; later it offered a full four-year arts course, which would give graduates a University of Toronto degree. The college had expanded by that time and had dropped the word *Methodist* from its title. It had also made the former Edmonds residence into

Courtesy New Westminster Public Library #855. Leslie T. Hill Collection.

6

its Ladies Building. The college closed in 1936, and their fine buildings were demolished.

The Hill Houses

~ 6 ~ *Idlewild faced Fourth Street near the corner of Fourth Avenue. The massive piece of property has since been divided into many smaller lots, with the buildings' ages correlating to when lots were sold off. This circa 1910 photograph is of Idlewild's lounge, or dayroom, and it appears to be well-used as a family room, even by today's standards. This is evident by the newspapers, magazine, books, etc., and the casual feel of the room. The large mantelpiece in the back is reported to have been made by the Wintemute Furniture Factory and is made of beautiful curly maple.*

The two Mr. Hills were brothers from Nova Scotia, and both were engineers. The idea of having their homes together on one city block, facing different streets, must have appealed to them: they could feel a sense of a larger piece of land and of privacy even while in a city. Together they built two Hill Houses.

Their shared property comprised the land between the 400 and 500 blocks, between Fourth and Fifth Streets, broader at the northern end by Fifth Avenue and the southern end by Fourth Avenue. The two homes were at corners almost back to back: Idlewild was on the 400 block of Fourth Street, and Dunwood was at the 400 block of Fifth Street.

Dunwood was the home of A.E. Hill, who was a city water engineer. Idlewild was the home of Albert J. Hill, a civil engineer whose business partnership, Hill and Kirk Engineers, was located within the Guichon Block on Columbia Street. His firm had been employed in surveying the proposed CPR terminal in Port Moody. The *Columbian* on October 6, 1906, reported that Albert had narrowly escaped death when he was struck by an express train at Mission Junction. Even though he was hard of hearing, he was able to jump off the track when the train was five feet away, escaping with only three broken ribs and a broken nose.

The brothers jointly employed the architectural firm of Maclure and Clow in 1891 to build them houses in the Queen Anne style. Idlewild was the more elaborate of the two and cost $4,000 to built. Dunwood was a more subdued home, at a cost of $2,800.

~ 7 ~ *Both homes were magnificent, but both were demolished in 1974. This image of the demolish-*

7

Courtesy New Westminster Public Library #1097. *Columbian* Newspaper Collection.

ment of Dunwood on May 6, 1974, was taken by Columbian *photographer Basil King. This demolition shocked the residents of Queens Park. They could not believe it could happen so easily. Out of this event, the New Westminster Heritage Preservation Society was formed.*

Courtesy authors' collection 19.PC.21

8

Central School/ F.W. Howay School, Royal Avenue and Seventh Street

~ 8 ~ *The school pictured in this unused postcard has undergone various name changes and alterations over its lifespan, and is clearly visible in many of the early photographs of the city as a landmark building. It began as only the centre block, without any of the wings visible in the picture.*

The school began in 1893 and was listed in the B.C. Directory only as "Public School — Royal Ave. & 7th St." The name changed to Central High School in 1895 and remained that until 1898. By 1899 it was known simply as Boys Central. In the early 1900s, the two wings were added, with the east wing being known as Royal City High School. The first listing of a combined school included Boys Central and Girls Central. When the Duke of Connaught High School was opened, the students of the Royal City High School moved into it. The school then continued as Boys Central and Girls Central, with each having their own wing.

In time, the school was renamed the F.W. Howay School. Frederick William Howay (1867–1943) was born in London, England, but moved to New Westminster, where he became a famous judge and the pre-eminent B.C. historian of his time. He is buried in the Fraser Cemetery. The school was closed on June 30, 1949, and its 360 students moved to the new Vincent Massey Junior High School at Eighth Avenue and Eighth Street. It was eventually taken down, and the site was redeveloped. Today it is the Royal Towers Hotel Casino's property.

Ewen House, 740 Carnarvon

Alexander Ewen was born in Scotland, arriving in New Westminster in 1862, at the age of thirty-two. Ewen, older perhaps than many of the immigrants arriving in British Columbia to start a new life, was experienced in the workings of a fish processing and canning operation. In 1870, he started his first cannery in Annieville, a slough across from Annacis Island. He used cans that were hand-made. This first site of Ewen's cannery is at the location of the current

Fraserport bulk loading facility. By 1876, Ewen, along with a partner, purchased a ready-made operation, a cannery in New Westminster. This cannery was located on Front Street, which at this time was on the waterfront.

The Ewen family's first home was a modest one-storey wooden home located at 762 Columbia Street. Its location was near his cannery, and in 1899, after the Great Fire, it would become the Windsor Hotel. It was one of two Ewen homes lost in that inferno. This first home was satisfactory enough to both Alexander and Mary Ewen that they stayed here for five years with their three daughters, Adelaide, Isabella, and Alexandria, all of whom had been born in New Westminster.

By 1885, the Ewen family had moved up the hill one block and into a more upscale residence at 740 Carnarvon Street. It was this second home that was substantially enlarged and improved upon by Ewen.

Courtesy New Westminster Public Library #2721. Isabella MacMillan Latta Collection.

9

~ 9 ~ *This drawing of the Ewen house from 1890 was very likely rendered by G.W. Grant's company during the fulfilment of their commission.*

In 1890 he retained the services of architect George William Grant, instructing him to more than double the floor space and to make all the substantial embellishments in keeping with the family's prominence in the city. A talented architect, Grant was able to meet and even excel these high expectations with the new Ewen home.

Courtesy New Westminster Public Library #2726. Isabella MacMillan Latta Collection.

10

~ 10 ~ *This image of the home taken in 1894 shows the final result. The Ewen family are posed on the grounds of their new home. (Left to right) Isabella (by first stone pillar), Alexandria (between second and third), Adelaide (between third and fourth), Mary (on a chair in front of the porch), and Alexander (on porch railing).*

Building out from a simpler two-storey late Victorian, the home was enlarged by adding two ornate towers on the side facing the river. This would have afforded Ewen a stately and comfortable place to view the action on the waterfront. These towers resulted in the closing of the front and back porches, requiring new front and back entries to be built. Grant enlarged the house with a new two-storey wing extending up the hillside. On this was built the third tower and the intricate double balcony over the new front doorway.

This fine home was completely reduced to ashes in the Great Fire — one of the most substantial private homes to be burnt to the ground. The Ewens then moved away from the city centre up the hill.

Alexander Ewen had already purchased two unsurveyed islands for his potential future operations and had fortunately moved his cannery from the Front Street waterfront area some years before the Great Fire. One reason he made this move was because the city had grown up around his cannery, and townspeople complained of the strong smell of fish where Ewen smelled only money. On the 740 Carnarvon site, the Russell Hotel was built in 1906, and it still stands today as the College Place Inn.

Chapter 20

This Single Moment

All photography captures a momentary image that cannot be duplicated, and change is constant. A photograph borrows and tucks away less than a second. It makes us reflect on the past and what its people and places were like, long after they have retreated from our sight. Photographs can also carry such a punch that simply seeing a certain photograph can stir up feelings and stop us in our tracks. This is what makes photographs so precious and what grants them the power to take us back in time.

New Westminster's Most Famous Moment

~ 1 ~ *A dramatic family moment.*

One photographic masterpiece that was taken in New Westminster is so well known and is viewed so universally that few people outside the city know that it was taken here. On October 1, 1940, Claude Dettloff, a photographer from the *Vancouver Daily Province* newspaper, had come to shoot the departure of the soldiers of the Duke of Connaught's Own Rifles from their encampment. Dettloff knew that the troops would be marching down the steep slope of Eighth Street. He set up his tripod and camera and waited for the troops to appear at the crest of the hill. He planned to get a dramatic shot of the line of troops, which would, from his position, appear as a six-block-long procession. The procession grew in glorious stature right before his already set camera. Suddenly, a little New Westminster boy cried out and ran from the crowd of onlookers.

His name was Warren "Whitey" Bernard, and he was five years old. Whitey had just spotted his father, and "the feeling of wanting to join in" completely took over him as he watched the line. According to his own account, "[I] was tugging and jerking at my mom's hand to get away and walk with my dad." Dettloff captured the moment, and he, the Bernard family, and providence created a masterpiece of time.

The image, "Wait For Me, Daddy," became the most famous Canadian picture of the Second World War, a symbol of the pain and hope of all those touched by the war.

1

Courtesy New Westminster Public Library #2066. Joan (Dettloff) Macpherson Collection.

Warren "Whitey" Bernard, who is approaching his seventieth birthday, was interviewed for this book. According to Mr. Bernard, or Whitey, as he still prefers to be called, the photo shaped his life in ways that he only much later was able to fully realize. Looking back over the past sixty-five years of his life, the photograph was always metaphorically with him.

He does not remember the actual day, but he can clearly remember what it felt like to go to school the next day after having his picture on the front page of the newspaper. However, "it was not as big a deal then as it would be now," said Whitey. "There was a war on, and the media was not seen yet as greatly important as it would become." There was no instant celebrity for Whitey.

However, the image travelled worldwide, and was eventually chosen as *Life* magazine's photo of the week. Whitey said that it was not a staged shot for the purposes of morale-building or positive propaganda. "It feels real, because that's what it is, people can tell that," he said. His mother had held him back from the very beginning of the troop parade, which was headed to Columbia Street (behind Claude Dettloff and his camera) before crossing the train tracks and then boarding the former CPR pleasure cruiser *Princess Elaine*, now refitted for troop transport. His mother was worried that Whitey would rush across the tracks and become lost in the large crowd at the waterfront waiting to see the ship off. It was when he saw his father that he pulled with enough strength to break away into the camera's frame.

The mother and son later went together to the waterfront to watch the ship sail off to "either Hong Kong or Singapore." Instead it went to Nanaimo ("Loose lips sink ships," was the watchword of the time).

His father, Jack Bernard, was thirty-two years old when he shipped out. He had been born in Summerland and married Bernice, born in Keremeos, in his hometown. In 1935, the couple "had a major row" over Jack's plan to enlist with the Duke of Connaught's Own Rifles and travel to the Lower Mainland while the now pregnant Bernice stayed in Summerland. She insisted on going, and there they went together.

With his father now in Nanaimo, Whitey was asked to do more. He became a spokesperson for the Victory Bond drive and appeared before crowds of war industry workers as a morale builder. He was taken out of school for two or three weeks, and about five times a week he would participate in the bond drive events. These would occur during lunch at one of the major industries, where the workers would watch a vaudeville-style show that included singalongs of songs like "Mairzy Doats," tap dancing, and comedy. "The clincher was me at the end," said Whitey, "when a curtain at the back of the stage would open to reveal a copy of the photo, about three feet by six feet, and I would come out in shorts and say something like, 'Buy bonds, please, and bring my daddy home.'" Bond salesmen were at tables around the stage, and sales were brisk and misty-eyed. He remembers meeting many of the stars of radio and the silver screen at these shows, and as he did so his confidence grew. He remembers the show at Burrard Dry Dock best of all, because the crowd was especially large and loud, as Jack Benny was the headliner. "I was the subject of some envy for that one," said Whitey.

In Nanaimo, Jack Bernard and the other men were sorted as medical records arrived and skills and training were assessed. "Some of the men were too old, or too young, or had bad backs and such," said Whitey. "My father had trained in the militia in the Okanogan with the B.C. Dragoons, a cavalry unit, so he was promoted to sergeant and assigned to a tank unit. He was sent to England's Camp Aldershot in 1941. On D-Day his battalion would fight all the way from Normandy and on through France, Belgium, Holland, and Germany."

Jack Bernard did make it home, but according to Whitey, "He was not the same man who went away, and was not my dad when he came back … too much had changed here as well." The end of the war also marked the end of the marriage of Jack and Bernice Bernard. Both eventually married others and led separate lives. Jack eventually worked as a salesman at a Vancouver sawmill. Bernice worked during and after the war in a number of places, including Pacific Mills in Ocean Falls, Vancouver Island, and B.C. Laminated Floors in Vancouver.

Whitey Bernard ended his childhood in Vancouver, and as an adult he moved to Vancouver Island, opened a gas station, got married in 1969, and became the father of four.

"I can speak as easy to five as I can five thousand, that I owe to the War Bond Drive, and the photo," said Whitey. Well settled and greatly esteemed in his Vancouver Island hometown, his self-assurance led him to success in business and in local politics. He was asked to run as an alderman and was elected the first time out. He was elected several times more as well, being an alderman, then mayor, and an alderman again. He has now retired, and is still going strong.

The Asian Community

~ 2 ~ *Riverside Apartments in New Westminster's Chinatown, circa 1946.*

2

Courtesy New Westminster Public Library #2373. Lillian (Draper) Francis Collection. Photographer: Cloyde Draper.

The Riverside Apartments on Royal Avenue between Tenth and Eleventh streets in 1946 were amongst the last remnants of what had been one of the earliest and largest Chinatowns in North America. It thrived from the 1890s until the early 1930s. The first Chinatown had included portions of Columbia, Front, McInnes, Agnes, and McNeely streets. The 1898 Great Fire had burnt out much of their early businesses, and after the fire, their property was taken over by the predominantly white business elite, who could afford to rebuild quickly. The Chinatown population from the affected downtown area was displaced northwest to areas including Royal Avenue's 700 to 1200 blocks, and below. The directories of homes and businesses of the early 1900s provided names, addresses, and occupations of citizens of the city, but the businesses within the Chinatown region had entries that would simply read "business, Oriental," and homes were given an even simpler designation: "Oriental."

The Riverside Apartments photo has a note attached to it with "Chinese Nationalist League" on it, and this sign can be seen just to the left of the Orange Crush sign. The league met within this building. Also listed within the Riverside Apartment block is the Chong Sing Grocery Company (formerly Sing C. Grocery), whose entrance can be seen just below the Orange Crush sign where its awning has been tied back. The store's front windows are located between the two Sweet Caporal cigarettes advertisements.

The building to the right of the apartment is a two-storey residence and business, although it is unclear how it is being used at the time of this photograph. Other addresses within the building at this time were E. Ginarson at 1031 Royal Avenue and "Orientals" at 1035. The Riverside Apartments soon burnt down, spelling the end of New Westminster's Chinatown: gone and almost completely forgotten. The property has since become a high-rise condominium site.

~ 3 ~ *A roundup of seized Japanese boats clustered together offshore of the western waterfront of New Westminster, 1942.*

Courtesy New Westminster Public Library #1238. Vancouver Public Library Collection, #3191. Photographer: L. Frank.

3

Genuine concern of a Japanese sneak attack on the West Coast soon reached a paranoid pitch after the attack on Pearl Harbor on December 7, 1941. It had come when least expected, argued some, and it would be much worse if it were discovered too late that even a few of the many Japanese fishers and waterfront workers were actually enemy agents or Imperial sympathizers who would organize should such an attack happen. Pamphlets such as "Are The Japanese Interested in B.C.?" concocted plots and presented false evidence that fuelled the flames of mistrust and racism. Amongst some British Columbians there was also greed and envy of the economic success of many Japanese fishers on the coast. The fear was shared in Ottawa, which on January 14, 1942, passed Order-in-Council PC365, creating what it called a "protection area" 160 kilometres wide up and down the West Coast. The intent was that all Japanese people aged eighteen to forty-five be removed to work in the camps near Jasper, Alberta. The "protection" was further extended by another Order-in-Council in late February 1942, authorizing the removal of "anyone of the Japanese Race" from the coast to be interned, even if they had been born as Canadian citizens and/or their families had been in Canada for generations. A total of nearly twenty-two thousand people were relocated by November 1942. Their material assets on the coast including homes and boats were seized and held by the federal government for protection from theft or vandalism. New Westminster had a good number of Japanese citizens, especially in the fishing and canning industry, and particularly in Queensborough. By early 1943, the war cabinet decided that to help subsidize the cost of Japanese relocation and internment, the material assets of those interned should be sold at auction, with the profit from the sales going to the government. Seeking redress for these actions is still a hot political issue.

~ 4 ~ *Pamphlet: "Are The Japanese Interested ..."*

Courtesy authors' collection.

4

Other Single Moments

~ 5 ~ *Demolition of the 1912 Royal Columbian Hospital, October 6, 1972. The* Columbian *wrote, "It looks like a scene from an 'end-of-civilization' movie. Nurse Kathleen Josey started her career at*

Courtesy New Westminster Public Library #512. *Columbian* Newspaper Collection. Photographer: Basil King.

5

the hospital in 1952 and knew the old wing of the Royal Columbian Hospital well. She took a nostalgic walk through the ruins Thursday. Bulldozers will have levelled all that remains by mid-October. Photographer Basil King used a fish-eye lens for the picture."

~ 6 ~ *Drawing of 1910 Masonic Lodge, Agnes Street. The cornerstone of this Oddfellows Masonic Building was laid by the Grand Master, David Wilson, on March 31, 1899. The ceremony involved members of the local lodges, together*

Courtesy K.A. Freund-Hainsworth Collection. Artist: Katherine Freund-Hainsworth.

6

with the Grand Lodge and visiting brethren from Vancouver, Chilliwack, and Mission. The president of the Masonic Temple Company, J.T. Scott, gave an address of welcome to the Grand Master. The first lodge was started in 1862 in the Hicks Hotel. The first building's cornerstone was laid at Lorne and Columbia streets in August 1887, but on April 15, 1891, it was destroyed by fire. The second building was rededicated at the same corner on December 27, 1892, only to be destroyed in the 1898 Great Fire. This building was their third temple, located at the juncture of Lorne and Columbia streets. The lodge then moved to a new address on Agnes Street, built in 1910, which they still occupy.

~ 7 ~ *The Grand Master of British Columbia, A.F. & A.M. laid the cornerstone of the Carnegie Free Library on October 1, 1902. The Carnegie Library stood on Library Square, which was the block bounded by McKenzie, Carnarvon, Lorne,*

Courtesy New Westminster Public Library #2979.
Photographer: W.T. Cooksley.

7

and Agnes streets. The current courthouse is located on the site of the former Carnegie Library, which was taken down in 1958 when the library's new building opened uptown on Sixth Avenue.

~ 8 ~ *YMCA building during construction,1910. The YMCA building was located at 514 Royal Avenue (near Sixth Street, and right across from the current city hall building). The building cost between $25,000 and $30,000, and the architect was Charles Henry Clow. Clow had lost all of his possessions in the 1898 Great Fire, and had to rebuild his life stone by stone. By 1910, he was back on his feet again running a very successful solo operation. Much earlier in his career he had worked in partnership with Samuel Maclure, but there was an abundance of partnership opportunities available to them, and they had gone their separate ways after March 1891. The YMCA building remained on this site until January 1964; it was eventually replaced by apartments.*

Courtesy New Westminster Public Library #2375.
Mary Bovee Collection.

8

~ 9 ~ *The 1900 post office building at the corner of Sixth and Columbia streets, dressed up in its patriotic finery for the visit by the Duke of Connaught on September 21, 1912. Decorating buildings in such a way was popular at this time. Today, the only time buildings are decorated with this much exuberance is in the month of December.*

Courtesy New Westminster Public Library #209.
Columbian Newspaper Collection.

9

~ 10 ~ *Dated September 30, 1908, this image is taken from a souvenir postcard. This ceremony occurred within Prospect Park, which later became part of the Pattullo Bridge approach, overlooking the Fraser River. The unveiling is for the pedestal portion of the monument presented. It was not until August 4, 1911, that the actual bust of Fraser was unveiled. Only the pedestal was installed in time for the one hundredth anniversary of Fraser's journey past the Royal City, with the bronze bust taking approximately twenty months to arrive in the park. The unveiling of the bust-less, Fraser-less plinth took place anyway, with Richard McBride, B.C. premier from 1903 to 1915, doing the honours in his hometown. McBride was born in New Westminster on December 15, 1870, and had practised as a lawyer before being elected to the legislature in 1898. Within two years, he crossed the floor to become the leader of the Opposition, and then premier — the youngest in B.C. history at thirty-*

Courtesy New Westminster Public Library #1765.

10

two years of age. St. Ann's Academy stands proud behind the ceremony. It is also particularly amusing that St. Ann's tower's clock face is observing the ceremony, appearing like a wide-open eye, surprised at the fact that the bust of Fraser is indeed absent. Only in the physical form is Fraser absent, as his spirit is brought alive by the attendees.

~ 11 ~ *On October 24, 1946, 130 parking meters were put into operation on Columbia Street between Fourth and Eighth streets in New Westminster's downtown core. The police sergeant in the photo's right is William "Red" Fraser, who started with the New Westminster Police Department in 1939, retiring in 1969. The law-abiding citizen to the left is unknown and could have been a city employee or a reporter. It is very likely that these were in fact the first parking meters in B.C., and it cost only pennies to feed them.*

~ 12 & 13 ~ *Winners of the best-dressed doll contest held during the Provincial Exhibition in 1927. Mayor*

Courtesy New Westminster Public Library #3098. Dan Mott Collection.

11

Courtesy New Westminster Public Library #2804. Herbert Spencer Elementary School Collection. Photographer: Stride Studios.

12

Courtesy New Westminster Public Library #2803. Herbert Spencer Elementary School Collection. Photographer: Stride Studios.

13

Arthur Wellesley Gray (1913–1920 and 1927–1933) is handing out the prizes, a box of Pauline Johnson chocolates each, to the second, third, and honourable mention prizewinners proudly holding their beloved dolls. The girl wearing the dark clothes standing by herself is the first-place winner. Her name was Annie Ross.

~ 14 ~ *A "larger than life" apple stands with these boys selling apples as a fundraiser for the Kinsmen organization on what they called*

Courtesy New Westminster Public Library #3116. Dan Mott Collection.

14

Apple Day, circa 1944. Events such as this were very popular fundraisers in the 1940s. The post office is directly behind with the old city hall to the right. Mayor William M. Mott would have more than likely crossed over Columbia Street from City Hall to give support to the boys and the big apple by posing for a publicity shot while buying one of the little apples. The Boy Scouts in New Westminster, and within other parts of the country, still conduct annual fundraising Apple Drives.

Courtesy New Westminster Public Library #2660. Isabella Thornton Collection.

15

~ 15 & 16 ~ *These two images show an informal parade of circus elephants followed by camels headed for Queens Park in 1953. They are passing through Sapperton, near McBride School. Even after the loss of the Provincial Exhibition in 1929, the park's tradition of festivals and interesting events continued to take place, and still does so today.*

Courtesy New Westminster Public Library #2661. Isabella Thornton Collection.

16

Afterword

Our History Is a Shared Legacy

A Legacy Given

On the winding road of historical research, many fascinating facts about human nature wait to be discovered. One clear fact about humanity is our deep desire to leave our mark somewhere in time. After the development of photography and its public use in 1839, the world began an interesting change — humanity had just discovered a superb new method of marking its presence for posterity. The word *photography* is taken from the Greek meaning "writing" and "light."

Most people chronicle the high points of their lives. Some people have also been chronicled publicly as outstanding figures in their communities, while others have been momentarily captured in photographs that change lives forever because they happened to be in the right place at the right time. The search for the past is generally pursued through written records. However, this is usually because visual historical records either have not yet been discovered or are assumed to not be in existence, but when one is discovered it can be a researcher's gold mine. Whether discovered through happenstance or at the end of a long period of research, the perfect photograph can have an amazing and almost magical effect. It is a great moment that can be shared and enjoyed by both the historical magician and the keen audience.

Public libraries are wonderful facilities. They have an outstanding mandate of protecting, preserving, and storing all kinds of records (not just books) for the public to access, thanks also to the philosophy and generosity of people like Andrew Carnegie.

~ 1 ~ *Unknown photographer in Queens Park.*

Courtesy New Westminster Public Library #3307. Faye West Collection.

1

When New Westminster opened its first library, it had as its first collection a selection of books from England chosen by Sir Lytton himself, donated by the remaining former Royal Engineers, and many other books, ten written royal speeches from the queen, and a photograph album donated by Governor Seymour. The library opened its doors — by consensus as a public facility, not as a privately funded one — on August 15, 1865, and soon after a museum was organized connecting itself with the library in a natural partnership. The facility's holdings included examples of Native peoples' handicrafts and geological samples that were put on display. The combined philosophies and influences of public and archival resources make the New Westminster Public Library's historical photographs collection a rarity today. In the present climate of provincial and public institutions, it is becoming more and more difficult for the general public to freely access historical collections. The difficulties in accessing history through these sorts of institutions, which do include some libraries as well, hinders historical legacy from freely serving the public.

Courtesy New Westminster Public Library #883.

2

~ 2 ~ *Pattullo Bridge opening, November 15, 1937. Some of the photographers are Charlie Stride, Dave Buchan, Howard Hume, and Alfred Knight. Standing third from the left in the front is Smokey Smith, recipient of a Second World War Victoria Cross.*

From the seed of that first photograph collection 140 years ago to the present library's collection of approximately 3,500 historical photographs, the New Westminster Public Library still "lends" this public legacy to its citizens. This is where we start our praises of gratitude, as this book in its form would not exist without the library. Hand in hand with the "public" library philosophy is the fact that history should be shared and accessible to everyone.

Also, great praise and thanks goes to the New Westminster Museum and Archives, which has shared with the library and the general public its own historical photographic collection. When we embarked on this book after exploring the library's vast collection, we found that during our research schedule we barely got through the library's extensive collection. We unfortunately had to leave a huge number of important and beautiful photographs out of this book, simply due to the sheer number of them. However, we are already planning our next book, where we will once again take up these treasures and plan out our time at the museum and archives as well as at the library.

Courtesy New Westminster Public Library #3248. Albert Fox Collection.

3

~ 3 ~ *1939 group portrait of Charlie Stride and the employees of Stride Studios, which was in business from 1920 to 1968.*

We are grateful to the city's ancestry for leaving these glimpses of themselves in photographic and written records, and for taking the time and making the effort to preserve such valuable records as a perpetual legacy for everyone. We are also indebted to those studio and darkroom photographers who, during the beginning years of the development of photography, worked out the bugs so that we could have these historical photographs today. There is much appreciation for all those amateur and professional photographers who worked in very difficult circumstances along with their cumbersome equipment. From those early days when the Columbian Detachment of Royal Engineers and visiting naval officers carried cameras to record the young province to the later travelling professional photographers who in their goals to make a living also served future generations with the benefits of inheriting these visual historic records, we thank you.

Giving a Legacy

Historical records needed the communal insight of people who nurtured and perpetuated the very survival of such a legacy. And equal praise and thanks goes to the many wonderful people at present who also add to the legacy of history with the belief that history must be shared. Thank you to those who have photographed, written about, talked about, preserved, and enriched New Westminster's past. Thank you for the legacy that began with the people who passed through the rooms and walked the paths of yesterday, who in turn have perpetuated the events that shape today's traditions through the fellowship of sharing history.

~ 4 ~ *Photographers at Queens Park in 1916.*

Courtesy New Westminster Public Library #2124. Mr. and Mrs. William Johnston Collection.

4

Gratitude goes to all the known and unknown photographers, past and present. To the many individual donors, past and present, of the photographs that make up the city's library and museum collections, and specifically to those of you whose photographs are included in this book, we thank you from the bottom of our hearts. Thank you to the wonderful people who came forward in the last few years with their own collections of great photographs, fascinating stories, and introductions to other people with stories to tell.

Thanks to city staff Leslie Gilbert, Steven Scheving, and Susan Anderson for your enthusiasm and direction. Thank you to Mayor Wayne Wright and to the City Council, the Community Heritage Commission, the Historical Society, the Preservation Society, and all at Timeless Books for support with our book project.

Thank you to Lon Mandrake for sharing his and his father's magical and amazing history with us and generously allowing us to put his photographs in this book. Thank you to Joan Macpherson for generously allowing us to put her father, Claude Dettloff's, photograph "Wait For Me, Daddy" in the book. Thank you to the little boy in the photograph, Warren "Whitey" Bernard, for your wonderful insights. Thank you to Patricia, Frank and Connie, Karen and Rick, and Mary Gardener for being great guides to our neighbourhood, introducing us to everyone, and keeping us up to date about what is happening in the area. Thank you to Lani, Tim, Ben, and Michael for being just around the corner from us. Also, thanks Tim for your portraiture skills and being the middleman between us and slide projectors. Thank you to Don and Evelyn Benson for your keen sense of the English language, your poetic words, and for putting up with our crazy schedule. Thanks to Lori for lending us her grandparent's neat old-fashioned slide projection screen. Thanks to Rob and Derek for shovelling snow off our sidewalk, and for Derek running over to our house with food and stories of the outside world while we wrote. Thanks also to Rob and Lori, Steve and Geraldine, Sweetie's at the Quay, and Sami's on 12th Street, for feeding us and making us laugh. Thank you to Gerry Thomson for sharing history with us, and for being quickly forgiving every time we were late to meet you. Thank you to Jaimie McEvoy for also sharing history, specifically on the Brow-of-the-Hill, and for being our computer crackerjack. Thanks to Don Luxton for your interest, and for giving support.

~ 5 ~ *The staff of the* Columbian *newspaper celebrating its one-hundredth anniversary on August 12, 1964.*

5

Courtesy New Westminster Public Library #3067. Willa Robinson Collection.

Thanks to the *Columbian* newspaper. Thanks to Connie Smart and Mr. Moor for sharing photographs and stories of their families. Thank you to Jim Hutson, for being the Heritage Godfather. Thank you to Wendy for your poetic words, written and spoken, and for your understanding. Thanks to Terry Julian and Alan Woodland for facts and inspiration. Thanks to Brigadier General Herb Hamm (Retired) and Colonel Morgan (Retired) for fact-checking and stories. Thank you to Steve at Foto Fun. Thank you Dan, for all of your great, inspiring, and understanding voice messages. Thank you to Nicole and Randolph for directing us to New Westminster. Thank you to Chad and Mary Beth and Sophia and Isobel for calling us on Sunday mornings to give us support and understanding from England. Thank you to the Parental Unit for your love, patience, computer, friendship, and book advice. Thank you in many ways to Suzy, Paul, Shaun, Connor, Doug, and Thuy, with a special, slightly late but not forgotten, Happy Birthday to our nephew Shaun. To Dale Bull, whose birthday has never been forgotten in twenty-seven years until this book came along. Thanks also to Paul for being the healthcare provider to one of our computers. Thank you Karin, Ian, Wes, and Elise for your undying love, interest, and understanding, and also to Wes for lending us photos of himself. Thank you to Susan and Hank for rum cake. Thank you to D'Anne for laughs, love, and contract advice. Thank you to our friends and family for forgiving us while we put this book together, and for welcoming us back when it was done.

To Dad, Joy, Grandma Kate, Aunt Edie, and Grandma and Grandpa Freund: Thank you (from Kathi) for leading me to my past and for giving me to the future. Thank you Grandpa Frank for seeing the good in us and for sharing history, hope you "enJoy" the book.

Love and thanks to Patricia for sharing with us and introducing us to Marie Dorothy Spooner Bilton. And love and thanks to Dorothy, because she let us into her heart and family, and gave us the thread to sew this book together. Also, thank you for all of your historical facts that have always led us in all the right directions, you are always right.

Thanks to the kind gatekeepers and guides of the New Westminster Public Library Reference Department: Wendy Turnbull, Ann Lunghamer, Stephanie Crosbie, Heather Goodwin, Rosemary Keelan, Mary Ann Janzen, Margo Lane, Lorna McAdam, Sunday Scaiano, Gina von Sivers, and Chief Librarian Julie Spurrell. And a special thanks and a historical salute to Archie and Dale Miller for your support, advice, concern, interest, friendship, and more, and for sharing history with us so this book could be brought up to be a good child.

Thank you in so many ways to Kirk Howard, Tony Hawke, Beth Bruder, Anne Choi, Kate Walker, Ali Pennels, Andrea Pruss, and Jennifer Scott — and all at Dundurn who work behind the scenes.

They say it takes a village to raise a child; well, it took our village to raise this book. Thank you.

Bibliography

Books

Adolph, Val. *In The Context of its Time: A History of Woodlands.* Vancouver: The Government of British Columbia Ministry of Social Services, 1996.

Anderson, Edna. *Queensborough Reflections.* July, 1989.

Akrigg, G.P.V., and Helen B. Akrigg. *1001 British Columbia Place Names.* Vancouver: Discovery Press, 1969.

Bingham, Janet. *Samuel Maclure Architect.* Ganges, B.C.: 1985.

Breen, David, and Kenneth Coates. *Pacific National Exhibition: An Illustrated History.* Vancouver: The University of British Columbia, 1982.

The British Columbia Hydro Power Pioneers. *Gaslights to Gigawatts: A Human History of B.C. Hydro and its Predecessors.* Vancouver: Hurricane Press, 1998.

Brown, Craig, ed. *The Illustrated History of Canada.* Toronto: Orpen Dennys – Lester Publishing Limited, 1987, 1991, 1996.

Chambers, Lucy B. *The Court House of New Westminster.* New Westminster: Heritage Preservation Foundation of New Westminster, British Columbia Heritage Trust, 1979.

Conn, Heather, and Henry Ewert. *Vancouver's Glory Years: Public Transit, 1890–1915.* North Vancouver, B.C.: Whitecap Books Limited, 2003.

Davis, Chuck, ed. *The Greater Vancouver Book: An Urban Encyclopedia.* Surrey, B.C.: The Linkman Press, 1997.

Downs, Art. *Paddlewheels on the Frontier.* Cloverdale, B.C.: British Columbia Outdoors Magazine, 1967.

Duncan, Michael. *A Royal View.* New Westminster: New Westminster Chamber of Commerce, 1981.

Francis, Daniel, ed. *Encyclopedia of British Columbia.* Madeira Park, B.C.: Harbour Publishing, 2000.

Fleming, R.B. *General Stores of Canada: Merchants and Memories.* Toronto: Lynx Images Incorporated, 2002.

Gatensbury, Steve. *Queensborough: Images of an Old Neighbourhood.* Delta, B.C.: Sedge Publishing, 1991.

Graham, Stewart. *Yeah College!: A Story of Douglas College.* New Westminster: Douglas College, 1992.

Granatstein, J.L., and Norman Hillmer. *Prime Ministers:*

Ranking Canada's Leaders. Toronto: HarperCollins Publishers Limited, 1999.

Green, George. *History of Burnaby and Vicinity.* February, 1947.

Gresko, Jacqueline, and Richard Howard, ed. *Fraser Port: Freightway to the Pacific, 1858–1985.* Victoria B.C.: Sono Nis Press, 1986.

Grove, Lyndon. *Pacific Pilgrims.* New Westminster: Synod of the Diocese of New Westminster, 1979.

Hibben, T.N. *Dictionary of the Chinook Jargon, or Indian Trade Language, of the North Pacific Coast.* 1899. Victoria, BC: T.N. Hibben & Company Publishers, 1972.

Hill, Beth. Sappers: *The Royal Engineers in British Columbia.* Ganges, B.C.: Horsdal and Schubart Publishers Limited, 1987.

Julian, Terry. *A British Lion: The Story of British Columbia's Magistrate William Franklyn, M.L.A.* New Westminster: Signature Publishing, 1998.

Julian, Terry. *A Capital Controversy: The Story of Why the Capital of British Columbia Was Moved From New Westminster to Victoria.* New Westminster: Signature Publishing, 1994.

Kerr, Dale H. *New Westminster: Mayors and Members of Council, 1860–1997.* New Westminster: WordCrafters Writing Services, 1997.

Knight, Rolf. *Indians at Work: An Informal History of Native Labour in British Columbia, 1858-1930.* Vancouver: New Star Books, 1978, 1996.

Lai, Chuenyan David. *The Forbidden City Within Victoria.* Victoria, B.C.: Orca Book Publishers, 1991.

Luxton, Donald, ed. *Building the West: Early Architects of British Columbia.* Vancouver: Talonbooks, 2003.

Maiden, Cecil. *Lighted Journey: The Story of the B.C. Electric.* Vancouver: Public Information Department, British Columbia Electric Company Limited, 1948.

Mather, Barry and Margaret McDonald. *New Westminster: The Royal City*. Vancouver: J.M. Dent and Sons Limited, 1958.

McLeod, Anne Burnaby and Pixie McGeachie. *Land of Promise: Robert Burnaby's Letters From Colonial British Columbia, 1858-1863.* Burnaby, B.C.: City of Burnaby, 2002.

Miller, Archie, and Dale Kerr. *The Great Fire of 1898.* New Westminster: A Sense of History Research Services Inc., 1998.

Molyneux, Geoffrey. *British Columbia: An Illustrated History.* Vancouver: Polestar Press Limited, 1992.

Murray, Peter. *From Amor to Zalm: A Primer on B.C. Politics and its Wacky Premiers*. Victoria, B.C.: Orca Book Publishers, 1989.

Ng, Wing Chung. *The Chinese in Vancouver, 1945–80: The Pursuit of Identity and Power*. Vancouver: University of British Columbia Press, 1999.

Pethick, Derek. *Men of British Columbia*. Saanichton, B.C.: Hancock House Publishers Limited, 1975.

Pullem, Hellen C. *Queensborough*. 1975. New Westminster: 1989.

Rayner, William. *British Columbia's Premiers in Profile: The Good, the Bad and the Transient.* Surrey, B.C.: Heritage House Publishing Company Limited, 2000.

Rayner, William. *Images of History: Twentieth Century British Columbia Through the Front Pages.* Victoria: Orca Book Publishers, 1997.

Reksten, Terry. *The Illustrated History of British Columbia*. Vancouver: Douglas & McIntyre, 2001.

Rooney, Frances. *Working Light: The Wandering Life of Photographer Edith S. Watson*. Ottawa: Carleton University Press, Images Publishing (Malvern) Limited, 1996.

Rudolph, Elmer, ed. *Memories are Made of This…: Reflections of the West End and Connaught Heights Neighbourhoods.* New Westminster: Millennium Project, City of New Westminster, 2000.

Sanford, Barrie. *Royal Metal: The People, Times and Trains of New Westminster Bridge*. Vancouver: National Railway Historical Society, British Columbia Chapter, 2004.

Sangster, J. Lewis. *75 Years of Service: A History of Olivet Baptist Church, 1878–1953*. New Westminster: The Olivet Board of Management, 1953.

Scott, Jack David. *Century House New Westminster, 1958-1988.* New Westminster: Century House Association, 1989.

Scott, Jack David. *Four Walls in the West: The Story of the British Columbia Penitentiary*. New Westminster: Retired Federal Prison Officers' Association of B.C., 1984.

Scott, Jack David. *Once in the Royal City: The Heritage of New Westminster*. North Vancouver, B.C.: Whitecap Books Limited, 1985.

Taylor, G. W. *Builders of British Columbia: An Industrial History*. Victoria: Morriss Publishing, 1982.

Thirkell, Fred, and Bob Scullion. *Breaking News: The Postcard of George Alfred Barrowclough.* Surrey, B.C.: Heritage House Publishing Company Limited, 2004.

Thirkell, Fred, and Bob Scullion. *Places Remembered: Greater Vancouver, New Westminster and the Fraser Valley.* Surrey, B.C.: Heritage House Publishing Company Limited, 1997.

Thirkell, Fred, and Bob Scullion. *Vancouver and Beyond: During the Golden Age of Postcards, 1900–1914*. Surrey, B.C.: Heritage House Publishing Company Limited, 2000.

Treleaven, G. Fern. *The Surrey Story*. Surrey: Surrey Museum and Historical Society, 1978.

Usher, Dale E.A. (Ted). *Policing the Royal City: A History of the New Westminster Police Service.* Coquitlam, B.C.: Dale E.A. Usher CD, 2000.

The Vancouver Province. *The Way We Were: B.C.'s Amazing Journey to the Millennium*. Madeira Park, B.C.: Harbour Publishing, 2000.

Woodcock, George. *Amor De Cosmos: Journalist and Reformer.* Toronto: Oxford University Press, 1975.

Woodcock, George. *British Columbia: A History of the Province.* Vancouver: Douglas and McIntyre, 1990.

Woodland, Alan. *Eminent Guests*. New Westminster: Heritage Endowment Fund of the Corporation of the City of New Westminster, 2003.

Woodland, Alan. *New Westminster: The Early Years, 1858–1898*. New Westminster: Nunaga Publishing Company, 1973.

Archival Documents

A Souvenir of the Visit of Their Majesties King George VI and Queen Elizabeth to New Westminster, British Columbia. 1939.

British Columbia Provincial Association Conference, Grand Lodge Convention. Monday and Tuesday, July 17 and 18, 1939.

Goad's Atlas of the City of New Westminster, British Columbia. Map. Vancouver: Chas L. Goad Civil Engineers Co., 1913.

Golden Jubilee, May Day Celebration Official Souvenir and Programme. May 1920.British Columbian Co.

Key Plan of New Westminster, British Columbia. Map. 1907. Vancouver: Chas L. Goad Civil Engineers Co., 1914.

King George VI and Queen Elizabeth: A Record of their Coronation. Supplement to *Weldon's Ladies Journal*, Number 718. May 12, 1937.

New Westminster. Map. New Westminster: Parsons, RE, 1862.

New Westminster, British Columbia. Map. July 1897. Vancouver: Chas L. Goad Civil Engineers Co., May 1909.

Coronation Souvenir of Our Royal Family. Supplement to *Weldon's Ladies Journal.* No. 694.1937.

Pictorial Souvenir of the Coronation: For King and Empire. April 15, 1937.

Provincial Exhibition Prize List. 1919, 1921–22, 1925.

Souvenir of Her Majesty Queen Elizabeth. 1937.

Souvenir of the Royal Jubilee. Supplement to *Weldon's Ladies Journal.* April 19, 1935.

Vilstrup, A. *Golden Jubilee of the Alternating Current: Early History of the British Columbia Electric Power System in the Lower Mainland of British Columbia.* British Columbia Electric Railway Company Limited, March 20, 1936.

Periodicals

British Columbia Illustrated Review. Vol. 5, Number 1 (March 2, 1936).

British Columbia Telephone Company: Vancouver, Burnaby, New Westminster, North Vancouver, Richmond, West Vancouver. March 3, 1957.

Canada West Magazine. Vol. 7, Number 4, Collector's # 29 (1977).

Canada West Magazine. Vol. 7, Number 4, New Series (Fall 1983).

Henderson's British Columbia Gazetteer and Directory. 1889, 1891, 1899-1900, 1900–01, 1901–1914. New Westminster Public Library.

Miller, Archie, and Dale. New Westminster Historical Society. A Sense of History Research Services. 2002–2004.

Miller, Archie, and Dale. *Tapho-Files: A Newsletter for People Interested in Cemeteries.* A Sense of History Research Services. 2002–2004.

People Making History: Royal Columbian Hospital, 1862-1987. 1987.

The Preservationist: The Newsletter of the New Westminster Heritage Preservationist Society, Vol. 7, Issue 1 (Winter 2000/2001).

The Preservationist, Vol. 7, Issue 2 (Spring 2001).

The Preservationist, Vol. 7, Issue 4 (Winter 2001).

The Preservationist, Vol. 8, Issue 1 (Winter 2002).

The Preservationist, Vol. 9, Issue 1 (February/March 2003).

The Preservationist, Vol. 9, Issue 3 (August/September 2003).

Thomson, Gerald E. "A Baby Show Means Work in the Hardest Sense: The Better Baby Contests of the Vancouver and New Westminster Local Councils of Women, 1913–1929". *British Columbia Studies*, 128 (Winter 2000/2001): 5, 22–36.

Williams' British Columbia Directory. 1882–85, 1887, 1890, 1892–95, 1897–98. New Westminster Public Library.

Wrigley's Vancouver – Victoria and British Columbia Directory. 1919–35. New Westminster Public Library.

Newspapers

Benson, Don. "The Fraser River: B.C.'s highway of the 1800s." *The Record.* July 15, 1998.

Benson, Don. "Riverboat pilots fierce competitors." *The Record.* July 11, 1999.

Benson, Don. "Old Scores: Wall will pay tribute to unsung city athletes." *The Record.* October 4, 2003.

Benson, Don. "Old Scores: The glory days of New West lacrosse." *The Record.* November 27, 2004.

Caranci, Julia. "Pricey Europe trip gets downsized." NewsLeader. July 24, 2004.

"Celebrating 90 years of progress." *NewsLeader.* May 21, 2003: 13, 15.

Chow, Wanda. "Havin' a Blast." *NewsLeader*. May 17, 2003.

Chow, Wanda. "Royal City's link to its military past." *NewsLeader.* February 14, 2004.

Hilborn, Dan. "Wallet in cannon for 25 years." *The Record.* June 9, 2004.

McManus, Theresa. "Rolling out the big guns." *The Record.* June 9, 2004.

McManus, Theresa. "Bosa buys site." *The Record.* May 22, 2004.

Miller, Archie and Dale. "Our Past." *The Record.* 2002–2004.

New Westminster Public Library. "Library Corner." *The Record.* 2002–2004.

New Westminster Public Library. The *Columbian* Newspaper Collection. 1861–1984.

Pappajohn, Lori. "Recalling life on Poplar Island." *The Record.* April 5, 2003.

Pappajohn, Lori. "Keeping May Day in the family for 90 years." *The Record.* May 17, 2004.

Pappajohn, Lori. "Hospital's history intertwined with city." *The Record.* May 22, 2004.

Pappajohn, Lori. "Bridge on the river Fraser." *The Record.* July 24, 2004.

Pappajohn, Lori. "Unveiling the city's gilded palace." *The Record.* November 27, 2004.

Pearson, L.M. "Centennial Scripts." *NewsLeader.* 2002-2004.

Robinson, Katie. "Kiwanis Club scrapbook contains 85 years of history." *NewsLeader.* November 3, 2004.

Thomas, Mia. "Weekend celebrates history." *The Record.* November 3, 2004.

Turnbull, Wendy. "Picture Puzzle." *NewsLeader.* 2002–2004.

Unpublished

Thomson, Gerald E. "The New Westminster Mat Day Ritual: A Continuous Cultural Tradition in the Far West of Canada." 2005. Submitted to *British Columbia Studies.* December 27, 2004.

Government Publications

British Columbia. Greater Vancouver Regional District Regional Parks Department. *A History of Sapperton*

Landing, 1859–1980. New Westminster: Queen's Printer, December 2002.

Non-print Sources

Miller, Archie, and Dale. A Sense of History Research Services "New Westminster Historical Society." General meeting lectures. New Westminster, 2001–2004.

Miller, Archie, and Dale. A Sense of History Research Services. City of New Westminster, New Westminster Museum and Archives. "Walking Tours — Lectures". New Westminster, 2001-2004.

Miller, Archie, and Dale. A Sense of History Research Services. New City of New Westminster, New Westminster Museum and Archives. "Cemetery Tours — Lectures". New Westminster, 2001-2004.

Miller, Archie, and Dale. A Sense of History Research Services. "Cemetery tour lectures and walking tour lectures." New Westminster, 2001–2004.

Index

A.G. MacFarlane & Co, Brokers 155
Albert Crescent 42, 117, 136, 140, 162, 197, 219
Alfred W. McLeod Ltd, Insurance, Loans, Real Estate and Retails 95, 151, 184
"Ancient and Honourable Hyack Anvil Battery" 158-160
Anderson family 47
"Apple Days" 237-238
Architects
    Bauer, Frederick J. 99
    Birds, Samuel R. Buttrey 117
    Clow & Welsh, 45
    Clow, Charles 45, 117, 223, 234
    Dalton, William Tinniswood 153
    Darling, Frank 148-149
    Eveleigh, Sydney Morgan 153
    Gardiner & Mercer 45, 49
    Guenther, Emil 75
    Grant, George William 106, 107, 154, 181, 222, 225-226
    Kennedy, James 211
    Macaulay, B. 48
    McCarter & Nairne 147
    McCarter, John Young 147
    Maclure, Samuel 68, 117, 142, 223, 234
    McKay, Thomas 220
    Mother Joseph of the Sacred Heart (Esther Pariseau) 101, 117
    Nairne, George Colvill 147
    Pearson, Lawrence 148-149
    Rattenbury, Francis 130, 146, 148
    Scott, Thomas Seaton 21
    Turnbull, William 220
    Welsh, Daniel 45
Ark (the) 20
Armitage House 47
Armoury 196, 198
Artists and exhibitions 80
    Plaskett, Joseph 52-53, 74, 104
    Turner, William 79
Banks/insurance companies 15, 42, 45, 46, 50, 58, 66, 78, 95, 130, 132-134, 146, 148-149, 151, 155, 184, 219, 222
Baxter's Motors Ltd. 143-144
Begbie Block 123-124, 213
Begbie, Judge 107-108
Bennett, Bill, Jr. 194
Benny, Jack 229
Benson, Don 122, 207
Bergen, Edgar 70
Bernard, Warren ("Whitey") 228-230
"Best Dressed Doll Contest, 1927" 236-237
Bilton family 53-54, 59, 66-67, 76, 137, 184, 189, 205-207, 214
Blackie Block 99
Bloomfield 45, 219
"Bloom Grove" 221
Bourne family 60, 215
Bowell family 47, 63
Bozyk, John 66, 133-134
Bradshaw, Chief George T. 133-134
Brackman & Kerr Building, wharf 123, 216
Bridges
    Fraser River Bridge 79, 108-110, 138, 167
    Fraser River Railway Bridge 92, 108, 138
    Pattullo Bridge 19, 38, 42, 47, 79, 110-112, 235, 240

Queensborough Bridge 8, 9, 43, 200-201
Brine Block p 154-156,187
British Columbia Electric Railway Company, Ltd. (see also Streetcars) 19, 35, 61, 85, 92, 133, 140-142, 152, 170, 180, 222
British Columbia Lumber Mill 152
British Columbia Mint 148
British Columbia Penitentiary 21-24, 36, 82, 134, 138, 215
British Columbia Proclamation 10, 18-19
Brownsville (see also Surrey) 11, 14, 15, 37
Brow-of-the-Hill 42-44, 53, 242
Brunette Sawmill 29, 139
Burrard Dry Docks 229
Brymner family 219, 132
Buchan, John (Lord Tweedsmuir) 187, 188
Burr Block 60, 61, 65, 75, 123, 124, 130, 143, 213,
Burr, Raymond William Stacey 65
California State Telegraph Co. 13
Cambridge, J.J. 162
Camilla Gilbert 92
Canadian Pacific Telegraph Company 154
Canneries 27, 30-36, 43, 46, 92, 138, 224-225
Carlisle, Chief 123, 124
Carnegie Free Library 14, 95, 96, 105-106, 218, 233-234
Cave-Brown-Cave, Beatrice 75, 162-163
Cemeteries 64, 65, 66, 116-117, 200, 215, 224
Central Livery Feed and Sale Stable 137, 159
Century House 173
Chamberlin Jewellers 156
Chelsea Lodge (McLeod House) 49-50,
Cheyne House 48-49
Chinatown 211-213, 230-231
Chong Hee Market 168
Chong Sing Grocery Company 231
Churches 13, 20, 47, 52-54, 78, 103-104, 126-127, 146, 153, 162, 169, 210-211, 222
Churchill, Winston 184, 186-187
City Hall
- Buildings 65, 85, 97-99, 105, 125, 162, 193-194, 197, 207, 215, 234, 237-238
- Early functioning and elections 98
- First mayor of New Westminster 98
- Motto 98
- President of New Westminster 98

CKNW Radio Station 193
Collins's Overland Telegraph 13
Collister family 57-58, 60-61, 67, 142-143, 156
Colonial Assay Office 148
Columbian Detachment of Royal Engineers (see also Sappers) 10, 13, 18-21, 24, 42, 68, 74-75, 82, 90, 99, 148, 153, 158-162, 197, 240-241
Columbian newspaper building 211
Confederation 21, 138, 158
Copp's Shoes 216
Courthouse 66, 106-108, 126, 129, 234
Crake family 170-171
Crescent Beach 169
Cricket Pitch 82
Crimean War 114, 197
Crown Colonies 10, 18-19, 21, 24, 63, 108, 114, 186,
Cunningham Trapp Hardware Co. 49
Cunningham family 94, 164
Customs House 211
Dave McWaters' Happy Gang Dance Band 77-78
Dawe's Shipyard 91, 164, 201
Dean, Charles 134
Department stores 51, 71, 147, 151, 152, 156
Derby 10, 19
Devon Café 154
Doctors 12, 18, 46, 66, 155-156, 179, 211,
Douglas Block 206-207
Douglas, James 10, 18-19, 148
Dreamland Dance Hall 77-78
Dufferin stagecoach 184
Duke of Connaught, HRH Arthur William Patrick Albert 82, 102, 140-141, 187, 196, 198, 224, 228-229, 234
Dupont Block 79
Edgar House 48
Eickhoff family 83, 149-150
Edward VII, King 11
Edmonds family 59, 66-67, 122, 133, 221-222
Elliott, Gilbert John Murray-Kynnynmon (Earl of Minto) 83

English folk dancing 162-163
English, Marshall Martin 36
Ewen family 27, 30-33, 36, 43, 46, 51-52, 56-57, 100, 152, 153, 201,224-226,
Evers, Muni 194
Explorations, 1700s 10
Fader, Elijah J. 153
Fales, W.E. 105, 149
Falk, Lee 70
Farmer's Home 211
Federal Building 108
Fillmore, Maria 76
Finlayson, Kathleen 160, 165-166
Fire, the Great 42, 45, 51, 75, 79, 98, 99, 104, 106, 107, 117, 121-130, 132, 138, 184, 186, 193,196, 212, 213, 225, 226, 230, 233, 234
  Contributing factors 123-124
  Hyack Fire Brigade 123
  Miracle of St. Mary's Hospital 117
  "Phoenix rising" 129-130
  Reverend Shildrick's wheelbarrow 126
  T.J. Trapp's dynamite 128-129
  Vancouver Fire Department 123
Firefighting, early 115-116, 183-184
  "Fire King" 115, 158-159, 161
Firsts, for British Columbia
  Hospital in mainland B.C. 117
  Parking meters 227, 236
  Public book collection 104
  Stone building 78
Firsts, for Canada
  City in Western Canada 19, 98
  Longest line of streetcar track 140
  Royal Tour of Canada 188-191
  Woman president of the Canadian Medical Association 66
Firsts, for New Westminster
  Automobile driver 57
  Business on Columbia Street after the Great Fire 128, 149-150
  City Council meeting after the Great Fire 98
  Church service 103
  Firefighting helmet 116
  Firing of Anvil Battery 159-160
  Hyack Anvil Battery uniform 160
  Mayor 98
  Ore carrier from New Westminster to Belgium 92
  Paid mayor 98
  Paid police officer 114
  Police Inspector 114
  President 98
  Saloon in Sapperton 153
  Schools 99
  Shipment to leave New Westminster with B.C. produce 28
  Standard store hours 146
  Streetcars 140
  Telegram 13
  Wrecking truck driver 57
First Nations 9-10,33, 90, 187, 200
  George, Chief Dan (Teswahno) 85, 193-194
First World War 56, 64, 75, 76, 93, 125, 117, 164, 198-201, 204, 207
Flu Pandemic of 1918 117
Fort Langley 10, 19
Fort Victoria 10
Fraser Port 36
Fraser, Simon 10, 235-236
Fraser River 7-9, 19, 28-29, 33, 36, 84, 92, 108, 123-124, 138, 167, 171, 197, 201, 235
  Floods 118-120
  Geography of 7-9
  Gold Rush 10, 21, 29, 63, 114, 148
Freemasons, New Westminster 46, 50, 63, 233-234
Freund, Augusta and Alexander 151-152
Galbraith House 83, 203
Gastown 138
Geo. Adams Grocery 214
George V, King 11
George VI, King 161, 185, 188-190
Gifford, T. 83, 84, 156
Gillander House 44
Gilley Bros. Co. 38, 59, 91
Gilley family 39, 59, 67, 75, 91, 98, 167
Gilley, Janet 67-68, 167
Globe House Dry Goods & Millinery 39, 154
Goad's Atlas of the City of New Westminster 15-16
"The Golden Mile" 149-150, 152
"Gold Mountain" 90
Government House 20, 24, 162
Govier, Ann 168, 206-207
Granville, Town of 138
Gregory-Price Ltd. 151
Guichon Block 223
Green, Sergeant S.M. 67

Gray, A. Wellesley ("Wells") 85, 204, 237
Hamber, Eric Werge 161
Hastings Saw Mill 161
Heaps Brick Company 201
Heaps Engineering Company 92-93, 201-202
Heaps Timber 201
Heaps family 201
Hendry, Aldyen Irene 161
Hendry, John 57, 161
Hicks Hotel 78, 233
Hill & Kirk, Engineers 223
Hill Houses, "Dunwood," "Idlewild" 75, 222-224
Hitchcock, Alfred 65, 188
Holbrook Block 216
Holmes Block 155-156
Hong Kong, fall of 202
"Honeymoon Heights" 42, 174
Hospitals 12, 18, 22, 24, 42, 47, 76, 91, 94, 101,116-118, 138, 189, 216, 219, 232, 233
Hotels 75, 78, 99, 133, 137, 138, 152-153, 158, 193, 211, 216, 224-226, 233
Howay, Justice Frederick William 224
Hudson's Bay Company 10
Hyacks 77-78, 115, 123, 125, 158-160, 161, 213
Hume, Frederick J. 165-166, 173, 187, 202
Hutson, Chief William 114-115
Imperial Munitions Board 200-201
Independent Order of Oddfellows (IOOF), Grand Lodge of B.C. 170, 233
Indiana Traction Company Station, Indianapolis, Indiana 142
Irving House Historic Centre 13, 14, 52
Irving, Captain William 12-14, 29, 122
Jackson, Toby 187
Jamieson, the Reverend Robert 13, 99
Japanese 33, 202, 231-232
Jardine House 46-47
J.J. Johnston House 45, 60, 61, 100, 143, 161, 166
J.J. Johnston 65, 67, 100, 142-143
J.J. Johnston and Son Insurance Company 45
Joseph P. Crane, General Store 100
Josey, Kathleen 233
Kynvet de Kynvet 37-39
Keary family 68, 69, 170, 216
Kelly (S.J.) Woodworking Company 49
Kiwanis Club, New Westminster 170, 173, 203
Knights of Pythias 46, 50, 170
Lacrosse 46, 83-86, 179
    Mann Cup 83-85
    Minto Cup 83-86
Ladner, Thomas E. 36
Lanternslides 31-33
Laurier, Sir Wilfrid 213
Lavery Block 132, 133
Leopold Park 207
Lexy Ewen's doll 51-52
Life Magazine "Photo of the Week" 229
Librarians 56, 58, 95-96, 104,106, 194
Libraries 13, 14, 33, 52, 58, 63, 69, 95-96, 104-106, 125, 166, 191, 194, 213, 218, 233, 234, 239
Lincoln, Abraham 13
Lindbergh, Charles 59
Local Council of Women, New Westminster 179-180
Logging 29, 37, 67, 90-91, 201
Longshoremen 92
Lord Lytton 18, 19, 240
Lytton Square 116, 147, 211
MacKenzie Brothers, Dry Goods & Crockery 154
MacKenzie King, William Lyon 188-190
McBride, Arthur H. 21
McBride, Richard 21, 82, 184, 235
McLeod family 49-50, 75, 95, 151, 184
McMillan family 58, 83
McNamara, John 134
McNaughton, Emma 78
McQuarrie & Mitchell Milliners 61, 62, 150
McQuarrie, Edmonds & Selkirk Law Offices 59, 67
McWaters, Dave 35, 77-78
Mandeville Block 154
Magicians 68-72
Mandrake, Leon 68-72
"Maple Leaf Forever," Buchan version 187-188
Maritime fur trade 10
Masonic Temple Company 233
May Day 45, 57, 64, 157-158, 160, 161-168, 181, 189, 192
    First children's election of May Queen 162

First May Day car 57
First May Day that all schools participated 162
First maypole dance 161
First May Queen and Suite 161
First sites for May Day 162
Origins of 161
Melrose, the 132, 218-219
Military 10, 18, 19, 61, 64, 158, 160, 187, 195-199, 202, 207, 240
Miller, Archie and Dale 33
Miner, Billy ("Grey Fox") 132
"Miss Canada Sales Campaign" 203
Moody Park 42, 172-173
Moody, Colonel Richard Clement 10, 18-21, 42, 90
Morey, Sergeant Jonathon 114
"Most Patriotic Girl," 1917 204
Mott Electric Co. Ltd. 86-87, 111, 193, 237, 238
Mouse's Ear Fish & Chips 154
Murchie, Daniel 64
Mowatt, John 61
Munitions Board 200-201
My Heart Soars 194
My Spirit Soars 194
Naming of New Westminster 19
New Westminster Board of Trade 50
New Westminster Fire Department 115-116, 158
New Westminster Harbour Commission 36
New Westminster Heritage Preservation Society 43-44, 223-224
New Westminster Heritage Preservation Society Annual Heritage Homes' Tour & Tea 44-45
New Westminster Historical Society 33
New Westminster Marine Railway Co. Ltd. 201
New Westminster Police Department 67, 114-115, 132-134, 236
New Westminster Street Railway & Vancouver Electric Railway and Light Company 140
North Road 138
Odin family 57, 58, 142, 143-144
Oddfellows Masonic building 233
Opera 73, 74-77
Orchestra 73, 74 -75
Oven's Blacksmith Shop 98, 159, 160
Pacific Coast Terminals 36
Pacific National Exhibition (Vancouver) 176, 177
Pacific Veneer Company Ltd 202
De Havilland Mosquitoes 202
Parsons, Captain R.E. 20
Peacock family 56, 104,
Pearson, Lester Bowles 191-192
Pattullo, Thomas Dufferin (see also Bridges) 38, 110-111
Penitentiary 17, 21-24, 25, 36, 82, 134, 138, 189, 215
Peterson family 48
Photographers
Bovill, W. 56, 211-213
Brooks, Edward Coley 35
Brown, W. 99
Buchan, Dave 240
Cooksley, William Thomas 91, 169
Cornish, John Charles 198
Crofton Studio (see also Dibble, Bob) 116, 168
Dettloff, Claude 207, 228-229
Dibble, Bob (see also Crofton Studios) 116, 193, 194
Fox, Alice (née Ringstad) 168
Glover, Randy 221
Hacking, Frederick Lewis 163-164
Hume, Howard 240
Kandid Kamera Snaps 151
King, Basil 221, 224, 233
Knight, Alfred 240
Leash, Homer Ellsworth 164
LeBlanc, Don 8
Merrill, Arthur Lawrence 30
Notman, William McFarlane 10
Photogelatine Engraving Co. Ltd. 36
Ritchie, Samuel J. 86
Spooner, Frederick Marvin 189
Stride Studios 61, 94, 164, 168, 187, 240, 241
Thompson, Samuel Joseph 36, 56, 130
Universal Photographers Co. (see also Stride Studios) 61, 221
Wadds Bros. 156
Photography 10-11, 31-33,59, 60, 61, 151, 221-212, 228, 239-241
CPR Photographic Car No. One 11
Pioneer Cricket Club 82
Pinkerton's Detective Agency 134
Plaskett, Reverend Canon Frank Joseph 52, 53, 104

Poplar Island 8, 9, 200
Poplar Island Shipyards 153, 200-201
Post Office buildings 68, 108, 125,158, 213, 234, 238
Powell Block 211
Public Hospital for the Insane 23-25, 76, 138-139
Public Market 28, 105, 116, 128, 146-147
Preservationist, the 43-44
Prospect Park 197, 220, 235
Providence Orphanage 101, 117, 218
Provincial Asylum for the Insane 17, 23-24, 82, 106, 189
Provincial Exhibition 69, 80, 85, 106, 149, 164, 167, 175-183, 186, 204, 218, 236, 238
Provincial Hospital for the Insane (see also Woodlands) 23-25, 138-139
Provincial Land Registry Office 48
Queensborough 8, 9, 19, 30-31, 42-43, 62, 92-93, 100, 118-120, 143, 152, 193, 200-201, 232
Queens Park 42-43, 45-49, 66, 69, 80, 85-86, 106, 136, 160, 162-166, 167, 168, 17-172, 176-183, 186, 189-190, 224, 238, 239, 241
Railways 19, 36, 92, 110, 133, 138-139, 176, 189, 201
Reichenbach family 128, 149, 150, 162
Reliable Furniture Company 50-51
Relief work 79,173, 196
Ritter, John and Tex 193
Riverside Apartments 230-231
Roads, early 17-18, 20, 36, 68, 90, 135, 137, 167, 209-210, 212, 215
Robbery 66, 131-134, 219
Robson, John 24
Rose Shop, the 168
Royal Agricultural & Industrial Society of B.C. 176-177, 184, 186
"Royal City" 19
Royal City Builders'Awards 47
Royal City Café 146
Royal City Cannery 138-139
Royal City Mills 92
Royal City Navigation Company 29
Royal City Planing Company 46
Royal Engineers' Camp 10, 12, 24, 42, 75, 153, 158, 161
Royal Hudson 189-190
Ryall Drugs 214
St. Clair 39-40
Sailing ships 28-29
"Salmonbellies" 83, 85
Sally Shop 168, 216
Sangster family 199, 203
Sappers 10, 12, 18, 19, 20, 21, 42, 75, 99, 137, 153, 158
Sapperton 12, 42, 52, 117, 133, 153, 170, 202, 214, 215, 238
"Saving Stamps for Victory Dance" 203
Sayer family 166
Schaake Machine Works 93, 99, 201
Schools 56, 59, 65, 66, 71, 79, 82, 94, 99-102, 117, 155, 162-164, 171, 176, 179, 182, 191-192, 198, 220, 224, 238
Scott, John Thomas 63-64, 98, 162, 233
Sea otter fur trade 10
Second World War 93, 125, 166, 202, 203-204, 205-208, 228, 240
Seddal, Dr. 18
Selkirk, T.R., (K.C.) 59, 67
Sharp, Cecil 162
Sheepshanks, Reverend Mr. John 103, 210-211
Shildrick, Reverend Mr. Alfred 126-127
Shipbuilding 91, 200-201
Shopping, early habits and traditions 145-146, 149, 155, 215, 216
Sikhs in New Westminster 62, 187
Sillitoe, Bishop Acton Windeyer 103, 162
Sisters of the Order of St. Ann 161, 219, 221, 236
Sisters of Providence of Charity 101, 117
Smallpox 116-117
Smith, "Smokey" 240
"Sockeye Run" 176, 177
Sons of Scotland 169
Soroptomist Club 203-204
Spalding, Captain William (RE) 108
"Spirit of Childhood" 58-59
"Spirit of St. Louis" 59
Spooner family (see Bilton family)
Sports 81-87
Stagecoach travel and coach houses 137-138
Sternwheeler steamships 29-30, 123, 201
Streetcars (see BCER) 42, 43, 83, 92, 122, 140-142, 143, 146, 152, 180, 213, 214
"Stump City" 11, 64

Sturgeons 9, 33-36
Sullivan, Judge Harry 67
Surrey (see aso Brownsville) 8, 11, 37, 108, 124
Tarasoff, Wendy Faith 207-208
Taxidermy, Victorian interest in 51-52
Temperance Hall 211
Theatres 65, 69, 70-71, 73-77, 167, 216
39 Steps 188
Thomson, Dr. Gerald 158, 162, 179
Thornton family 61
T.H. Smith, Dry Goods 155
Tidy, Ann 162
Tinley, Captain 197
Tip Top Tailors 48
Totem poles 172, 182
Townsend, W.B. 115
T.J. Trapp's Hardware 49, 127-128, 129, 214
T.J. Trapp's stolen roadster 133, 134
Trapp building 216
Trapp family 59, 66, 84, 101, 129, 198
Trapp Motors Buick and Pontiac 71
Trudeau, Pierre Elliot 192-193
Van Horne, William 138
Valley Lumber Yards 47
Vaudeville 68, 69, 216, 229
Venables, P.J. 33
VE Day 206-207
Victoria 10, 18-19, 20, 21, 23-25, 83, 130, 140, 148, 169, 178
Victoria, Queen 18, 19, 42, 159, 160, 187
Victory Bond efforts 203, 229-230
Victory Heights 173-174
Wagner, Mildred 68
"Wait for me, Daddy" 207-208, 228-230
Walsh, Johnny 64
Warwick family 60-61
Webster Building 78
Webster, J.A. 78
West End 42, 75, 132, 173-174, 200
Westminster Iron Works 93-94
Westminster Modern Business School 155
Westminster Quay 28, 192-193
Westminster Trust Building 46, 59, 68, 95, 151, 216
White, Reverend Mr. E. 103
White Rock 72, 162, 163, 169
Wilkinson family 48-49
William John Shoe Store 104
Wilson, family 218-219
Wintemute's Furniture Company, family 50, 52, 83, 223
Woodland, Alan 194
Woodlands 24, 25, 106
Woods, Justice R.S. 67
World Roller Skating Championship 78
Ying Tai & Co., General Merchants, Local Contractors 212-213
YMCA Building 84, 87, 125, 213, 234